PELICAN BOOKS
A880

THE ACCIDENTAL CENTURY

Michael Harrington was born in 1928 at St. Louis, Missouri, and educated at Holy Cross, Yale and the University of Chicago. He was associate editor of *The Catholic Worker* from 1951 to 1953. His social work at the Catholic Worker House in New York led to studies of American industry, social alienation, and institutionalized poverty. A member of the Socialist Party since 1953, he has participated in the civil rights and disarmament movements of the past decade. He is chairman of the board of the League for Industrial Democracy and an adviser to the government on problems of poverty and unemployment.

Mr. Harrington is best known for his earlier book, THE OTHER AMERICA, which provided the intellectual stimulus underlying the national antipoverty programs of the Kennedy and Johnson Administrations. THE OTHER AMERICA is also published by Penguin (S223).

BY MICHAEL HARRINGTON

The Other America
The Accidental Century

THE ACCIDENTAL
CENTURY

MICHAEL HARRINGTON

PENGUIN BOOKS INC
BALTIMORE • MARYLAND

Penguin Books Inc
3300 Clipper Mill Road, Baltimore, Maryland 21211

This edition first published 1966 by arrangement with
The Macmillan Company, New York

Reprinted 1967

The author wishes to thank the following
copyright holders for permission to reprint previously published material:

T. S. Eliot for lines from "Choruses from 'The
Rock,'" from *Collected Poems 1909-1962*, published by Harcourt, Brace & World, Inc.; Hannah Arendt for *The Origins of Totalitarianism*,
published by Harcourt, Brace & World, Inc.;
Revolt of the Masses, by Jose Ortega y Gasset,
copyright 1932 by W. W. Norton & Company,
Inc., copyright renewed © 1960 by Teresa
Carey; *Voices of Silence* by Andre Malraux
published by Doubleday & Company, Inc.

FOR Stephanie

CONTENTS

ACKNOWLEDGMENTS

At the outset, I want to recognize the intellectual, moral, and practical support of the Center for the Study of Democratic Institutions. I hope what follows will be a contribution to its vital discussion.

The inspiration for this book derives from a living tradition rather than from any formal experience of education. For better or for worse, it is the product of American radicalism: of what I have learned from the thoughts and deeds of the best men and women of the labor, civil-rights, and, above all, socialist movements. These have been my post-graduate university.

In particular, I owe a deep debt to Max Shachtman who tutored me in the rich intellectual heritage and the immediate relevance of the labor and socialist movements; to Norman Thomas, who is for me, as for so many other Americans, an example of moral integrity and humane political conviction; and to Bayard Rustin, a man of extraordinary courage and wisdom who taught me that American Negroes are not simply raising the issue of race but of the future of democracy itself.

And just behind these three, there are others, too numerous to name, American radicals who today count themselves in thousands and who, if there is to be a hope for tomorrow, will become millions.

THE ACCIDENTAL CENTURY

1

The Accidental
Revolution

In the twentieth century, something enormous is being born. And something enormous is dying. This book is about what is dying. It is about the contemporary decadence.

For more than fifty years, the Western world has haunted itself with rumors of its own death. Some said that the life of the instincts was being smothered, others that the spirit had become dry and brittle. There were those who recoiled before militant poverty and the revolt of the masses and those who feared the corruptions of affluence. Theologians announced a crisis of faith, secularists a crisis of reason.

W. B. Yeats wrote that things fall apart, the center will not hold. Paul Valéry said that the traditional values are "no longer sacred; or else . . . nothing but sacred," and that, "Once destiny was an honest game of cards which followed certain conventions, with a limited number of cards and values. Now the player realizes in amazement that the hand of his future contains cards never seen before and that the rules of the game are modified by each play."

The conservative, Wilhelm Roepke, spoke of a "limitless relativism," "an immeasurable moral and internal decadence"; the man of the Left, Albert Camus, asked if society could live without either grace or justice. A Catholic philosopher, Bochenski, held that a three-century epoch was coming to an end and said of the moment, "One can compare it to the great crisis which, at the time of the Renaissance, gave birth to modern culture." The Russian mystic, Berdyaev, proclaimed, "The old faith in reason is impotent in the face of the irrational forces of history," and the great German sociologist, Max Weber, wrote of his generation, "it might truly be said, 'Specialists without spirit, sensualists without heart, this nullity imagines that it has reached a level of civilization never before attained.'"

Usually, social doom was foretold fearfully, as an inescapable fate. "As death comes after life," Spengler prophesied, "civilization is the inevitable destiny of culture." For him, and for many others, this formula meant the triumph of a mechanized, rootless existence ("civilization") over the rich organic life ("culture").

And yet, a decadence is often a birth. If there is a historical rhythm of decline and fall, there is also one of decline and rise.

In Huizinga's *Waning of the Middle Ages*, for instance, there is a famous description of the medieval twilight in which "It was, so to say, bad form to praise the world and life openly. It was fashionable to see only its suffering and misery, to discover everywhere the signs of decadence and the near end—in short to condemn the times or to despise them." Yet these dark, terrible days were also the prelude to the Renaissance; they were the throes of both death and life. For Henry Adams, there was a sense in which America had become decadent by 1840; the hallowed verities of his Massachusetts aristocracy were in decline. Yet for most historians after Adams, the period signified the beginning of the victory of American capitalism and the emergence of the most dynamic nation the world has ever known.

In this context, this is a hopeful book about decadence. It focuses upon what is dying in order to understand the new life which is possible. It ends, not upon a note of despair, but tentatively, in search of what is being born.

Decadence is a moody and connotative word more than it is a precise term, which is why it can be used, as here, suggestively. In an influential German tradition (seen in the sociology of Tönnies, the philosophy of Nietzsche, the early writings of Thomas Mann, the historical speculation of Spengler, and so on), decadence means the destruction of the human community by the inhuman city. In a French and English literary usage, it is the ennui of the sensitive poet confronted by the banality of material progress. Others implied the idea rather than define it. For Freud, society grows at the price of instinctual denial, and the more man conquers nature, the more he represses himself. The existentialists see the threat in the supremacy of essence, of sterile categories of reason (and, particularly, of scientific objectivity) over life. Marx predicted that the capitalist fabric would burst out of its inability to contain the capitalist technology.

All these theories have their substantial content and many of them will be examined in the course of this book. In this analysis, however, the vantage point is a particular view of history and society. What is decadent in the contemporary

West (always keeping in mind that there is much which is not) derives from an accidental revolution.

This accidental revolution is the sweeping and unprecedented technological transformation of the Western environment which has been, and is being, carried out in a casual way. In it, this technology is essentially under private control and used for private purposes; this situation is justified in the name of a conservative ideology; and the by-product is a historical change which would have staggered the imagination of any nineteenth-century visionary. In following their individual aims, industrialists blundered into a social revolution. There is indeed an invisible hand in all of this. Only it is shaping an unstable new world rather than Adam Smith's middle-class harmony.

In one sense, this represents a familiar process. History, after all, has always been stumbling into new social systems. The Industrial Revolution and the capitalist economy were neither anticipated nor planned. The English of the seventeenth century thought that their upheaval was over theology, the French of the eighteenth that theirs was over philosophy. In retrospect, each event had more to do with the rise of a business civilization than with either God or Man.

But this comforting analogy misses the very essence of the accidental revolution. The older ideologists and utopians were victimized by their ignorance of the limits of the possible. They sought divine commonwealths and secular salvations which were impossible of achievement. Where these conscious revolutionists of the past proposed visions which outstripped reality, the unconscious revolutionists of the present create realities which outstrip their vision. In the first case, it is history that is sad, in the second, man.

THE ACCIDENTAL REVOLUTION

As a result of this development, cracks opened up in every ideology and philosophy. Conservatives unwittingly made a revolution, but it was not the one the revolutionists had predicted, and the antagonists were mutually bewildered. Religious thinkers reported the progress of godlessness, but the fact did not seem heroic to atheists. Literacy increased, making many educators fearful, since its uses seemed anticultural; the people asserted themselves and the traditional democrats became uneasy. There was perplexity on all sides. And many decadences were thus discovered.

What is in decay in these theories is not so much the past as the future. To be sure, some conservatives nostalgically looked back to the golden days of happy hierarchies that never really existed. But, as shall be seen, the more serious idea of decadence is that the West no longer senses either a City of God or of man in the middle or long distance. It has lost its utopia to come rather than its golden age that was. And this is the meaning of the term intended here: the present decadence is the corruption of a dream rather than of a reality.

The city is a prosaic, and crucial, case in point of the accidental revolution. To the Germans it was the very climax of decline. More broadly, it is one of the most accessible examples of the contemporary predicament. In what follows, a fairly familiar description is summarized as an illustration of the not-so-obvious workings of the accidental revolution.

In the last decade or so, social scientists have invented a word to describe a new stage of urban life: Megalopolis. In part, this term reflects the sheer and tumultuous growth in the population of cities. In 1800, there did not exist a city of a million inhabitants, and London, with 959,310 citizens, was the largest concentration of people on the face of the earth. By 1850, London numbered two million; by 1910, there were eleven places in the world with over a million inhabitants; by 1930, twenty-seven which had exceeded that limit. And the trend, of course, continues.

In and of themselves, these quantities gave rise to the Malthusian theory of decadence. Population, it was said, would outstrip food supply; the birthrate was a harbinger of social death. If these fears have diminished in the advanced nations of the West, which are the subject of this book, they have become more plausible on a global scale. In the characteristic mode of the accidental revolution, science makes more existences possible, but casually, without bothering with the consequences.

But the main thrust of the concept of Megalopolis in the advanced lands does not derive from the Malthusian fear. It defines a new system of Western social relations. As the cities grew, more and more people—the fortunate ones— left the central city and went to the suburbs. Urban life expanded from the old industrial center, leaving decaying areas in its wake, and migrated to the new, low-population fringes. Eventually, even the factories joined in the pattern, and a vast system of highways supported two huge streams of daily traffic, the blue-collar out-commuters hurrying to the margins, the executive and white-collar mass speeding to the downtown business area. Because of the vast, sprawling spaces involved, mass transportation became more costly and inefficient, and a supercongestion became a normal feature of life. (Throughout this book, the preponderance of evidence will be American, but that is only because the United States, as the most technologically advanced nation, shows the farthest flung trends of advanced society in general.)

These events also transformed the landscape. In the United States, Megalopolis defined urban continuums hundreds of miles long (for instance, from Boston in the North to Washington, D.C., in the South). The city, like man, no longer had limits. It ceased to be a nucleus of civilization set in the countryside and reached out, obliterating the immemorial distinction between town and nature. As a result, man could not escape himself.

All this had profound consequences for every aspect of life. It tends, as I tried to show in my book, *The Other America*, to alter the very eyes of society. Those left behind in the central city—the aged, the racial and national minorities, the poor generally—drop out of the mind and sight of those riding the superhighways from suburbia to office and back. On a broader, economic level, entire regions were left, like neighborhoods, to rot and stagnate in the midst of rapid change: the American Appalachians, the English North, the Italian South. Intimately, Megalopolis, and particularly its automobile, helped to rearrange the structure of family life and played a major role in the destruction of the traditional sexual ethic.

The nineteenth-century seers had argued that such fundamental changes in the human environment would create different kinds of people. This happened. But, typically, the new personality types did not correspond to the old hopes any more than the new society did. There is, for example, that most unlikely revolutionary creation, the teen-ager.

Teen-age is not a chronological phenomenon—there have always been young people between twelve and twenty— but a historical one, the product of the accidental revolution. As a result of Megalopolis and the technological culture which it incarnated, there appeared a generation of adolescents with leisure, money, and mobility. They constituted a huge market, and tastes were duly fabricated for them. And they had a radical impact on the very quality of social life.

America was, of course, the land of the teen-age pioneers. But as American standards of living began to spread throughout the West, so did the styles of the American young. The teen-ager, an afterthought of social history, became a more genuine example of the "new man" than any of the calculated personalities which the Communists held up for emulation. The Russians discovered that even totalitarianism could not keep out jazz and cool music. And there were other kinds of people invented in the United States and exported to Europe: the organization man, the suburban housewife, and so on.

One of the most important aspects of this chaotic emergence of unprecedented ways of living and artificial countrysides was that it was governmentally encouraged but not democratically planned. In the United States in the postwar period, huge Federal subsidies were granted to the suburban rush of the middle class and the rich. An express Congressional commitment to a broad, low-cost housing program for the poor was made in 1949 and then usually ignored. In a good many instances, the impoverished slum-dwellers, and the Negroes above all, were the prime victims of an urban renewal which was supposed to help them. In

England during the fifties, there was a parallel policy of official support for office buildings and automobile congestion and against homes and quiet. By the early sixties in Paris, the telltale Megalopolitan apartments looked down on the gray, working-class *banlieues*. (Marc Paillet, in his 1964 study, *Gauche, Année Zéro*, estimated the annual French deficit in new housing units at 150,000 out of 500,-000 required.)

It took the power of society to facilitate changes of such a magnitude. Yet, even though the collectivity was deeply involved in the causes and effects of Megalopolis, there was never a free, thorough debate on the transformation. The priorities of the future were derived from the *status quo*, which satisfied neither the conservatives nor the revolutionists.

The resulting continuity of Megalopolitan problems within the West provoked like-sounding indictments. In America, Lewis Mumford wrote of "the increasing pathology of the whole mode of life in the great metropolis, a pathology that is directly proportionate to its overgrowth, its purposeless materialism, its congestion and insensate disorder . . . That sinister state manifests itself not merely in the statistics of crime and mental disorder, but in the enormous sums spent on narcotics, sedatives, stimulants, hypnotics and tranquilizers to keep the population of our 'great cities' from coming to terms with the vacuous desperation of their daily lives and the even more vacuous horrors that their rulers and scientific advisers seem to regard as a reasonable terminal for the human race."

And the British social critic, C. A. R. Crosland, said, "Greedy men, abetted by a complaisant government, are prowling over Britain and devastating it. . . . Excited by speculative gain, the property developers furiously rebuild the urban centers with unplanned and tawdry office-blocks; so our cities became the just objects of world-wide pity and ridicule for their architectural mediocrity, commercial vulgarity, and lack of civic or historic pride."

The coming of Megalopolis wrote a cruel denouement to many a nineteenth-century vision. For what happened was that a revolution took place without conscious revolutionists.

Megalopolis and the age it represented constituted a most radical restructuring of the experience of life itself. There has truly been a "devaluing of all values" as Nietzsche said there would be. But the event did not summon up a new race of stoic and aristocratic supermen. The barbarians who acted in Nietzsche's name would have been despised by their master. Capitalism had, as Marx announced, been unable to contain its own technology within the bounds of its traditional theory and practice, but it had not been succeeded by a socialist leap into freedom. In short, the material transformations have exceeded the wildest imaginings of the science and social fiction of the last century—and so has the conservatism of men. Instead of emancipated proletarians, as in Marx, or sensitive slaveowners as in Nietzsche, there are teen-agers, organization men, suburban housewives.

How had this come to pass? Through technology, some answered, mistaking a precondition for a cause.

It is a cliché that the West (and throughout, I will take the term to mean Europe and America) has been undergoing a continuous technological revolution in this century. In Henry Adams' curious, but revealing, metaphor, time is speeding up, history is becoming volatile, like water in the transition from ice to liquid to steam. Around 1900, Adams calculated that the next, and decisive, phase in the process would take place in the middle of 1917, which was a remarkable intuition no matter how eccentric his method. But, whatever point of departure one chooses, it is clear that during the last sixty or so years Western man has been refashioning reality and, often without noticing it, himself.

And technology was, of course, a basic element in this revolution. First the symbol was the railroad. "We who lived before the railway," Thackeray wrote, "and survive out of the ancient world, are like Father Noah and his family out of the Ark. The children will gather around and say to us patriarchs, 'Tell us, Grandpa, about the old world.'" Then came the automobile, both as a mighty achievement of mass production and as a social force in its own dynamic right. And then the airplane and then the rocket and no one knows what next. There was a succession of technological floods, and each new generation looked back to its youth like Father Noah.

As John Maynard Keynes put the radical character of this development: "At some epoch before the dawn of history—perhaps even in one of the comfortable intervals before the last ice age—there must have been an era of progress and invention comparable to those in which we live today." Between that hypothesized burst of primitive ingenuity and the eighteenth century, Keynes said, "there was no very great change in the standard of life of the average man in the civilized centers of the earth." Then, with gathering momentum, man in the last two centuries changed himself more basically than at any time since the beginning of recorded history. To cite a typical prodigy, in Colin Clark's figures, net income from manufacturing in the United States rose by 4,500 percent between 1860 and 1953.

And all the signs point, of course, to an acceleration of this process in the future. In 1960 a group of scientists (Nobel Prize winners, members of the Moscow Academy of Science, and others) predicted the state of invention in the year 2000. Voyages to the moon, they said, would be normal, and there would be inhabited artificial satellites. The population of the world would have increased fourfold and stabilized. Seawater and rocks will yield all necessary metals, and knowledge will be accumulated in electronic banks and transmitted directly to the human nervous system by means of coded electronic messages. And genetics will allow the scientific planning of the personalities of the next generation.

There is no need to prolong the recital. The miraculousness of technology is a popular article of Western faith. Henry Adams long ago realized that the modern dynamo was an alternate principle of civilization to the medieval Virgin—only he did not understand how soon the dynamo would become old-fashioned. And yet, it is not machines, but the uses dictated to them by men which create new societies. The responsibility for the accidental revolution is human, not inanimate.

In order to understand this fact, it is necessary to speak of capitalism. This will come as an embarrassment to many in the West, and particularly in the United States, for there is a strong tendency to doubt or ignore the existence of such a system. (Some of the reasons for this attitude will be discussed shortly.) To others, the introduction of the term is an announcement that caricature will follow, another one of those dreary, monomaniacal reductions of the complexity of life to statistics about production.

A few things should be made clear. The private despairs, the aesthetic creations, the personal psychologies of these times are not simply the reflection of an economic system. They are, indeed, not "simply" any one thing, for they are always complicated, and they often have their own autonomies and cannot be understood without being taken seriously on their own terms. At the same time, these arts and inner selves do not take place in a void but in a given century and in a century that would not let any man alone. The various aspects of decadence cannot be turned into functions of the economy and neither can they be grasped without relating them to this dynamic and momentous part of contemporary life.

To talk of capitalism as an economic system is the first step away from fatalism. If it is the machines alone which have created all these changes, then the best that one can do is to pray to the computers and production lines that they will become more benign. Such an approach leads to a modern animism that invests technology with the spirits that once inhabited trees and storms. But if it is man's use of machines—the economic system—that is responsible for what is happening, then the direction of events can be altered. And that is a basic premise of this optimistic study of decadence.

There is no question that Western capitalism has changed enormously from the nineteenth-century model. Some of these transformations are analyzed in Chapter 3. Child labor has long been legally abolished, most of the sweatshops are gone, there has been a persistent decline in the length of the working day, and so on. In addition, the night-watch-man state of the *laissez-faire* ideal has given way, in one degree or another, to the welfare state in every advanced nation. In the place of the robber baron and the plutocrat—"I owe the public nothing," J. P. Morgan said—there is the corporate technocrat giving speeches on the social responsibility of his firm and the partnership of capital and labor, whether hypocritically or not.

Yet, however genteel these modifications have made the system, the basic allocation of resources is still made in the pursuit of profit. Production decisions are reckoned in terms of private advantage without reference to social consequences, at least so far as that is politically possible. There is a considerable literature which examines this calculus of gain and how it has been altered by the separation of ownership and management in the corporate collective. But, whatever theory one chooses, the corporation has not become philanthropic or democratic. In one way or another, the executive, no matter how responsible, is paid for making money and not for guiding technological change in a humane and decent way.

Without getting into unnecessary arguments, the force of this aspect of the accidental revolution can be put in terms of a familiar distinction. It has long been recognized that under capitalism there can be a divergence between the private and social cost of a good or service. In the dear, dead old days, this divorce appeared manageable and measurable. A railroad, in its pursuit of profit, would start a new line. It would cost so much money for the materials, the engineering, and the land. But then, there would be another cost. The sparks from the train would injure trees bordering the track. Who was to pay, the company or the farmer? That was a relatively easy issue, and it could be settled in the courts. The new line would destroy the beauty of a valley and deprive an entire town of its view. That was more distant, less amenable to the assignment of responsibility.

But now, as the twentieth century advances, a chasm opens up between private and social cost. The production of automobiles plays a role in changing the structure of the family, sexual mores, and polluting the very air men breathe. The private decision of real-estate developers to ring a city with carefully zoned, relatively expensive suburbs exacerbates racial tensions, segregates education on the basis of color and class, modifies the urban tax base and consequently the political order, and embitters the experience of old age for those who are left behind.

Take an example of this same phenomenon involving an entire geographic region. In Appalachia, the post-World War II decision of the coal companies to automate had the most profound consequences. The new technology of strip and bore mining literally tore up the very landscape, decreased mining employment by almost two-thirds, made various forms of traditional agriculture impossible, eroded the land-tax basis of the already inadequate school system, drove hundreds of thousands of people into cities and an urban life for which they were totally unprepared, and even dangerously changed the very quality of the water that flowed down into the reservoirs of the Tennessee Valley. But the courts held that corporations had the private right

to work this public havoc because of contracts that had
been signed at least a generation before anyone had the
remotest idea of what they would come to mean. (All this,
and much more, is documented in Harry Caudil's brilliant
book, *Night Comes to the Cumberlands*.)

This is one way of saying that the contemporary technology is, of its very radical nature, social. If it is left within
a context of private, often hit-or-miss, decision-making, that
is not so much free enterprise as it is the rule of corporate
bureaucracy in the public sphere. And it is precisely this
mechanism which gives the present revolution its accidental
quality. The cause of change—a personal or corporate investment in gain, a private cost and profit—stands in little
or no relation to the effect—a new order of human life.

One of the most glaring examples of this reality has
already been cited: the heedless speculation in land and
building which has characterized practically every postwar
Western nation. (An exception, like Sweden, receives its
privileged position precisely from the conscious intrusion
of a public motive in this area and from a large, cooperative
housing sector.) And so the desperate needs of slum-
dwellers are sacrificed to the profitable luxuries of middle-
and upper-income homes.

In the market sector, there is a gigantic apparatus designed to mask this corporate egotism. Through one of
society's most important educators, the advertising industry,
all of the techniques of science are used for the private
socialization of the public taste. The consumer's "free"
choice is thus engineered and calculated as far as is possible
so that it will coincide with the highest profitability to the
producer. The influence of this carefully wrought value

system increases as one descends the social class ladder. As in all things, the poor pay the highest cost and give aid and comfort to the rich.

In any case, the growing chasm between private and social cost, the corporate control of a technology which is essentially public, called into question a most basic assumption of Western thought: that man frees himself through reason. Each new invention, like the automobile, television, nuclear power, space rockets, was a triumph of the human intelligence. But the totality of these innovations, with all of their revolutionary consequences, was an increasingly puzzling, even mysterious, society. As the parts became more ingenious and minutely calibrated, the whole became more irrational to those who had unwittingly fabricated it. The legend of one of Goya's *Caprichos* etchings—"The dream of reason produces monsters"—seemed as much social science as surrealism.

Spengler's famous book popularized one version of the resulting bewilderment, but it rested upon a fragile analogy. In the *Decline of the West*, what was happening had always happened. History, like biology, was moving through the immemorial cycle of birth, maturity, and death. Max Weber was much more profound. What was happening had never happened before. Technological progress was achieved by a radical method of breaking life up into specific functions which could be measured and engineered. In such a sub-divided existence, there was no vantage point for the comprehension of the whole. Bureaucratic, scientific man was losing his intellectual hold on reality even as he pragmatically conquered it.

It is still possible to counterpose a hope to these pessimisms of Spengler and Weber (and their themes are present in most of the contemporary dooms). The accidental revolution could become conscious of itself, and the future would thus be chosen rather than submitted to. To make this hope anything more than a wish, it is necessary to understand the attack that the twentieth-century genius mounted upon it. And this is a main purpose of this optimistic study of decadence.

In attempting such an anatomy of the various destinies assigned to these times, a typical excess of the century emerges at the outset: that it has supported two, seemingly contradictory, apocalypses, one gentle, the other violent.

The profound revolution manifest in Megalopolis came into existence without the intervention of masses in the streets. It can stand as a case of the gentle apocalypse. The violent apocalypse is relatively simple to define. Lenin referred to it when he declared the post-World War I period to be an epoch "of imperialist war and proletarian revolution." Change was to proceed by the road of cataclysm. And between 1914 and 1945, the West went through two world wars (which had the shattering aspect of a civil conflict within a common heritage), inflation, a general collapse of the economic system, the rise and fall of fascism, the most bitter and intense class struggle, and, finally, the discovery of a bomb which could annihilate mankind and render the world uninhabitable. It seemed, as one poet put it in September, 1939, that a culture had been driven mad.

In addition to these incredible transformations within the West, the globe itself was in furious change. And though the analysis of this book limits itself to trends within Europe

and America, the international context should at least be
sketched in as background. Along with all the other reasons
for fear and doubt, the West in this period lost its unquestioned rule of the world. In 1914, the white countries
were secure in their hegemony over the nonwhite masses
of the earth. The inferiority and passivity of the colonial
peoples was almost taken for granted. Four or five years
later—the turn of the Chinese Revolution toward anti-
imperialism in May, 1919, is as good a symbolic date as any
—that was no longer true. Europe and America, to be sure,
retained their political and economic power and hardly
saw in a Chinese student demonstration the beginning of a
momentous end. But, it became increasingly clearer, some
hundreds of years of white dominion were drawing to a
close.

This turning point was not, as André Malraux has pointed
out, simply political. Up until the reentry of the nonwhite
millions into history, it was logical to assume that the cultural standards of the West were as superior as its technology. "Decadence" was anything that departed from the
classic, Mediterranean tradition. But then, simultaneously
with the loss of Western internal conviction, the formerly
subject cultures forced their way rudely into the century.
Suddenly, African masks were no longer the fetishes of
primitives but an art about demons that had a reference for
the advanced nations.

Indeed, the violent apocalypse can be traced in art as well
as in history. A writer like Thomas Mann is a typical case
in point. The times literally took him by the scruff of his
neck, transforming his novels as well as his politics, ultimately leading him to conjure up the Devil in order to ex-

plain what his native Germany was doing to itself. Mann was not alone in his shock. The aesthetic revolution had begun even before the First World War, and the Philistines were right for the wrong reasons in considering the radical dissolution of traditional forms as the harbinger of a new relativism.

Between the two wars, the arts were implicated in upheaval like everything else. Dada discovered that tone of inspired mockery that still persists. The Surrealists attempted the wedding of Freud and Marx, dream and technology. There were atonalism, abstraction, the modern dance, and many other departures. If one knew nothing of these years from history, their apocalyptic character could be inferred from their art.

The response of two sensitive men, the one a Czech novelist, the other a British scholar, can stand as a documentation of this point. After World War I, the haunting modern genius, Frank Kafka, remarked, "The war has opened the flood gates of chaos. The buttresses of human existence are collapsing. Historical development is no longer determined by the individual but by the masses. We are shoved, rushed, swept away. We are the victims of history."

And, writing in the 1930's from the very midst of the violent apocalypse, Gilbert Murray said, "There is something wrong. There is a loss of confidence, a loss of faith, an omnipresent, haunting fear. People speak as they never spoke in Victorian days of the possible collapse of civilization." The Victorians, Murray asserted, had a cosmos (it included the nebular hypothesis, the theory of evolution, the liberating potential of science, a sort of Christianity, and a concept of the gentleman); the moderns have a chaos.

In economic and political terms, the climactic moment of the violent apocalypse took place in the 1930's. That decade provides an older, more dramatic, example of the accidental revolution than Megalopolis: the paradox of starvation through glut. The West had achieved the highest technical proficiency in the history of man. There were desperate, crying needs which demanded fulfillment. There were idle resources, material and human, which could have satisfied them. Yet society could not put its industrial capacity and its people to work to meet these obvious necessities. In Germany, the failure led to fascism, and in the rest of the Western world to sharp class conflict. Wealth had labored to produce hunger; empty factories brooded over the men who had made them but could not use them.

Murray's fears are signed with the mood of those times. They are the sentiments of an educated British gentleman but, in different forms, they were shared by people in every Western nation. This was the stuff of the violent apocalypse, the experience that led many to consider the "possible collapse of civilization." At such a time, the idea of decadence was not academic and scholarly, but political. It was an intellectual element in the growth of revolutionary mass movements on the Right and Left, and communists, socialists, and fascists all spoke of the decadence of the bourgeois society.

And yet, it is important to realize that this explosive and unstable period is related to the quiet revolution of Megalopolis. Paul Valéry was one of the first to recognize that there were two decadences possible in the twentieth century. The first would see "a depression of intellectual values, a lowering, a decadence comparable to the one produced at the end of antiquity; culture abandoned, masterpieces become incomprehensible or destroyed. . . ." This prophecy was in the mood of Gilbert Murray. But then, Valéry also saw another terrible option: "the application of industrial methods to the production, evaluation and consumption of the fruits of the spirit would end by transforming the highest and most important intellectual virtues . . ." And this is an intimation of the gentle decadence.

At first glance, there is little connection between the thirties and the sixties, between the Depression and class struggle on the one hand, and prosperity and internal stability on the other. Yet, these are two modes of the accidental revolution. In each instance, technology is more thoughtful and creative than men. In the case of the violent apocalypse, the failure to control the work of man's hands led to mass unemployment, fascism, war, a rending of the Western social fabric. This caused many people to talk about revolution, usually without making one. In the gentle apocalypse, Megalopolis and similar developments occurred behind the backs of those whose lives they transformed. People made a revolution without talking about it.

Practically everyone in the West today recognizes that a violent apocalypse took place in the period *entre les deux guerres*. But now, it is said, all that is past, and talk of revolution or basic change is hopelessly outdated. Through modifications in their structure, the advanced nations have brought the economic demons under control and can now attend to the aesthetics of social life. The profundity of Megalopolis challenges such a complacency. But beyond the statistics, it is important to understand the reason behind this refusal to notice that human existence is being remade.

And here again, Friedrich Nietzsche is relevant. In an 1888 polemic against Wagner, the German philosopher wrote: "What characterizes the literary decadence? It is that the whole no longer has life. The word becomes sovereign and leaps up out of the sentence, the sentence reaches out and obscures the page, and the page comes to life at the expense of the whole. . . ."

Nietzsche's literary judgment can be translated into a description of much of social thought today. In it, "the page comes to life at the expense of the whole." The large ideas about society's alternatives have faded into the background. The tiny increments of change are minutely examined; their sweeping, radical sum is all but ignored. Between the two wars, and particularly in the thirties, this was not the case, mainly because the Nietzschean prediction of upheaval was so obviously true. With the breakdown of the Western economy and the barbaric retrogression in Germany, history was ransacked for explanations. Significant sections of the population debated and struggled over the order of things to come.

In the post-World War II years, this all changed once more. The revolutionary hopes of the European Resistance were cruelly disappointed, the United States did not return to the conditions of the Depression. As a result, some social scientists in the fifties and early sixties talked of the "end of ideology." The old debates had, they said, become sterile. In part, these thinkers were reacting to some of the oversimplifications of the thirties. In part they expressed a general mood of relative economic and political satisfaction.

It is difficult to grasp a revolutionary evolution, which

is what the gentle apocalypse is. In the thirties, it was a question of a storm; in the sixties, it is one of a deep sea change below the social surface. And both moments are the expression of the same persistent turbulence of the twentieth century.

Now that a revolution is indeed taking place in every aspect of social, economic, and political life, such concepts as capitalism, socialism, and democracy are relevant. There is an imprecision to such generalities, but there is also an imprecision to sociological minutiae, and at the present a more dangerous one. To attempt to anticipate in outline form the large idea which makes up the main argument of this study: The accidental revolution has resulted, not in this or that loss of faith, but in introducing doubt and contradiction into every Western creed, secular or religious. In time of gentle apocalypse, such as the present, it is possible to ignore such a convergence of crises or to treat them pragmatically. The revolution is going its casual way, there are no Western *coups d'état* to take a position for or against, and one can hope that the situation will be blundered through. Still, it is of some consequence that capitalism, socialism, democracy, religion, and atheism have simultaneously become problematic. This fact might become even more urgent tomorrow if, as can never be discounted in this century, the revolution would once more become revolutionary.

Here are some of the decadences with which the modern world is concerned.

Adam Smith has been stood on his head. In the classic theory, the invisible hand of the market directed the sum total of private and individual decisions toward a common good. This was the element in the Western economic creed

hat made it something more than a rationalization for
greed. According to this view, the market not only resulted
n the most efficient use of material resources but strength-
ned the freedom of choice of the citizen and ultimately
created the happiness of the largest possible number of people. Thus, capitalist man was accomplishing moral and
political virtue as well as observing economic reason when
he vigorously pursued his personal gain.

The mystical equilibrium of this theory was never real-
zed in reality. Yet, in a rough way the activity of the entrepreneurs did raise the level of the entire society. It was,
to be sure, necessary for the people, and particularly the
workers, to sacrifice and struggle in order to achieve their
share of the new wealth (it was not delivered to them by
the market mechanism). But there was still some sense to
the Smithian equation of the public and private gain.

But the growing divergence, and even conflict, between
private and public cost has converted the capitalist economy into the near opposite of Smith's description. Not only
do the individual decisions add up to a revolution rather
than a harmony, but they often dissatisfy their successful
makers. One of the wriest spectacles of the age is that of
businessmen lamenting the "socialistic" drift of the system
which has made them richer year by year (or, in the
thirties, denouncing the anti-Depression measures which
were designed to save them). This amounts to a confused,
corporate acknowledgment that the old rules no longer
apply.

So capitalism no longer explains the capitalist reality.
Indeed in more than one sense the most efficient anticap-
italists inside the Western world are the businessmen.

Socialism is in a different kind of crisis. In the patristic

statements of the nineteenth century, the socialist father
argued that utopia had become practical. In the past, the
said, the good society was a dream of poets and philosopher
as well as a persistent, but impossible, instinct of the mass
But with the Industrial Revolution, history turned a cor
ner. For the first time ever, the production of genuin
abundance was within the technical competence of man. A
a result, there was a material basis for human decency. An
with the appearance of the modern working class, driven t
economic and political organization by the necessities o
daily life, a social force had come into being that would b
impelled toward the theory and practice of justice.

For a considerable time, the socialist hope seemed to b
coming true. A huge, revolutionary movement grew up i
Europe, and Karl Liebknecht could cry out in the Germa
Revolution at the end of World War I, "We are stormin
the gates of heaven!" But then, the workers in the West di
not seize power, confusion and fascism came, and, mor
recently—this is the gentle apocalypse of the labor move
ment—the changes in the manpower structure of Wester
society have begun to reduce the absolute and relative num
ber of direct producers. It is now possible to think of
cybernated age that will dispense to a large degree with th
blue-collar men on the assembly line, with clerks, and eve
middle-level executives.

Yet, at the same time that the political will of socialism
seemed to falter, the basic argument which had originall
inspired the movement grew in force. The means of pro
duction, the nineteenth-century socialists had asserted, ar
social in character, increasingly interdependent, and becom
ing collective in fact if not in law. But the ownership, man

gement, and guidance of them (and from the point of view of this theory, it makes no difference which of the three preceding terms one chooses to emphasize) remain private. In order to direct this technology humanely, it is necessary to place it under democratic social control. This thesis grows more apt every day. Thus, at that point at which the socialist vision has become all the more compelling, the number of people who take it with political seriousness in the West seems to have declined.

One element in this socialist crisis has implications for the very concept of economics and society itself. The change in the manpower structure of the West, the recent shift (mainly in America) from mass production by men to mass production by machines, threatens some of the culture's most cherished economic, psychological, and ethical assumptions. Immemorially, it has been assumed that economics is concerned with being economical—with the use of scarce resources. It is this premise which has motivated the Western obsession with efficiency. Now, this conventional wisdom, as John Kenneth Galbraith has called it, is less and less descriptive of a society which has the potential to produce more with fewer workers.

Every President of the United States since Harry Truman has proclaimed that it is the duty of the citizen to consume. The statement is usually made in the course of creating the details of economic policy, yet it is fraught with the most important ethical and psychological implications.

Another related crisis is that of democracy. In the nineteenth century, it was thought that the growth in social wealth and literacy would produce a more democratic population with a higher set of values. However, a series of recent analyses have suggested another denouement: that as a result of these changes, the West has created a new kind of mass society in which education and an increased standard of living have the effect of pulling culture down to the lowest common denominator. And there are now those who look back nostalgically to idealized days of aristocracy.

The character of contemporary technology seems to reinforce this antidemocratic trend in modern life. Part of the manpower revolution is the division of the society into the highly skilled and the highly unskilled. With so much economic, political, and social power concentrating in computerized industry, the question arises, who will do the programming? Who will control the machines that establish human destiny in this century? And there is clearly the possibility that a technological elite, perhaps even a benevolent elite, could take on this function.

Profound shifts like these cannot, of course, be confined to the economic and political sphere. Up until the twentieth century, religion had spoken to men who were haunted by plague, famine, and natural disaster. Within the last hundred years, large portions of these traditional domains of God have been mastered by science. It is difficult to pray for rain when the meteorologists can predict it and, in some cases, even precipitate it. So the question arises, where does God live now? With man more and more ubiquitous, with nature transformed from a mysterious given into a product of the human will, divinity is in crisis.

But the confusion of the religionists has not resulted in the triumph of the atheists. In the old calculus of godlessness, the irrationality of religion had been imposed upon man because of his impotence in the face of the world. Once the external environment was understood, man would no longer require the solace of an imagined God. Yet, it has been characteristic of the accidental revolution that the more the various aspects of society have become rationalized, the more the totality of society seems to be inexplicable. If the awesomeness of the world that God was once said to have created has declined, the opacity of the world that man has made has increased. And this new mystery is all the more bewildering since it cannot be blamed on, or justified by, the supernatural.

One could go on listing crises almost indefinitely, yet the main point should be clear by now. The chasm between technological capacity and economic, political, social, and religious consciousness—the accidental revolution, in short—has unsettled every faith and creed in the West. This has led many people to a sense of decadence. The theories that express this mood relate to every aspect of human life. They embrace psychology, religion, ethics, and art, and there are important things to be seen from each of these specific vantage points. But in a complex way, the accidental revolution is party to every one of these developments.

The result of this process, the summary paradox, is that these most conscious and man-made of times have lurched into the unprecedented transformation of human life without thinking about it. And in a sense, this century, this scientific, technological, and utterly competent century, has happened accidentally.

In the description of decadence and the accidental century that follows, I have made no attempt to be neutral. In an age such as this, when change is epidemic, the present does not hold still long enough to be studied with archeological objectivity. Today is always partly tomorrow and can only be understood in movement, futuristically, speculatively. So let me state my bias openly. The hope for the survival and fulfillment of the Western concept of man demands that the accidental revolution be made conscious and democratic. And to argue this requires a restatement—or, perhaps, to borrow a word from Pope John XXIII, an *aggiornamento*—of the socialist ideal and the socialist possibility.

2

Images of Disorder

". . . It is the time when uprightly and in pious sober wise, naught of work is to be wrought and art grown unpossible without the divel's help and fires of hell under the cauldron. . . . Yea, verily, dear mates that art is stuck and grown too heavy and scorneth itself and God's poor man knoweth no longer where to turn in his sore plight, that is belike the fault of the times. . . ."

DOCTOR FAUSTUS

Thomas Mann belonged to the Devil's Party.

This is not primarily because he made Satan the last theologian of an unbelieving age in *Doctor Faustus*. Neither is it simply another way of saying that he participated in the rediscovery of the irrational and demoniac which took place in the arts and politics of the twentieth century. Rather, it is that Mann, like Shelley's Milton, could not join the side of the angels even when he tried to do so. Darkness and disintegration were his flesh-and-blood fact; hope was his abstract wish.

In this, Mann was typical of many of the most significant writers of the century: the Devil's Party is a major camp of modern genius. It is composed of those who could give aesthetic form to chaos, but not to order. It is found in the breakdown of narrative time as in Joyce, in the battle of memory against death in Proust, in Kafka's agnostic theology.

The Devil's Party arose because more things fell apart in the last half-century than were put together.

Of all the great writers of the Devil's Party, Mann is the most relevant to a study of the contemporary decadence. He lived through all the unnerving transitions of the period: the turn of the century, World War I, the stultification of the German middle class, the rise of fascism, World War II, and the Cold War. Not only did he write of these incredible times; the times wrote his life as if it were one of his novels. In his tempestuous fusion of autobiography and art, the inability of a culture to understand its own revolution becomes personal and evocative.

Mann was dragged protesting into the twentieth century. In his native Lübeck, corporate efficiency shattered the patriarchal calm of merchant society. Mann took flight from progress, finding refuge in a resigned, ironic aestheticism. But then World War I made him a militant reactionary, and the peace moved him to the left of the Center. World War II forced him to go back, savagely and tenderly, to his youth and to try to find there the source of a national tragedy. He died undecided, hesitating between a desperate optimism and a weary pessimism.

Thus, every one of Mann's major works is a product of, and an insight into, an upheaval. He was, it has been remarked, a seismograph, delicately measuring the quaking earth of his century. It is in this guise that he is seen here. This is not to read his genius as a document in social statistics. His images of disorder—a water fight, an *omelette-*

en-surprise, a poisoned butterfly—are too haunting for that. Rather it is that his life and work are typical of the contemporary decadence in everything but their profundity.

Wars and revolutions provoked Mann to greatness, yet he was a failure in his own terms. Against his will and after he was forty, he was driven out of contemplation into the knowledge that his individual plight required a social solution. Still, his deepest affirmations were passing and private. Even when political involvement made him seem committed and positive, his imagination and emotions continued to subvert his own convictions. Like most of the great artists of his age, he was more at home with disintegration than with hope. He was of the Devil's Party.

For Mann, the bursting, shattering times in which he lived finally seemed a decadence. In the counterpoint of his fact and fiction, one discovers why, and the symbol maker is seen as the symbol of a generation.

I

If Thomas Mann had died before August, 1914, he would have been a particularly brilliant representative of a sensitive, selfish minority that was stranded by the twentieth century. The children of capitalist individualism, they were overwhelmed by the triumph of the capitalist corporation. They sought to disaffiliate from the technological and economic revolution their fathers had unwittingly begun. And since they were victimized by a success rather than by a failure, they gave a most paradoxical definition of Western decline. They protested against a dynamic decadence.

Thomas Mann dramatized this experience in a water fight.

Hanno Buddenbrooks, the last, sickly member of his house, is swimming:

He stood with his girlish arms up to the middle in the turbid water of the pool. . . . They, sure of their prey, came on with long splashing strides. They had muscular arms, those two young Hagenströms.

The Buddenbrooks family, once sturdy and respected leaders of the merchant oligarchy, have been crushed by modern, efficient competition. All that is left to them is a spindly, musical child (typically, for Mann, their economic and spiritual failure expresses itself in the very body of their heir). Now they are the prey of the Hagenströms who have adapted to the new business methods. The unequal water fight is between two versions of society.

Like Hanno Buddenbrooks, Mann came from a merchant family whose firm had defaulted shortly after its centenary. His world, as he later described it, was "socially speaking that of the patriarchal Burgher, spiritually speaking that of the individualistic Protestant subjectivity." * Its collapse led to the dark definitions of the water fight. The new social reality, like the Hagenströms, is muscular, predatory, and amoral. The artist, incarnated in Hanno, is sickness, spirit, failure, and sensitivity, a gifted survival of the older times. This knowledge is proud, since Hanno is a musician, Mann a novelist, and the Hagenströms could be neither. But it is wistful, too, since the outcome of the water fight is never in doubt.

* Throughout Mann's writing, one encounters the German word *Burger*. It does not mean bourgeois, indeed it is antithetical to that term. It defines the North German merchant oligarchy, the old-fashioned and religious tradition of the entrepreneur, as opposed to the latter-day capitalist. It is translated in this book as Burgher.

Mann's tension between artist and society, his conflict of spirit and matter, was not new. At the very beginning of the industrial system, poets and novelists had protested against its crassness and yearned for the earlier times in which they thought the artist had dignity. Yet these rebels —Blake, Keats, Hugo, Heine—were in active opposition. They participated in the very dynamism of the process they deplored.

But for Mann, and those of his generation who shared his mood, there was weariness, fatalism. They were alienated, not from a social revolution, but from a social maturity. As Mann himself described the process: "This is the way of the German Burgher: from revolution to pessimism, to a re-signed, power-protected innerness." Actually, the itinerary was not quite so inevitable. Mann's brother, Heinrich, hero-ized Zola, Ibsen, and Tolstoy, turning from the merchant past to the republican future. But for Mann and those like him in Germany, the household gods of disillusionment were Nietzsche and Schopenhauer. These thinkers were the companions of their interior exile.

But how can one defend the sober virtues of Protestant individualism by disaffiliating from the world? What makes the child of merchants the champion of a sickly musician?

This problem was evident in the way that Mann picked and chose the Nietzsche who was to influence him (in this century, almost everyone has his own, private Nietzsche). He was not at all concerned with the activist side of the philosopher, with the partisan of the future and the prophet of the *Übermensch* who predicted that the chaos would give birth to a star. He was fascinated by Nietzsche as the "psy-chologist of decadence." For Mann, the shattering of the

oligarchic society occasioned sadness, not anger, and the
turn of the century was filled with "the ethical air, the
Faustian flavor, Cross, Death and Grave."

With Schopenhauer, Mann's equivocation was not in the
interpretation of the master. Schopenhauer's theories were
a sort of metaphysical version of the water fight between
Hanno and the Hagenströms. But here, the difficulty for
Mann was even more profound. In the name of entrepreneurs he had been turned into a mystic.

Schopenhauer's world is essentially dark. The philosopher
describes it as an "enigmatic force and energy," a place
"where hope is never satisfied or extinguished." Reality is
not reasonable, it is will, it is muscular like the Hagenströms.
As a consequence the thinking man can never master it. Reason is the recognition of this fundamental irrationality, it is
as helpless as Hanno. Once man understands that he is caught
up in a blind energy, he transcends it. There is light in the
darkness.

Like Mann, Thomas Buddenbrooks discovered Schopenhauer; like Mann, he was both attracted and repelled by the
experience. It was Thomas Buddenbrooks' misfortune to
preside over the beginning of his house's failure. In the midst
of the turmoil, he comes across a volume by Schopenhauer.
For a moment, "the alternating of light and darkness held
him." (This Schopenhauer image was to obsess Mann all his
life.) Buddenbrooks even accepted his own death, finding
release in the act of resignation. But the mood passes and
Thomas Buddenbrooks thinks of Schopenhauer's philosophy: ". . . it is too much for my sense of being a Burgher."
He never looks at the book again.

This is the first of Mann's flawed affirmations. In the de-

fense of the old values he, like Thomas Buddenbrooks, had
been driven to contemplation. But then, withdrawal was as
much a denial of the ancient merchant verities as an up-to-
date corporation. As a result there was a feeling of guilt and
uncertainty in Mann's first reaction to catastrophe. On the
one hand, he stood for the traditional truths, and the Hagenströms were efficient decadents. But, on the other hand, his
hopeless, nostalgic commitment to the ethics of the past had
transformed him into their very opposite: an uprooted
artist. He detested the Hagenströms for their amorality; he
secretly admired them for their success.

It was this ambivalence that provided Mann with his fundamental literary pathos until 1914. His stories focused on
outcasts, cripples, fanatics, artists, Hanno in a dozen cos-
tumes. And yet, Tonio Kröger, the *"bourgeois manqué,"*
knew in his isolation that ". . . it is the normal, respectable
and admirable that is the kingdom of our longing; life in all
of its seductive banality." More tragically symbolic of this
conflict, Gustave Aschenbach, "the poet spokesman of all
those who labor at the end of exhaustion," pursued the
beauty of a young boy in Venice to the point of his own
death. The *bourgeois manqué* becomes, in effect, a suicide.

In August, 1914, Mann's pessimism, like every other ideology in the Western world, took a sudden turn. The essential analysis remained as nostalgic as ever, but its practical
conclusion changed from ironic withdrawal to belligerent
militance. The water fight had become World War I, and
the values for which Hanno Buddenbrooks had stood were
transferred to the German Army.

Mann now proposed to hold back the future by force of
arms.

Until the war, Mann's definitions were personal, even social, but never political. To be an artist was to choose values, to stand for a defeated morality in an amoral world. It was also a fate, the product of an evolution that had sundered the old Protestant-merchant unity of righteousness and power. But the refugees of sensitivity who emerged from this process were, like Mann, spectators in an unfriendly century, not participants. Politics would have been a betrayal of their only consolation, their "innerness."

Then with World War I, Mann learned that he could not hide from contemporary history, even inside himself. In a sense, his prewar alienation had been comfortable and his tragedy satisfying. He had been something like his master, Schopenhauer, who had argued for suicide while eating at a lavish table. Now, his pessimism became the practical principle of the world outside. Not simply Lübeck, but Europe itself, was breaking down.

Under the pressure of crisis, the ideals for which Hanno Buddenbrooks had pathetically struggled were projected as the war aims of the German nation. The enemy was no longer the Hagenströms within, but the Hagenströms from without: France, England, and, later, America. The verities were still music, spirit, and Protestant piety, only now they were incarnated in the Kaiser's troops rather than in a sickly child.

In his book of World War I essays, *The Observations of an Unpolitical*, Mann announced, "The difference between spirit and politics is contained in the contrast of culture and civilization." Germany was culture, music rather than literature, the organic community of the folk. The Allies were politics, civilization, logic rather than life, the rootless masses of the great cities. Something like this distinction had been implicit in *Buddenbrooks*, but there it was parochial and North German. Now, Mann made it an explanation of the entire world and, by way of patriotism, entered into one of the central traditions of contemporary cultural despair.

Throughout the nineteenth century, there was a conservative existentialism which protested against the rationalization of life in a machine society. In England, Burke was one of its figures, in France, Baudelaire. But in Germany, industrialism was both late in coming and extraordinarily rapid once it arrived. There seemed to be no possibility of resistance, and the conservative protest acquired a distinctive quality: fatalism.

In the 1880's, Ferdinand Tönnies expressed this mood when he developed one of the most important contrasts in modern German, and even Western intellectual, history. He distinguished *Gemeinschaft*, community, from *Gesellschaft*, society (the thought could be traced back in Germany to Paul de Lagarde-Boetticher, who had posed a similar antithesis as early as 1853). In the community, "that which binds men together is seen as a real and organic life," in society, "as an ideal and mechanical formulation." Community is vital and natural, society an artificial construct. Community, Tönnies concluded with seminal fatalism, inevitably degenerates into society, and the harbinger of decline was the great city, the center of the antifolk.

Germany produced the most doom-laden statement of this theory, yet its corollaries and analogues appeared throughout the West at the turn of the century. There was a generalized reaction against the mechanistic ideologies of the nineteenth century and the machine civilization that had given rise to them. In France, there was Bergson and his *élan vital*, in England, Pierrot and *fin de siècle*, in the United States the wry but predictably more optimistic pragmatism of William James. Mann took up the German and fatalistic variant in his opposition of "culture and civilization."

In Mann's World War I patriotic polemics, this distinction is used to attack democracy (which counts heads rather than divining the incalculable will of the folk community), French rationalism, American efficiency. As a result of this analysis, he became more and more sympathetic to the Russians, even though they were enemies, and in particular to Dostoevsky and his equation of Roman Empire, Catholic Church, and socialism. He exalted music as against literature, spirit as against reason.

The Bohemian had become a militant conservative. Toward the end of his life, Mann looked back and spoke of "a close relationship which we have every reason to ponder: that of aestheticism and barbarism." He was talking about what could have happened to himself. For this theory of decadence which led Mann from the fringes of society to its Right Wing was to lead others far beyond, into fascism itself.

Before 1914, the distinction between community and society could minister in a genteel way to the mercantile, old-fashioned critics of the new capitalism. It allowed them a certain aristocracy, an identification with art and spirit as against the corporation and power. Then, under the pressure of the war, this theme became a rallying cry of the conservatives, a critique of the democratic pretenses of the Allies. But as the crisis deepened in the inflations and depressions of the peace, the irrationalist, antidemocratic thesis became a powerful weapon for attacking the breakdown of postwar capitalist economic rationality. So it was that in 1934, Alfred Rosenberg told Hitler at a Nazi conference, "You, mein Führer, have rescued from oblivion the works of Nietzsche, Wagner, Lagarde and Dühring—works which foretold the doom of the old culture."

Aestheticism had turned to barbarism, a sensitive, nostalgic theory of decadence had, under the revolutionary conditions of the time, helped promote a brutal, armed decadence. Hanno Buddenbrooks had become the Kaiser; and the Kaiser had become Hitler.

Thomas Mann, to his eternal credit, refused this terrible logic. By the time it had arrived at its monstrous conclusion, he had turned upon the theories of his early years. But at the end of World War I, his course was not so clear, for his world was in shambles. "One must become contemplative," he wrote at that time, "read and understand Spengler, and realize that the English-American victory is the civilizing, utilitarianizing and rationalizing of the West." Mann had left contemplation to take up politics, and within five short years he had been driven to the contemplative fatalism of Oswald Spengler and the *Decline of the West*. But the times had by no means exhausted its surprises, for Mann or for anyone else.

II

History literally played a joke upon *The Magic Mountain*. It took a book which had been intended as a brief comedy and turned it into a massive tragedy without an ending.

The Magic Mountain was first conceived in the comfortable prewar days. In 1912, Mann accompanied his sick wife to a sanitarium at Davos. Out of the experience he decided to write a "satyr play" on the world of cosmopolitan tuberculars. As he then imagined his project, "A simpleminded hero, a droll conflict between macabre adventure and bourgeois sense of duty—the outcome was not decided but would surely be found. And the whole would be easy and amusing and not take much space."

The outcome was not found; history would not allow it. The war transformed the "droll conflict" into a somber meditation on human destiny. The "incalculable subversions" of the peace, as Mann called them, thrust him into the midst of a chaos which he could render but not master. At the novel's end, the hero simply disappears. And throughout, the affirmations are few and uncertain, the meanings ambiguous, the issues carefully, even schematically, posed and then left unresolved. The times, in Mann's own phrase, had "palsied" his imagination.

Looking back upon *The Magic Mountain*, Mann described it as "an ideological challenge to many cherished things, a withdrawal from dangerous sympathies, enchantments and temptations—a farewell address and an attempt at self-discipline." The "farewell address" was a rejection of the past, not a proclamation of the future. That is why it is constructed out of doubts rather than affirmations. That is why it has no real ending. It was as if Mann, caught in the spiritual desolation of the peace, had decided to fabricate, carefully and beautifully, a ruin.

And yet, these irresolute symbols were a striking act of realism. Precisely because of its utter fidelity to the confusion that gave it birth—a bewilderment that was part of history and not simply a failure of the author's person—*The*

Magic Mountain became one of the richest and most revealing works of its time.

Thus, *The Magic Mountain* is a work of anguished agnosticism. Everything is in question, for everything is its opposite. In *Buddenbrooks,* decline was sickness, power was health, and if reality was sad at least it was straightforward. Now catastrophe is so total that even nature is a liar. Arriving at the sanitarium, Hans Castorp thinks that his cousin Joachim "looks as if" he had just come back from maneuvers. Actually, he is sick unto death. When Castorp's mother dies, the moment first seemed to be a fit of laughter.

Dr. Krokowski generalizes the theme. Hans, on arrival, claims that he is perfectly healthy. The doctor replies, "Then you are phenomenon worthy of study. I, for one, have never in my life come across a perfectly healthy being." And Hofrat Behrens explains the paradoxical theory behind the clinic. The air on the Magic Mountain helps the disease it is supposed to cure: "it begins by speeding it up, in that it revolutionizes the whole body; it brings the latent weakness to the surface and makes it break out."

Such contradictions obsess this novel. The X ray reveals a rounded arm: it is "like a pale and misty envelope, within which there stood out the sharp clear nucleus—the skeleton." Even the coming of warm air is but a disguise for frost like "an *omelette-en-surprise* holding an ice within the hot froth of the beaten egg." In short, the entire world has become a sort of dialectical nightmare. There are no more certitudes.

These lies of nature and the weather are related to an even more puzzling malignancy: that man has been sickened by history.

The novelist, speaking in his narrator's voice, describes

the plight of people like Hans Castorp: "Now if the life about him, if his own time seem, however outwardly stimulating, to be at bottom empty of such food for his aspirations; if he privately recognizes it to be hopeless, viewless, opposing only a hollow silence to all the questions man puts; . . . then in such a case a certain laming of the personality is bound to occur, the more inevitably the more upright the character in question; a sort of palsy, as it were, which may even extend from his spiritual and moral over into his physical and organic part."

This definition of the disease of history is part of the farewell address, for in it Mann takes leave of the nineteenth-century Romantic theory of the artist. In his old view, sickness was something aristocratic, a sign of genius, a mark of the sensitive few. Now, it is an infection of society and of the times themselves. Mann has moved from the poetic suicide of Gustave Aschenbach in *Death in Venice* to the sufferings of an engineer. And Hans Castorp is, at times at least, an anti-Romantic. He thinks of the ending of *Aïda:* "What was it, considered with the eye of reason, that was happening here? Two human beings, buried alive, their lungs filled with pit gas."

Two other characters, Settembrini and Naphta, also demonstrate how history took Mann by the scruff of his neck.

Throughout the *Observations*, the "Civilizations-Literat" appears as a traitorous enemy and a figure of scorn. As Mann describes him, he is "the man of the spirit, of the pure and beautiful, radical and literary spirit; he is thereby the man of words, of the pure and beautiful, the radical and literary words . . ." In real life, the Civilizations-Literat was Mann's Francophile, leftist brother, Heinrich. In fiction, he was immortalized as Settembrini.

But toward the end of the *Observations*, the focus of derision changes from the Civilizations-Literat to a new enemy: the Gothic man. He appears at the moment when Mann fatalistically realizes that "the five hundred year epoch of Burgher tolerance is coming to an end." The gravedigger of the cherished society is the Gothic man. Where the Burgher had been a "tolerant, doubting, individualistic person," the Gothic man is "the man of the new intolerance, the new anti-humanity of the spirit, the new closedness and determination, of belief in belief; he is the fanatic man."

To Mann's Protestant mind, this fanaticism was bound up with the pre-Burgher authoritarianism of the Catholic Church. To his literary mind, as influenced by Dostoevsky, there is a connection between Roman Catholicism and revolutionary socialism, both seeking an imperium, a new Rome. This is the context of the curious fact that Naphta in *The Magic Mountain* is both a Jesuit and a partisan of a mystical dictatorship of the proletariat.

On balance, Mann's novel prefers Settembrini to Naphta. This in itself is a sign of how his concern was shifting from the prewar enemy, the rationalist and humanist, to the postwar danger, the totalitarian fanatic. And yet, even though Settembrini is somewhat sympathetic and Naphta a suicide, the old humanist remains a figure of gentle derision. His verbose good intentions are simply not equal to the mysteries of life and death one encounters on the mountain. Mann had defined a new enemy—but he had not found an effective opponent for him.

And this ambiguity is related to the strange fate of the various theories incarnated in this book. None of them works.

Hans Castorp stays at the sanitarium for years, and there is no sign that he is any better. He leaves when the war starts, and there is no sign that he is any worse. The liberal rationalist, Settembrini, is for a society of health through social reform, yet he remains a bumbling figure who omits the *élan* of life from his calculations. Naphta embraces the irrationalities which Settembrini ignores, but he is a fanatic, Gothic man, and his prescriptions for living lead him to suicide. The doctors, Behrens and Krokowski, think of disease in terms of great sophistication, and still they cure no one (or rather, their successes are accidental). Even spiritualism is considered as a possible answer (and Mann himself was in the early twenties involved with spiritualists). A seance is taken quite seriously, but it reveals, like the X-ray machine with which it is compared, death in the midst of life.

In such a world, how does one affirm? Settembrini's liberalism, Naphta's religious dictatorship of the proletariat, the theories of the doctors, these all fail. Hans's love affair with Clavdia is abortive. The decaying figure of Mynheer Peeperkorn is a powerful presence, but he can hardly speak and, like Naphta, kills himself. Thus, Mann's corrosive agnosticism leads him to question and destroy the past, but it cannot achieve a real hope of redemption.

Yet on two occasions, Mann seeks an affirmation. Each time it is like the experience of Thomas Buddenbrooks and his discovery of Schopenhauer. There is a momentary feeling of exaltation and acceptance, but it passes.

In the first attempt at yea-saying, Castorp is studying biology and asks himself the huge question, "What then was life?" He answers by a series of ingenious paradoxes: life is "a form building (made possible by the over-balancing of its instability, yet controlled by the laws of growth inherent within it) of something brewed out of water, albumen, salt and fats which was called flesh, and which became form, beauty, a lofty image, and yet all the time the essence of sensuality and desire."

Toward the end of his meditation, Castorp projects his bewilderment into the very center of being. "Life itself? Was it perhaps only an infection, a sickening of matter? Wasn't that which one might call the original procreation of matter only a disease, a growth produced by morbid stimulation of the immaterial?" Finally, Castorp is exhausted by his own speculation and falls asleep. And life, in the mythic guise of a woman, comes and kisses him.

This symbolic conclusion resolves nothing. The woman is Mann's agnosticism made mysterious, the personification of the world as will, of life as an unknowable, but undeniable, fact. But the very structure of the symbol betrays its basic weakness. Mann has a wraith incarnate flesh and blood; his woman is as insubstantial as Milton's God.

The second attempt at affirmation is more explicit. Lost in the snow, Hans has a vision. First he states the terrible discovery which Mann, and Europe, made during the First World War: "I have dreamed of man's state, of his courteous and enlightened state; behind which, in the temple, the horrible blood sacrifice was consummated." And then, he goes on to fashion a synthesis:

"Disease, health! Spirit, nature! Are these contradictions? I ask, are they problems? No, they are not problems and neither is the problem of their aristocracy. The recklessness of death is in life, it would not be life without it—and in the center is *Homo dei* between recklessness and reason, as his state is between mystic community and individualism . . . In this state, he must live gallantly, associate in friendly reverence with himself, for only he is aristocratic and the counterpositions are not at all." And finally, "For the sake of goodness and love, man shall let death have no sovereignty over his thoughts."

Mann has to make this affirmation momentary. He himself has described the crisis as social, with man sickened by history. Yet, his hero can reach no higher than an individual act of courage: man must "live gallantly." His vision reasserts the prewar ethic of the few, the mystic, resigned few, in a postwar world where, by Mann's own definition of Castorp, it is utterly inadequate. Thomas Buddenbrooks' revelation was fitful because it was too much truth for his Burgher spirit; and Hans's realization is passing because it is not enough truth for the post-Burgher upheaval.

So it is that *The Magic Mountain* has no ending. World War I comes, Hans leaves the sanitarium, and, in the middle of a battle scene, "in the tumult, in the rain, in the dusk, vanishes out of our sight." And the novel itself concludes, not with a statement, but with a question: "Out of this universal feast of death, out of this extremity of fever, kindling the rain-washed evening sky to a fiery glow, may it be that Love one day shall mount?"

Thus, the farewell address trails off in an unresolved ambiguity. Hans Castorp had come to the sanitarium for a brief visit; he stayed for years as a patient; he left to go to war and it is not known whether he is cured or not; he vanishes. And the same plot line applies to Hans Castorp's author. He came to the Magic Mountain as a visitor, to write a "droll conflict"; he stayed with the book for years, a patient infected by history; and he leaves it not knowing whether he has cured himself or not. Only Mann, unlike a fictional hero, could not simply vanish in the rain.

Yet, with all of these marvelous irresolutions, *The Magic Mountain* goes as deep as any novel of its period. Perhaps its most radical aspect, its insight on the history of the war and the peace, is that its hero is ordinary. It had been easy, and romantic, enough to describe the alienation of the exceptional few from the vulgar and healthy majority. That was a tame, posturing theory of decadence which could serve to symbolize the idyllic tragedies of prewar Europe. But now, no one was whole, neither Hanno Buddenbrooks nor the Hagenströms. Decadence was felt, not as a personal fate, but as the human condition.

III

Between the two wars, Mann adopted his strangest literary and political position: hope.

At first, his reversal took the modest form prefigured in *The Magic Mountain* and his correspondence of the early twenties. The most fanatic enemy of the old values was no longer the reformer, the Civilizations-Literat. Now it was the fascist, the new Gothic man, and Mann united with his old liberal enemy in the face of the danger. As the crisis deepened, his transformation became more complete. Immediately before Hitler's rise to power, Mann, who had once found the efficient capitalism of the Hagenströms a menace, was advocating united action with the Social Democrats. A few years later, he was drawn into the Popular Front and even adopted a socialist rhetoric, a belief that man's conscious and rational activity could create a just society. He was now to the left of his old foe, the Civiliza-tions-Literat.

By 1932, Mann had changed so much that, in effect, he launched an attack upon his own youthful convictions. "The Burgher is lost," he wrote, and will lose touch with "the new or coming world if he cannot bring himself to part from the life-destroying, easy-going ideologies which still condition him . . ." What were these ideologies? In part they were a "decadent and provincial soulfulness," i.e., the point of view of Buddenbrooks and almost everything Mann wrote until 1914. The new world is inevitable, and it will be "the social world, the organized, planned and unified world . . ."

It was in this period that Mann wrote *Joseph and His Brothers*, his "humorous song of mankind," a work which lies outside the bounds of this analysis (except to note that, with all its psychological and anthropological complexity, the God of the Old Testament is a sort of New Dealer, advising compensatory government action to deal with crisis: the grain is stored in the good years and dispensed in the lean times). But, as it turned out, Mann's new hope failed to prevent the rise of fascism and World War II.

So there was a new cataclysm, and it summoned up Mann's strangest hero: a madman.

IV

The protagonist of *Doctor Faustus*, Adrian Leverkühn, makes a pact with the Devil, willfully contracts syphilis with a prostitute, and finally goes utterly mad. On the sim-plest level, the novel can be read as a political allegory on the fate of German culture. The story is told in flashbacks from the midst of World War II. Leverkühn's ultimate collapse is recounted at the same time that Nazism is going up in flames. The narrator, Serenus Zeitblom, is a Catholic who lays a particular stress upon the most Gothic-Protestant and apocalyptic aspect of the German past. There are descriptions of the salon irrationalism of the twenties which contributed to the rise of Hitler (once more, the link between aestheticism and barbarism).

Given such a reading of *Doctor Faustus*, one would agree with the communist critic, Georg Lukacs, that Mann is here tracing the terrible political consequences of the "power-protected innerness" he himself had lived in his earlier years. In this perspective, *Faustus* would appear as a direct continuation of Mann's Popular Front activity, as a powerful, symbolic work of antifascism.

And yet: Thomas Mann declared that he was more sympathetic with Adrian Leverkühn than with any of his heroes.

He even went further. "Leverkühn is, so to speak, an ideal type, a 'hero of our times,' a man who bear the sufferings of an epoch." And the book is not simply an attempt to deal with Nazism, but nothing less than an expression of "the situation of art, of culture, yes, of man, in this utterly decisive epoch of ours."

How does a mad composer, ravaged with disease and in a pact with the Devil, become "a man who bears the sufferings of the epoch"? Any answer, clearly, must involve a most extreme, despairing definition of an epoch and its sufferings which can be ideally incarnated in an insane genius.

Leverkühn is, of course, a victim of his century. Where history infected Hans Castorp, it drove the musician mad. Yet that would not qualify the latter for Mann's sympathetic identification. It would justify the detached compassion that Castorp received from Mann, but little else. And indeed, the author's involvement with his insane protagonist goes much deeper than a concern for a casualty of historical determination. There is a sense in which Adrian Leverkühn is Thomas Mann.

In *Buddenbrooks*, the world was sad, and art was a refuge from it. By the time of *The Magic Mountain*, the world had become a dialectical nightmare, and it was impossible to know whether it was sad or not. In *Faustus*, the world is so mad that madness is the only sensible reaction to it.

The old definition of decadence as the triumph of society over community, of *Gesellschaft* over *Gemeinschaft*, returns in tragic form to define the situation. As a young man, Leverkühn had learned a distinction between cult and culture from his first mentor, Kretschmar. In the period of cult, art is in the service of God and religion; in the time of culture, it has become an end in itself. It must find a new dedication.

"But there is no other alternative to culture," Leverkühn's friend Zeitblom remarks, "but barbarism." And Leverkühn answers, "Barbarism is only the contrary of culture within a system of values determined by culture itself." And, a little later, "It will become necessary for us to become much more barbaric if we are once again to be capable of culture. Technique and comfort. With these one *speaks* of culture, but one does not have it." The rest of Leverkühn's artistic life is a development of this tactic of seeking culture by way of barbarism. His compositions are filled with parody and irony, his human voices sound like musical instruments, his instruments like a chorus of men and women.

In the world which believed in God, Leverkühn demonstrates, music could be the subjective expression of a harmony which was believed to exist outside of man. But in a completely secular world, devoid of transcendence and filled with war and upheaval, what ground is there for harmony? Conventional beauty is a lie, the artist is faced with unrelieved chaos, the dark spirits are a daily experience, the Diety is not. Then art must be pre-God—or, which is the same thing, post-God,—for all the assumptions of Beethoven's *Ninth Symphony* and Western culture have been destroyed. The aesthetic is made out of ugliness, if it is serious, since ugliness is all that remains. And to make sense out of the mad world, it is necessary to traffic with insanity.

Mann mediates this desperate view of art and life through the symbol of a butterfly.

Early in the novel, Leverkühn and Zeitblom receive a lesson in the cunning of nature. There is a butterfly, Hetæra Esmeralda, which is diaphanous and which survives because, in flight, it seems to be a petal in the wind. Other related species mimic leaves even to their imperfections. And finally, out of this development, there emerges a pair of butterflies: one is poisonous and proclaims the fact by flying slowly and being beautifully visible; the second copies the markings and speed of the first but is not poisonous.

Each butterfly strategy involves adapting to a terrible environment in order to survive in it.

When Adrian Leverkühn sleeps with a prostitute he knows to be syphilitic (for this is now the savage image of how spirit couples with matter), her name is Esmeralda. After that, the composer builds all of his musical compositions around the letters that spell Hetæra Esmeralda, the butterfly-prostitute. In his final, mad speech, Leverkühn once again conjures up the butterfly and the prostitute as the very image of his pact with darkness.

"Esmeralda" is the final, tragic unity of the opposition of spirit and matter, community and society (here cult and culture) that Mann first discovered in Lübeck. Until the First World War, the tactic of the alienated spirit was aloofness. With *The Magic Mountain*, Mann began to realize that he could not flee into any refuge. Now, from the shambles of World War II, art's penetration of reality has become a sought-after infection rather than a fate like Hanno Buddenbrooks' sickness. Beauty is the intercourse of a composer and a diseased prostitute, of the human spirit and a world which is sick at its very core. But more than that, like the butterfly Esmeralda, spirit must mimic its terrible environment in order to survive, or else announce its disease. Madness is the strategy against a mad history.

And yet, Mann attempts an affirmation. As with Thomas Buddenbrooks' and his Schopenhauer or Hans Castorp in the snow, it is a passing moment. He describes the *Lamentations*, the last, utterly negative work of Adrian Leverkühn:

Here towards the end I find that the utmost accents of mourning are reached. . . . One group of instruments after another retires, and what remains, as the work fades on the air, is the high G of a cello, the last word, the last fainting sound. Then nothing more: silence and night. But that tone which vibrates in the silence, which is no longer there, to which only the spirit harkens, and which was the voice of mourning, is so no more. It changes in meaning; it abides as a light in the night.

This is Schopenhauer set to imaginary music: the terrible, inexplicable world of tragic will is transcended precisely because it is accepted in all of its irrationality. But, as in *Buddenbrooks* and *The Magic Mountain*, the instant of optimism vanishes quickly. There follows, not a "light in the night," but a scene of madness. It is the summary of Adrian's view of art and man in the twentieth century with which this chapter began. And it is worth restating, now that its import has been placed within its context:

It is the time when uprightly and in pious sober wise, naught of work is to be wrought and art grown unpossible without the divel's help and fires of hell under the cauldron. . . . Yea, verily, dear mates that art is stuck and grown too heavy and scorneth itself and God's poor man knoweth no longer where to turn in his sore plight, that is belike the fault of the times. . . .

This is not Mann's last book, but it is his most extreme statement of what he sees as the contemporary decadence. The distance between this cry of Adrian Leverkühn's and Tonio Kröger (which is to say, the younger Mann) is four decades of upheaval. In that period, time has made a full, and devastating, circle, destroying not only the old community but the new society which was its adversary. Nothing reasonable is left, not even the familiarity of one's enemies.

Tonio Kröger had led a life that "some people rightly considered . . . one of the signs of decay." His voyage, compared to Leverkühn's, was a pleasure trip. Alienated and isolated, he was near enough to the commonplace to yearn for "the normal, respectable and admirable that is the kingdom of our longing." In him, and in Mann's first world view, decadence was more poignant than anything else.

In between Tonio Kröger and Adrian Leverkühn, Mann
saw ordinary engineers infected with the illness that once
had belonged to the chosen few, yet still there was hope
that love would follow upon the fever. In *Faustus*, even that
tentative optimism is denied. The time of cult (community)
in which art and man served God is gone, but then that
was true from *Buddenbrooks* on. But the triumph of society,
of the Hagenströms, when art and man were to serve themselves, has proved an illusion as well.

At least the old foes were part of a rational, if sad, opposition. Now they explain nothing, for they are victims too,
Of the ancient world of Lübeck, there remains not even
the victory of its destroyers. And the only response to such
chaos is a sophisticated barbarism, art coupling with the
diseased, prostituted reality, infecting itself.

Thus, even though *Doctor Faustus* narrates, and even ana-
lyzes, the rise of fascism, that is not the main point. (After
the Second World War, some of Mann's German critics
attacked him on the grounds that his early writings had prepared the way for the political tragedy described in his
book, and that he therefore had no right to indict fascism!)
The breakdown which brought Hitler to power drove
Leverkühn mad. But the latter's reaction to the crisis was
not Nazi membership but rather music. Mann's novel accounts for both fascism and Leverkühn, two very different
consequences of the same collapse of institutions and values.

It is in this context that one can understand Mann's identification with Leverkühn. There are elements in the composer's biograph that are taken from Mann's life (Adrian's
childhood home of Kaiseraschern is, in many respects,
Lübeck; some of his work experiences correspond to those

involved in the writing of *Buddenbrooks;* and so on). But more basically, Mann is a party to his own fiction. The imaginary narrator, Serenus Zeitblom, writes of Adrian and relates the progress of his madness to that of the war—which is exactly how Mann wrote the book. Adrian Leverkühn is driven to the Devil in order to comprehend his age. So, in writing *Doctor Faustus,* was Thomas Mann.

And Mann's ultimate image of disorder, his deepest despair, is in the life of Adrian Leverkühn. As his end approaches, the composer wants to "take back" Beethoven's *Ninth Symphony.* This act of renunciation is directed against "that for which men have fought, in the name of which they have attacked the Bastiles of their oppressors, that which the great visionaries have announced with exultation. That must not be! It must be eradicated! I want to eradicate it!"

On the surface, this might seem to be cultural Nazism, the fascist contempt for art and man's struggle for liberation. But it is the opposite of that. Leverkühn is passionately dedicated to the great tradition in music. What drives him mad, in part, is the thought that the essential optimism of Western humanism, typified by Beethoven's concluding Hymn in the *Ninth Symphony,* has now been rendered decadent by events. So terrible is reality that it turns the entire European tradition into a lie based on the assumption of a harmony that does not exist. Only darkness can comprehend such darkness. One must "take back" the *Ninth Symphony* in art, for history has already done so in life.

Adrian Leverkühn is not simply a spokesman for Thomas Mann. Yet in this tragic scene, he states that profound and hopeless sense of decadence which overwhelmed Mann, and a good part of a Western generation, during and immediately after the war.

V

Felix Krull, a bellboy, and Diane, a lusty, wealthy writer are in bed together.

While making love, Diane says to Felix, "J'adore d'etre humiliée! Je t'adore! Oh, je t'adore, petit esclave stupide qui me déshonore . . ." And a little later, "The intellect longs for the non-intellect, that which is alive and beautiful dans sa stupidité, in love with it, oh in love with it to the point of idiocy, to the ultimate self-betrayal and self-denial, in love with the beautiful and the divinely stupid, it kneels before it, prays to it in an ecstasy of self abnegation, self degradation, and finds it intoxicating to be degraded by it . . ."

This is one of Mann's last attempts at affirmation. In some ways, it is a near parody of the act of darkness with Hetæra Esmeralda which started Adrian Leverkühn on his way to madness. Once again, spirit is in pursuit of matter. But, this time, Mann does not view the scene from the point of view of the anguished, outcast poet, but rather from that of the partisan of life—a confidence man. The novel, *Felix Krull*, is his Tempest; or perhaps better, a hymn to the Hagenströms.

In all of Mann's previous affirmations, his most positive note was that of a weary, momentary existentialism. But Felix Krull—a Sunday's child—is a happy existentialist. He had wondered whether it was important to "see the world small, or to see it big?" The great men, he thinks, "field marshals, statesmen, empire builders, and other leaders who rise through violence above the masses of mankind must be constructed to see the world small, like a chess board, or they would never possess the ruthless coldness to deal so boldly and cavalierly with the weal and woe of the individual." Felix, on the other hand, regards the world as "big": as made for enjoyment, not reconstruction.

And finally, Felix asserts that "Life's being only an episode predisposed me in its favor." In this, he is the perfect Schopenhauerian, only with a sense of humor. He transcends the irrationalities of life by accepting them, and accepting them joyously. In this, he suggests another Mann character, Mynheer Peeperkorn. Peeperkorn had been the sheer force of will and life, but seen at a moment of disintegration and age. Krull is the young Peeperkorn, which is to say he is Mann's resignation made with a smile rather than sadly.

And yet, Mann did not fully believe his own character. He could not. He could dream Krull, wish him, fantasize him, but he could not really be convinced by him. After all the upheavals, he could find relief in the figure of the "confidence man" of life, but not a resolution of his own pessimism. Toward the very end of his days, in an essay on Schiller, Mann summarized his odyssey of nearly eighty years:

The past half century has witnessed a retrogression of humanity, a chilling atrophy of culture, a frightening decrease in civility, decency, sense of justice, loyalty and faith and of the most elementary trustworthiness. Two world wars, breeding brutality and rapacity, have catastrophically lowered the intellectual and moral level (the two are inseparable) and left behind a state of disorder which is a poor safeguard against the plunge into a third world war which would end everything.

In spite of Krull, Mann had seen his century as small, as a tragic history rather than a lusty comedy.

VI

Here, then, is history seen from the vantage point of art and personal experience. As a German, Mann was particularly close to the dooms of his time. His nation went through two military defeats, two postwar havocs, the rise of modern barbarism, and the intense period of the Cold War, all within his lifetime. But these facts were not, of course, simply German. The incalculable subversions which Mann confronted shook the entire culture of the West. And these images of disorder tell, more than any chronicle or sociology could, how and why so many felt that a decadence was, and is, abroad in this age.

Mann's legacy involves much more than a political statement on the retrogression of humanity. It is composed of characters and moments which evoke, not simply the events of a revolutionary time and the shattering of so many values, but the emotional quality, the taste and touch, of that collapse. ("Poetry," Aristotle said in the *Poetics*, "is something more philosophic and of graver import than history, since its statements are of the nature rather of universals, whereas those of history are singular." So with Mann, whose fictions are truer than his theses.)

In the twentieth century of Thomas Mann, spirit had become sickly like Hanno Buddenbrooks, beauty and righteousness are set against power in an unequal battle. Nature and society have become a dialectic nightmare in which a woman's death seems to be a fit of laughter, and the warm wind is the harbinger of frost like the hot crust around the ice cream in an *omelette-en-surprise*. Genius, like a butter-fly adapting to its environment, imitates madness. And the old harmonies have become so irrelevant that, in the name of art, a composer must seek to take back the *Ninth Symphony*.

In the chaos which provoked these images, Mann continually sought a way in which to affirm. In all of his searching, he never lost the Protestant moralism of his youth in Lübeck. Yet, he never succeeded for more than a moment, his yes came and went like Hans Castorp's vision in the snow. Intellectually, he did come to the conclusion that there must be a new, consciously fashioned, society, that the Burgher must go forward rather than yearn for a return into the oligarchic past. In pursuit of this ideal, Mann signed manifestos and played a political role, yet he did not make a single, lasting symbol out of his convictions.

Even in *Felix Krull*, his most concerted attempt to invent a hero who was positive, Mann contradicted himself. Krull succeeds by seeing the world as meant for personal enjoyment, as big, and refusing the small perspective of those so disrespectful of reality that they seek to reconstruct it. This happy existentialism is the diametric opposite of the knowledge which Mann purchased at the price of so much anguish. Krull is an escape, not a solution.

Mann failed to answer the questions history thrust upon him, but then, history did not answer them either.

The artist, the moralist, cannot simply fabricate a harmony out of wish and will. Somehow, they must find their beauty and principles in reality, or at least potentially so. And here, Mann was pursued by the same demons as Adrian Leverkühn. If fact had become monstrous, if Lübeck and its verities had utterly vanished, if humanism had not stopped fascism and World War II, how could fiction be any less tortured? Leverkühn composed his *Lamentations;* Mann wrote his *Doctor Faustus.* Each made the same kind of a response.

In this aspect, Mann provides an insight into much of the aesthetic genius of his time. His contemporaries, too, were impelled toward demons and the primitive in order to cope with their days. Some went beyond Mann. The latter's books are, by far and large, in the formal tradition of the nineteenth-century novel. But there were those of Mann's colleagues who tore up the structure of language and the very sequence of time in order to render faithfully their experience. In either case, the greatest works of the half-century were generally written by members of the Devil's Party, but those more at home in the darkness than in the light.

Prophetically, during World War I, Mann said of himself that he was a "chronicler and illustrator of decadence." The description is apt in more than one way. He described the contemporary malaise and was one of the great literary pathologists of his generation. But more than that, the sickness of the century infected his autobiography as well as his art. Like Hans Castorp, he came to the Magic Mountain as a visitor and stayed as a patient.

And yet, it is precisely as a chronicler and illustrator of decadence that Mann is not decadent. He did not simply become ill of history like Castorp. He generalized his condition, he turned it into unforgettable images of disorder, he gave the events their "graver import" even with all their ambiguity. And if neither he, nor anyone else in his time, found answers to the questions suddenly thrust upon the West, Mann continued the great tradition though it was breaking down. To be faithful to so much confusion is an enormous positive accomplishment.

In this, his work is like the *Lamentations* of Adrian Lever-kühn. It does not contain affirmations, it is suffused with despair. And yet, the mere fact that he sought to comprehend so much darkness illuminates the age; it is a light.

This, then, is one man's brilliant account of how Western history felt in the first half of the century. These are some of the reasons why those years seemed to so many to be a decadence.

3

Capitalism:
The Cold Decadence

The average nineteenth-century prophet thought that capitalism would end volcanically. Its contradictions, it was said, would one day burst the system asunder.

Now, another metaphor may have become more apt: Capitalism is moving toward its end massively, imperceptibly, like a glacier. Its decadence is cold, not hot.

Thomas Mann's images of disorder were, from World War I on, evoked by the violent apocalypse. But in *Buddenbrooks*, he wrote of a less dramatic change, the defeat of the merchant oligarchs by the new businessmen. That development, which Mann only glimpsed, was but the beginning of a process: the pacific war of capitalism against capitalism, the gentle apocalypse. This quiet decadence persisted as a possibility when the economic breakdowns, revolutions, and counterrevolutions did not destroy the established order. And since its progress is recorded by statistical increments rather than by masses in the street, since it is gradual enough to allow the old rhetoric to mask the new reality, it is more difficult to observe than the collapse of a nation or the disintegration of a social class.

Three aspects of the cold decadence of capitalism suggest its character. The capitalist economy is destroying the capitalist civilization and personality; in the process, businessmen are building a collective society for private profit; and, as a result, it is the corporation rather than the Communist Party which is the major Western institution moving toward a convergence with the Soviet example.

I

The civilization of capitalism—not its economic mechanism, but its culture, its morality, its idealism—is being destroyed by the capitalist economy. The expropriation of traditional values is thus being carried out by unwitting businessmen rather than by revolutionary proletarians.

Historically, capitalism appeared as an ethic as well as a system of production. The competitive individual with his absolute right to private property served his fellowmen by seeking his own profit. It was the free market, an invisible hand fixing prices, allocating resources to their best use and so on, which vectored all the antagonistic personal greeds into a common good. In such a theory, the making of money was a virtue since it promoted individualism, innovation, and the wealth of the entire society.

In the Protestant version of the capitalist morality, riches were the reward of the righteously ascetic. In the French Physiocrat's view, private property was the very basis of freedom itself. As A. A. Berle summarized this doctrine, "if a man was to be free, able to speak his own mind, depict his own thought and develop his own personality, he would have to have a base apart from one that was politically or ecclesiastically organized and controlled." That base was private property.

The idyll described in these visions did not, of course, exist. The millions who were degraded in the teeming new cities were the victims of the accident of their birth rather than the products of an economic selection of the fit and unfit. They demonstrated this fact when they formed the labor and socialist movement and educated the wealthy in some of the fundamentals of humanity. And yet, there was some relationship between the workings of the economy and the righteousness felt by the entrepreneur. If business early learned the value of state subsidy and tariff protection, there was still competition. The invisible hand of the market regularly misallocated resources and precipitated depressions, but over the long run (with the modifications imposed upon it by the supposedly incompetent majority), more and more goods were manufactured and distributed.

Under such circumstances, it did not take utter hypocrisy or ignorance to profess the capitalist faith sincerely.

At the same time, the predictions of violent capitalist breakdown were tenable enough to corroborate the traditional socialist expectation. For most of the twentieth century it did indeed seem that the system would end apocalyptically. In the thirty-one years between 1914 and 1945, there were two world wars, the Russian Revolution, aborted revolutions throughout Central Europe. the Great Depression, Italian fascism, and the barbaric retrogression of Nazism. The data gave comfort to the "catastrophic optimism" of Karl Marx (the phrase is Raymond Aron's).

After World War II, however, events altered the classic perspective. The United States did not undergo its scheduled depression and instead reconverted to prosperity. This allowed it to subsidize the reorganization of capitalism in Western Europe. The renaissance of the Continental economy profoundly affected the labor and socialist movements. They largely abandoned the doctrine of the class struggle and accepted the welfare state and mixed economy as their ideal.

Capitalism enjoyed an unprecedented internal security from everything but itself.

It was in this period that the capitalist economy took the most vigorous measures against the capitalist ideology. And perhaps the twenty years of postwar capitalist success destroyed more of the capitalist ethic than the thirty-one years of intrawar capitalist failure. This was the process of the cold decadence.

The capitalist destruction of the capitalist ethic took place primarily through the private collectivization of the Western economy for minority profit.

A few anticipated this process and many have described it after the fact. The industrialist and mystic, Walter Rathenau, talked as early as 1917 (in a book entitled *Von Kommenden Dingen—Of Coming Things*) of an economy in which corporations would generate their own resources, free themselves from any real relation to the individual investor or the market, and become anonymous, self-sufficient automatons. Vatican sociology has often expressed a similar fear. In *Mater et Magistra*, John XXIII wrote, "In fact, by its own deep-seated and, as it were, intrinsic tendencies, free competition has almost destroyed itself. It has brought about a great accumulation of wealth and a corresponding concentration of economic power in the hands of a few 'who are frequently not the owners but only the trustees and managers of invested funds, which they administer at their own pleasure.'" (The quotation is from Pius XI in 1931.)

There are many statistical descriptions of this process and there is no point in rehearsing them at any length here. A few figures should suffice to outline a reality which is daily becoming more and more unmistakable. Their relevance to this chapter is that each one of these changes in economic structure marks an ethical event, the passing of a virtue.

In the place of the old competition, there is now a "corporate socialism" (the phrase is Estes Kefauver's) or a "collective capitalism" (Gardiner C. Means). Instead of a multiplicity of producers confronting one another in the market, there were in 1962 in America 500 corporations with $229.1 billion in sales—or more than half the sales and 70 percent of the total profit of the economy. The United States, as the most advanced industrial nation, became the most anticapitalist without knowing it.

This enormous concentration of corporate power had been particularly dynamic in the post-World War II period. Between 1947 and 1954, the 100 largest companies had increased their share of manufacturing from 23 percent to 30 percent; and the 200 top units controlled fully 37 percent of manufacturing. In American slang, one spoke of the Big Three in automobiles (actually, the Big Two and nearly the Big One), of the Big Four in steel, the Big Three in chemicals, and so on.

In 1964 the *U.S. News & World Report*, a conservative business magazine, announced that 25 percent of all American profit had gone to seven companies: General Motors, the American Telephone and Telegraph Company, Standard Oil of New Jersey, Texaco, Ford, Gulf Oil, and International Business Machines. In 1956, the same seven corporations had cornered "only" 16.6 percent of the profits. In short, the concentration of the rewards of production was even more acute than the concentration of the volume of production.

There were attempts to explain this development away by arguing that it had been accompanied by the diffusion of stock ownership. In part, this was simply much less true than the proponents of the thesis thought. In a 1963 National Bureau of Economic Research study, Robert J. Lampmann pointed out that 1.6 percent of the adult population of the United States held 82.4 percent of the publicly held shares. Insofar as a larger number of people did hold some stock, this represented a growth in the total of helpless, impotent small stockholders whose fragmented "ownings" had little to do with how corporations acted.

As a result of this concentration of corporate power, more and more companies were freed from the law of supply and demand. The most dramatic form of this development was the "administered price," in which the cost of an item on the market was determined, not by how much how many buyers were willing to pay, but in order to return a set profit. So it was that a Senate Committee in the 1950's revealed that General Motors "targeted" its profits for a "20% rate of return on the net worth after taxes at a predetermined level of production, or standard volume." Actually, the intention in this case was modest, since the company in question regularly reached profit levels of 25 percent and above.

Gardiner C. Means, one of the first American economists to theorize about this transformation, estimates that General Electric and Du Pont also have target rates of 20 percent after taxes, that Union Carbide seeks a 15 percent, and that U.S. Steel in the fifties increased its target from a traditional 8 percent to a goal of perhaps as high as 15 percent.

There is a most instructive irony in all of this, one which reveals how a businessman can be a revolutionist without noticing it.

During the New Deal, when much of management was talking of the destruction of cherished values, the Administration set up a National Planning Board. It explored the possibilities of "facilitative planning" (a rough equivalent of the "indicative planning" practiced in France, to be described shortly). In the course of its work, the Board developed production-consumption patterns which indicated how people would spend their money at different levels of economic activity and what the production and employment requirements would be at these levels.

Gardiner Means, who was the Board's Director of Research, notes that the main practical use of this technique by the Government was made during World War II. The military sector was analyzed in terms of production-consumption relationships, and input-output analysis was employed in one of the vastest industrial efforts of all time. After the war, some of these ideas survived, but modestly, in the Employment Act of 1946 and the activities of the Council of Economic Advisers.

But, and here the irony surfaces, the large corporations had become so huge that they could take up these methods which had been worked out for the national economy.

Thus, General Electric estimated the demand for electrical appliances at full employment, and then decided what proportion of the market it would plan to supply. This same company is one of the most politically conservative in the United States, and would be appalled if the Government were to emulate the planning techniques of the profit-making corporations, techniques which the Government itself had developed. General Electric, and many giants like it, had emancipated itself from most of the capitalist verities but not the capitalist rhetoric.

This contradiction in which businessmen consciously violate the economic laws that they proclaim is not limited to a few of the largest corporations. Texas oilmen, the most aggressive of America's millionaire conservatives, invest mightily in the propagation of *laissez-faire*, pure and simple, and especially simple. They are able to do so because they operate in an industry in which production is strictly controlled under law and with their support. The Farm Bureau, the organization which represents the wealthy American farmers who receive over $4 billion in annual subsidy, predictably opposes degrading "handouts" to poor farmers. This near-comic opposition of greed and principle is only one aspect of the historic corruption of capitalism by capitalism. Occasionally, though, someone does talk of the *Emperor's Clothes*.

In the thirties, Russell Leffingwell of Morgan's told an investigating committee, "The growth of corporate enterprise has been drying up individual independence and initiative. . . . We are becoming a nation of hired men. Hired by great aggregates of capital."

With the corporate giants able to remove price and profit

from the vagaries of the free market, they were also able to
collectivize inventiveness. In the United States, where military research and development played such a major role in
the postwar economy, some two-thirds of this technological
pioneering was financed directly or indirectly by the Government. In every Western nation, inventive genius had become rationalized through research bureaucracies.

A similar process took place in another area where business was theoretically supposed to submit to the judgment
of the free economy: the money market. In fulfillment of
Rathenau's 1917 prophecy that the corporation would be
able to divorce itself from the individual investor, the
American companies more and more raised their capital
from themselves. A. A. Berle has estimated that, from 1947
to 1956, the United States economy raised $292 billion in
investment funds. Of this enormous sum, 60 percent was
financed from retained profits, and 40 percent from "outside" the corporations. But even this latter figure was decep-
tive, since the "outside" was not primarily composed of
thinking, judging risktakers, but of insurance companies,
mutual funds, pension trusts, and other institutions whose
adventurousness is limited by law or tradition.

Some of the elements of capitalist collectivization, then,
are the concentration of economic power, the consequent
ability to "administer" prices to an economy rather than
responding to the law of supply and demand, the utilization
of profit targets and planning techniques, the statification
of inventiveness, and the abolition of risk in the money
market. Making money had been declared virtuous because
it promoted individualism, inventiveness, and the productive
taking of chances. Now, each one of these qualities had been

largely negated by the system. Adam Smith had thought that the corporation was hopelessly medieval, since it represented the anonymous control of someone else's money, and this contradicted the spiritual essence and genius of capitalism. By the mid-twentieth century, the corporation was capitalism.

This developing new system created new kinds of people.

In *The Lonely Crowd*, David Riesman perceptively described the personality evoked by the old reality and ethic. The "inner-directed" entrepreneur lived on a social frontier between feudalism and capitalism. He therefore consciously chose his individualism and his values, operating on a sort of internal gyroscope. In the twentieth century, however, wealth had become a function of manipulation and organization. There appeared the "other-directed" man, the team player who needed radar rather than a gyroscope, who took his values from others—when he could find them.

C. A. R. Crosland described a similar change in England. "The old style capitalist was by instinct a tyrant and an aristocrat who cared for no one's approval. The new style executive prides himself on being a good committee man, and subconsciously longs for the approval of the sociologist." In France, Pierre Bauchet has documented the way in which the new directors, bureaucrats of capital rather than entrepreneurs, find it natural and useful to integrate their "private" activities into a state plan.

But perhaps the most poignant case in point came to light in William H. Whyte's study of *The Organization Man*. Whyte wrote his book while working for *Fortune*, a business magazine. Though honest about the reality of capitalism, he is hardly its ideological opponent, and this led him to a hopeless contradiction. Whyte candidly described the way in which the corporation was invading, and consciously rationalizing, the very lives of its employees. Even the romantic concept of marriage, one of the great moral accomplishments of capitalist civilization, is bureaucratized as the company calculates a man's wife along with the rest of the assets and liabilities.

Having described this relentless progress of the organization, Whyte can recommend no resistance more profound than an interior aloofness. He counsels the young executive to be a sort of good businessman Schweik, defeating the system by disloyally playing its game. This individual act of disaffiliation is as far as Whyte can go, and thus the true believer in the individualistic truths of the old capitalist ethic becomes a fifth columnist within the actual capitalist economy.

In America, then, one can watch the cold decadence of capitalism as it transforms and collectivizes the executive personality. In Europe, however, these changes have become explicitly political.

France is the most illuminating example of this juridical denial of capitalist laws by capitalist economies. In the Paris of the early sixties, a conservative and nationalist general presided over the Fourth Plan and prepared the Fifth. His prime minister was a banker. They were both committed to a directed economy in which state planning is a means of mobilizing the entire society behind politically determined goals. They were also in favor of capitalism, or at least of extracting private profit from public effort. In this dual purpose of state plan and corporate gain, De Gaulle and Pompidou presented one of the most advanced instances of private collectivization.

The French Plan began immediately after the Second World War. In part, it was a culmination of the social consciousness of the Resistance; in part, it was a necessity imposed upon a war-torn nation which had to restore the very structure of its economy. By the mid-fifties, French planning had transcended both of the motives that presided over its birth. It had become conservative, or at least technocratic, rather than militant and plebian as in the Resistance ideal. And it was starting to plan in a context of relative affluence rather than that of poverty.

Even during the extreme parliamentary instability of the last days of the Fourth Republic, the French economy continued to register high rates of growth (annual increments of over 5 percent were common in the mid-fifties). When General de Gaulle took power, he inherited the accomplishments of the Plan and turned them into a vision of a paternalistic, directed, and planned economy which would restore grandeur to the nation. (He also developed a curious thesis of a classless France in which workers, peasants, and the bourgeoisie would no longer contend among themselves but be tutored, on television, by the Leader.)

The Plan which was at the center of this philosophy does not in any way change the system of ownership or profit in France. It is "indicative" rather than compulsory, and the businessman is free to ignore its suggestions. Indeed, as critics of the Plan like Pierre Mendès-France have documented, even the nationalized enterprises, like Renault or the public banks, often violate the very guidelines of the Government which "owns" them. (In a society dominated by private corporations, public corporations absorb the former's methods, morality, and immorality.) Yet, the Government's control of 50 percent of new investment is a powerful lever with which to secure conformity to the Plan.

On paper, there is a wide participation of all classes in the society in the planning process (this is the basis for De Gaulle's claim to a classless, cooperative France). In fact, the Fourth Plan was elaborated by commissions which were weighted over 90 percent toward businessmen and state functionaries—the distinction between the two categories is not always clear—and about 8 percent for worker and peasant unionists. Still, even if there were numerical equality between corporate and popular representatives, the businessmen would be at an enormous advantage. They command professional, paid research staffs and are thus in a position to understand and shape the Plan. The unions, by virtue of the very income and power structure of the society, count for less in these deliberations, whatever the representational mathematics.

The chief concept of the French Plan was, and is, a denial of one of the basic propositions of capitalist economics. Rather than allowing the "invisible hand" of the marketplace to determine the allocation of resources and rewards, the planners make a conscious and political choice of a growth rate to be achieved over a period of several years. Supply and demand are then adjusted to this decision, rather than the other way around. The result was a more harmonious development of the entire economy and an increase in the profit of the corporations that now have the state as a center for market research. But, as Gilbert Mathieu, the economic correspondent of *Le Monde*, noted in 1963, the relative inequities of income distribution increased between 1956 and 1961.

Indeed, there is a sense in which this maldistribution of income under the Plan is inevitable. When the state intervenes in an economy in which rewards are still assigned on the basis of private profit, then an increase in the general integration and efficiency of the society will benefit the rich. This might be offset by a vigorous and progressive tax policy, but this is certainly not the case in France (which, if anything, provides more scope for tax avoidance by the wealthy than the United States). As it is, one comes up with a system that combines the collective mode of planning with the private appropriation of money, a hybrid that moves away from both capitalism and socialism. And in terms of the distribution of wealth, the effect is for the entire community to subsidize those who are best off.

In American discussions, the embarrassing French example is usually countered with the German "miracle." In that country, it is said, the "social market economy" has observed the classic rules and prospered accordingly. However, as *Business Week* noted in the early sixties, the reality is a little less Adam Smithian than the claim: 55 percent of all investment in plant, equipment, and construction was financed by the state, and more than 40 percent of aluminum and more than 40 percent of auto, lead, and zinc production were also statified. (Accordingly to a high official of the French Commissariat du Plan, conversations between French and German planners in 1963 indicated that the two nations had an equal government intervention, albeit in different forms.)

Given such facts, it becomes somewhat more understandable that the British Conservative Party, in the name of anti-socialism, should introduce national planning in their country. As George Lichtheim concluded from this case and others, the directed economies of Europe "may still be capitalist" but they "cannot any longer be described as bourgeois." Capitalism is destroying capitalist motivation, ideology, and even personality.

In the United States, however, this process has been somewhat more disguised than in Europe. In the absence of open government planning, America has preferred to carry out its collectivizations in the name of something called "free enterprise." Ironically, the French Commissariat du Plan sends a technician to America in order to learn planning methods from the corporations. For in this country, the exigencies of production demand planning as much as in Europe, only the piety of tradition will not allow the word to be spoken openly.

Even so, in the mid-sixties there were signs that American theory would at least begin to catch up with American practice. A majority report of the Senate Subcommittee on Employment and Manpower in 1964 urged conscious planning. And in the Housing Message of 1964, President Lyndon B. Johnson declared, "By 1970, we shall have to build at least two million new homes a year to keep up with the growth of our population. We will need many new classrooms, uncounted miles of new streets and utility lines, and an unprecedented volume of water and sewage facilities. We will need stores and churches and libraries, distribution systems for goods, transportation systems for people and communications systems for ideas. . . .

"Now is the time to direct the productive capacity of

our home building industry to the great needs of the neg-
lected segments of our population. . . . In the tradition of
the long-established partnership between private industry
and community development, the Federal Government
should encourage and facilitate these new and desirable approaches."

Such a statement recognized that the housing needs of the
nation were so complex and interrelated that they required
both anticipation and planning. But, significantly, after the
Federal Government had accomplished what the free market was once supposed to do—direct a broad allocation of
resources—and after it had laid down the plans for the new
communities and provided their infrastructure, they would
be turned over to private builders for their profit. Here
again, innovation is collectivized and profit privatized.

While the Europeans were carrying out frank social planning for private profit, America was doing the same thing
shamefacedly. As a result, a conservative movement could
arise in the United States and, in the logical name of all the
hallowed truths, make the preposterous proposal to go back
to *laissez faire*. And many of the wealthiest businessmen
who supported this fantasy were themselves the most successful practitioners of the capitalist anticapitalism. The spectacle would be humorous were it not dangerous, yet clearly
a society cannot long pay such an astronomical price for its
rhetoric. Along with the old-fashioned virtues, the old-fashioned vocabulary will have to vanish.

In short, in the spiritual name of courageous, inventive,
and risk-taking individuals, bureaucratized corporations,
supported and subsidized by governments, were planning
in increasing independence of the laws of supply and de-

mand or the judgments of investors. Economic life was more and more dominated by anonymous collectivities, and a relatively few directors were making decisions that effected the existence of almost every citizen. The civilization of capitalism, its ethics, its morality, its philosophy, was being destroyed by the practice of capitalism.

And businessmen, without giving too much thought to the matter, were shaping new environments and new types of men.

II

If Karl Marx was the great prophet of the apocalyptic decadence of capitalism, of its violent breakdown, it was Joseph Schumpeter who most profoundly expressed its cold decadence. His feat was all the more remarkable in that he was a partisan, not a foe, of the system whose strange doom he described. He was, as Daniel Bell has said, that rare being, an economist with a sense of the tragic.

Indeed, one of the most remarkable things about Schumpeter is that he wrote his *Capitalism, Socialism and Democracy* in a time of the worldwide breakdown of the capitalist economy, yet he predicted that the system would be destroyed, not by its failures, but by its very accomplishments. Capitalism, he said, "through its very success undermines the social institutions which protect it, and 'inevitably' creates conditions in which it will not be able to live and which strongly point to socialism as the heir 'apparent.' " Setting aside for the moment Schumpeter's prediction of the coming of socialism, let's examine the thesis of the evolutionary subversion of capitalism.

Perhaps Schumpeter's most poetic statement of the theme

is contained in an analogy between the medieval warrior and the modern businessman. Among other things, the knight was rendered obsolete by a weapons technology, by guns which democratized the battlefield and made a peasant or an artisan as lethal as a prince. Similarly, the capitalist is the victim of a technological change which, and the notion has a poignance, he himself brings about. "Since capitalist enterprise, by its very achievements, tends to automate progress, we conclude that it tends to make itself superfluous— to break into pieces under the pressure of its own success. The perfectly bureaucratized giant industrial unit only ousts the small or medium-sized firm, but in the end it also ousts the entrepreneur and expropriates the bourgeoisie as a class which in the process stands to lose not only its income but also what is infinitely more important, its function."

Like the social psychologists who came after him, Schumpeter understood that these changes in structure implied transformations of personal and ethical values as well: "The capitalist process, by substituting a mere parcel of shares for the walls of, and machines in, a factory, takes the life out of the idea of property. It loses the grip that was once so strong —the grip in the sense of the legal right and the actual ability to do as one pleases with one's own . . . And this evaporation of what we may term the material substance of property—its visible and touchable reality—affects not only the attitudes of the holder but also that of the workmen and public in general. Denaturized, defunctionalized and absentee ownership does not impress and call forth moral allegiance as the vital form of property did."

The capitalist economy, Schumpeter realized, expropriated the capitalist civilization. "The scheme of values in capitalist society," he wrote, "though causally related to economic success, is losing its hold not only upon the public mind but also upon the 'capitalist' stratum itself."

At this moment in his analysis, Schumpeter developed a profound insight in the form of a confused prophecy and a bad definition. Socialism, he said, was the successor to that capitalist system which destroyed itself by accomplishing too much.

For Schumpeter, any society which centralized economic decision and in which the public sphere dominated the private was socialist. By reducing the term to a simple description of a way of organizing an economy, he narrowed, and radically so, the meaning that the socialist movement itself had given to its ideal. In Western European history and, above all, in the American socialist vision of Eugene Victor Debs, socialism stood for equality, solidarity, the elimination of class distinction, cooperation, and the fulfillment of democracy at least as much as for the nationalization of the means of production.

What Schumpeter did was to confuse socialism, which was and is a democratic program for a collectivist age, with collectivism itself (after the triumph of Joseph Stalin, the world Communist movement propagandized in favor of this same error). And yet, his very imprecision contains an important understanding on his part. "A society," Schumpeter wrote, "may be fully and truly socialist and yet be led by an absolute ruler or be organized in the most democratic of all possible ways." If one takes Schumpeter's "socialism" as a reference, not to the historical socialist dream of a democratic life, but to the collectivism which emerges out of capitalism, a significant truth appears.

Schumpeter understood that the political issue was not *whether* the future was to be collective, but *how* it was to be so. Collectivism could be the basis of the "most democratic" organization. It was not, as conservatives had held, inevitably cruel and totalitarian. But then, it could also support absolutism and authoritarianism. It was not, as some socialists had thought, inevitably benign and libertarian.

And so Schumpeter concluded on a note of profound ambiguity. Collectivism was inexorably being created by the "Vanderbilts, Carnegies and Rockefellers" more than by the revolutionary proletariat. But the social content of this irresistible trend, whether it would be egalitarian or dictatorial, humane or antihumanist, was not predetermined. The quality of the life of the future was still to be fashioned, and by men and not by economic patterns. In short, the question of freedom had been posed, not settled, by contemporary history.

III

Schumpeter's insight can be deepened by way of a further irony. The *laissez-faire* ideologists had always charged that any form of collectivism would inevitably be bureaucratic and unfree. Today in the West there is indeed the possibility for the emergence of such an anthill society. It is promoted by unwitting businessmen, the spiritual children of *laissez faire*.

The basis for this paradox is fairly simple to describe. Capitalists are now in control of the transition to a non- and anticapitalist order. Their training and background prepare them to carry out such a transition in the most confused and self-contradictory way. Left to themselves, the managers will create a bureaucratic form of collectivism and thus emphasize the convergence of the Western and Soviet systems much more effectively than any of the Communist parties of Europe and America.

The potential of this development comes more and more to the surface in the discussions of corporate "responsibility." A section of the business community, disturbed by the disappearance of any clear management responsibility to stockholders or to the law of supply and demand or to owners—or any other classic source of legitimacy for economic power—has been trying to decide to whom, or to what, the corporations owe fealty. For if the classic morality of private property no longer describes who rules, and should rule, what does?

Some of these theorists have come up with a most revealing answer, usually put affirmatively, happily. The corporation, they argue, is becoming responsible to the public. But if this is so, then the managers no longer fulfill the virtue of making money. Now, they are making public policy. And then, as an insightful observer put it, one is watching "the frightening spectacle of a powerful economic group whose future and perceptions are shaped in a tight materialistic context of money and things but which imposes its narrow ideas about a broad spectrum of unrelated non-economic subjects on the mass of men and society."

The ambiguities of this corporate collectivism are perhaps most accessible in the writings of A. A. Berle.

Berle's analysis is particularly important in that he writes as a friend of the capitalist order and proponent of the notion that the corporation must develop a conscience. In

1932, he had joined Gardiner C. Means in writing *The Modern Corporation and Private Property*, one of the very first empirical studies to hold that in the capitalist society the capitalist himself—the property owner—no longer managed his enterprise. In his place stood an administrator, an executive, who made decisions but did not own. Since this seminal analysis, many writers have developed aspects of the Berle and Means thesis of the separation of ownership and control in advanced capitalist society. And Berle has attempted to come to legal and ethical grips with the consequences of the system of "power without property" which he had helped define.

To whom are the managers responsible if ownership is no longer the source of their authority? Under the developed ideology of capitalism, it was possible for the manager not to own his enterprise, but then he was the agent of the stockholders and thus ultimately responsive to the claims of property. But if Berle is right in his factual description, the stockholders have become passive, have been excluded from the decision process, and the manager disposes of millions, and even billions, of dollars without being practically accountable to anyone.

Berle's answer to the theoretical problem inherent in this situation is straightforward. The corporation should, he affirms, develop a conscience. And in one way or another, major segments of American business have taken up this rhetoric, proclaiming through institutional advertisements that they are somehow trustees of the commonweal. One company, General Electric, raised this theme to the level of a corporate philosophy (called "Boulwareism") which combined community education with a concerted attempt to destroy trade unionism.

But then there is a basic anomaly in Berle's position, one which F. A. Hayek, among the best known of the contemporary defenders of the traditional capitalist wisdom, put bluntly: "So long as management is supposed to serve the interests of the stockholder, it is reasonable to leave control of its action to the stockholders. But if management is supposed to serve wider public interests, it becomes merely a logical consequence of this conception that the appointed representatives of the public interest should control management."

Hayek is right as against Berle in that the latter attempts to give a democratic legitimacy to the corporation—it is supposed to become an instrument of the people—but leaves it in the hands of a bureaucratic elite which is neither elected nor controlled by the people. Berle is right as against Hayek in that the traditional theory of the corporate rule of the stockholder applies less and less every day. In short, Berle's description of new forms of property is much more compelling than his vision of a new corporate ethic.

This confusion over the theoretical justification of the current system of production points to the kind of world which the corporation is, in fact, creating. It is not socialist, for, as Hayek notes, it is run by a managerial elite. It is increasingly not capitalist in the historically understood definition of the term, since it does not rest upon private property. It is a society whose trends are collectivist, and therefore anticapitalist, and bureaucratic and elitist and therefore antisocialist.

One might say that the corporation is moving toward a bureaucratic collectivist order, neither capitalist nor socialist.

When one leaves the ethical questions about this system

of "power without property" and moves on to more empirical description, the issues become clearer. Here it is possible
to determine the responsibility of the corporation as it actually manifests itself in day-to-day operation. A public
corporation, for instance, would show a political struggle
in its decision process. A corporation with a conscience
would demonstrate situations in which ethical considera-
tions overrode a calculus of gain. What, in fact, has been
the conduct of the corporation?

Predictably, all of these changes in the structure of the
economy have affected the way in which corporate decisions are made. In his authoritative *La Planification Fran-
çaise*, Pierre Bauchet describes the separation of ownership
and control in France. Then, in an analysis which applies
to the United States, he states some of the consequences of
this fact. The managers, he says, "seek less a profit of the
capitalist than a profit of the enterprise. The capitalist's
profit is traditionally identified with immediate financial
gain, while that of the enterprise develops over a long period
of activity: the first is based upon the conservation and increase of the wealth of the owners, the second upon aug-
menting the power of the firm . . ." It is, Bauchet believes,
because of this development that the corporations engage
in long-term planning and are even willing to integrate their
policies with those of the state. Their power is no longer
personal; it has become collective.

Gardiner C. Means has a similar description of the mode
of operation of the American corporation where "the directors . . . try to run it well for the same reasons that the
trustees of a great university seek to run the university
well . . ."

And yet, even though the old robber-baron psychology no longer operates, even though the aim is no longer a personal profit, the goal is still a private profit. Only now, the private recipient is not an individual or a family but the collective of managers itself. And the way in which this power has actually been exercised provides no warrant for the discovery of a corporate conscience.

Between 1958 and 1962, for instance, American manufacturers spent $13.3 billion on new investment—and let 18 percent of their productive capacity stand idle. Socially, one result of this pattern was to promote a high, chronic rate of unemployment. On a public or conscientious basis it would be impossible to justify such a squandering of resources, both human and material. But with their targeted profit rates, the corporations go on strike whenever they cannot gain their predetermined return. More than that, their targets are established on a long-run volume of production so they can make their money even while allowing their plants to work far under capacity.

The steel industry is an excellent example of this process. Dominated by a small group of corporations, it spent a fair portion of the 1950's running well under its capacity—and sometimes 50 percent under capacity. It was not that society had satisfied its social appetite for steel. Far from it. In the very same periods, unmet needs desperately required steel: low-cost housing, schools, hospitals, transportation systems, etc. According to the hallowed laws of the free market, the steel giants should have taken advantage of this demand by lowering prices, increasing volume, and thus creating a new market.

In reality, the steel corporations, particularly the industry leader, U.S. Steel, used this period to increase their targeted profits, as Gardiner C. Means suggests. They also increased prices, recommended wage restraint to workers whom they accused of being recklessly inflationary in their demands, and, when this curious concept of the public interest was mildly challenged by a Democratic President, reacted as if America had suddenly become a totalitarian society. All this took place in a sector of the economy whose decisions affect more of the life of the United States than most state governments and many acts of Federal legislation.

In short, the structures, techniques, and direction of the corporation have been more and more collectivized, and its policies are generally no longer made to further the interest of an individual or family. But the old principle of profit survives the passing of its ethical justifications and itself becomes collective, anonymous, and even more powerful. In the heart of the process, it is difficult to discern a conscience.

So far, the focus has been upon the collectivization of corporate production, personality, and decision-making. But there is another important collectivization: that of mass opinion and taste. This, of course, is accomplished by the most successful educational institution of contemporary capitalism, the advertising industry.

Much of the rage directed against advertising by intellectuals is unfair. These critics note that this industry has a systematic habit of degrading language, truth, and culture in general. They generally assume that this is primarily due to the personal corruption of those who direct the communications media in America. Yet this misses the more profound functions of advertising and implies the too simple theory that one is confronted by a conspiracy of traitorous college graduates. The reality goes much more deeply into the American economic system and the new, private collectivism.

The advertising industry now accounts for an expenditure of approximately $15 billion a year which puts it on a par with formal education as a social activity. As a standard text by S. Watson Dunn describes the situation, "Since the end of World War II, advertising expenditures have been rising faster than Gross National Product, national income, carloadings, or almost any barometer of business activity one might choose." Such a massive investment is clearly not made out of a Philistine hatred of culture.

Rather, this development takes place because the rationalization and collectivization of production require the rationalization and collectivization of taste. The child, in David Riesman's apt phrase, is turned into a "consumer trainee." And, as David M. Potter, one of the most perceptive commentators on the subject, has written, "advertising now competes with such long-standing institutions as the school and the church in the magnitude of its social influence." Just as the "free market" no longer allocates resources, determines prices, or raises the bulk of new investment funds, it no longer provides an open confrontation of buyer and seller. The consumer is taxed so that his own desires may be standardized enough to be run through a computing machine.

Even more basically, it is the role of advertising to make the misallocation of resources characteristic of corporate collectivism appear as the free choice of the society.

For example, the public sector of American life—health,

governmentally financed housing, education, transportation, and the like—is considered a great burden by most Americans. Yet, this sector contains some of the most important necessities of modern life and is a fundamental constituent of a standard of living. The private sector, on the other hand, is thought of as an area of freedom. Here one may bid for competing detergents made by the same firm, purchase planned obsolescence in automobiles and household appliances, and pay interest rates which are carefully designed for maximum deception. The private sector advertises; the public sector, by far and large, does not.

It takes money and ingenuity to convince people to invest in luxuries which they do not need and to ignore their necessities. It also makes money to do so. And it is the advertising industry that makes this misallocation of resources seem rational and freely chosen.

This instance, and the other cases of planned waste for profit, should serve to throw light on Berle's hopes for the coming of a corporate conscience. Whatever the institutional advertisements about the public responsibilities of business, the corporation acts to promote its private, but collective, profit. It imposes itself upon the people rather than responding to their needs, producing on a basis of targeted greed. It no longer follows the classic capitalist virtues, but it has managed to retain the classic capitalist vice of irresponsibility.

It is a somewhat confused recognition of this reality that leads Berle to one of his most surprising statements. Again, it must be emphasized that he writes as a defender of capitalism (and, in foreign-policy terms, as one of the more rigid American opponents of the Soviet Union). Yet he asserts,

"The private property system in production, which began with our great grandfather's farm and forge, has almost vanished in the vast area of the American economy dominated by this system [retained-profits financing and institutional investment—author's note]. Instead, we have something which differs from the Russian or socialist system *mainly in its philosophic content*" (emphasis added).

Even if one takes Berle's statement of the present convergence of the communist and capitalist systems as extreme, as I do, how is it that one can even talk of such a comparison? For if this were even a major tendency in the West, then the role of the Communist parties is being usurped by businessmen. To deal with this bizarre possibility, it is necessary to go back to some of the implications of Schumpeter's definition of "socialism."

In the Marxian version of the hot decadence of capitalism, the working class of the most advanced, technologically developed nations would seize power from owners who could no longer resolve the contradiction between the social character of the productive process and the private character of the system that directed it. History would make the capitalists weak and the workers desperately strong. Yet, it is quite possible that the movement toward collectivism (not socialism) in this century took place under the opposite conditions from the ones envisioned by Marx: in Russia, where the workers were weak; in the West, where the capitalists were strong.

If Russia in 1917 was ripe for a socialist revolution, it was almost totally unripe for socialism. Industrially backward, its tiny working class could, for specific historic reasons, lead the overthrow of the old order, but it did not have the numbers or the economic resources to build a new order. Lenin and Trotsky felt that their Revolution was only the beginning, that it was going to be rescued by socialist victories in the heart of Europe. That did not happen.

Instead, the first attempt actually to institute socialism was based upon the socialization of poverty rather than abundance. As Marx had predicted long before, such a project could not succeed democratically. The material basis for socialism was an already existent wealth, which was precisely what the Russians did not have. Stalin forced the restriction of consumption, feeding heavy industry rather than people. To exact such a sacrifice from the masses, he expropriated their political power and concentrated it in the hands of a bureaucratic elite with social and economic privileges.

The Russian rhetoric was socialist, the Russian reality was not. The state owned the means of production—but the people did not "own" the state. They could exercise such an "ownership" over the nationalized means of production only if they could determine who would direct them and with what policies. For them, democracy was the only title to social wealth, their equivalent of the capitalist stock certificate. Thus, the destruction of democratic freedoms by Stalin was not simply a denial of political rights but the end of the social and economic power of the people as well.

The new bureaucracy established its privileges through its totalitarian monopoly of political power. The bureaucrat played politics as the businessman plays the market—as a means to gain economic and social position. When the industrial backwardness of Russia was overcome, the wealth created by the labor of the many was concentrated in the hands of the few. This was a collectivization in the absence of a strong working class.

In the West, the bureaucratic and collectivist tendencies emerged from riches rather than from scarcity. The capitalist system automated and collectivized the old-fashioned capitalist out of existence, replacing him with a manager. The corporation bureaucrat became more powerful, but not as in Russia through a process of forced industrialization. His power grew as society was backing leisurely and unthinkingly into the future. The executive was a revolutionist but did know it. The resulting structure—and it is still far from finished—was not identical to the Soviet system or anything like it. In Russia there was totalitarianism; in the West, limited democracy; under communism, resources were allocated by direct and centralized political decision; under capitalism, by indirect, though increasingly centralized, economic decision.

And yet, there is a possible convergence of these utterly different histories. As the West becomes more collectivized under a managerial elite and Russia becomes wealthier under a political elite, the conscious, self-seeking decisions of a minority could become the basis of both economies. In terms of their evolution, there would be tremendous contrasts between General Motors and a Commissariat of Transportation. In terms of economic function and practice, the two entities could come to resemble one another more and more.

And what the two cases would share, above all, would be that their collectivization would have been accomplished without the active, directing participation of the great mass of the people.

Marx, and the early socialist movement, had based the hope for a libertarian collectivism on the way in which socialization would take place: through the revolutionary struggle of the democratic majority. It would be humane, he argued, because the people, and the workers in particular, would be driven to brotherhood out of a daily necessity which they would turn into a social virtue. They would join together in unions, in a political movement; they would counterpose their superior numbers and ethic to the superior funds and egotism of business. The secret of their triumph, and consequently of the society they would fashion, would be free cooperation.

But assuming the very real possibility that Western collectivism will be introduced by businessmen, then Marx's method would point toward dark consequences. The conditions of life, the practical necessities, of the executive are material gain, authority, direction. The capitalist who accidentally stumbled into the revolutionizing of society would imbue it with the only values he knows, and the worst traditions of the past and the grimmest potential of the future would be united.

IV

But one need not look so far into the distance in order to discern the cold decadence of capitalism.

Practically every ethical, moral, and cultural justification for the capitalist sytem has now been destroyed by capitalism. The idyll of the free market, risktaking, inventiveness, the social virtue of making money, all these have been abolished by the very success of capitalism itself. In some cases, most particularly in the United States, this contradiction between rhetoric and reality has led to the appearance of an atavistic "conservatism" which seeks to repeal the modern world. As a social and economic program, this is preposterous; as a political movement, it might threaten the very peace of the earth.

But, most basically, the problem of the cold decadence of capitalism is not that it represents the decline of the values and ideologies of the past. It is that this system will transform itself without really noticing the fact, and that the businessman as revolutionist will corrupt, not simply himself, but the society of the future as well.

4

The Decadence
of the Poor

The decadence of the rich is a fascinating disorder. In the twentieth century, it has evoked novels, plays, and films, among them at least one masterpiece, *Remembrance of Things Past*.

The decadence of the poor is, however, a more serious matter.

In one major Western tradition, the mass is thought of as somehow immune from the corruptions of the rich. Marcel Proust described the workingmen and women gazing through the window of the wealthy hotel at Balbec as spectators at an aquarium; the monied guests were exotic fish. He thinks, "it is an important social question to know if this wall of glass will always protect the festivals of the marvelous beasts, and if the obscure people who avidly watch in the night will not some day burst through and devour them."

For the sensitive, aristocratic French genius, as for Karl Marx, the people were excluded, separate, protected by their poverty from the dissolute life of the rich. And the social question was whether this mass would one day break the walls down in an act of fierce anger.

In his speculations on history, Arnold Toynbee puts this intuition in grand theoretical form. For him, one of the marks of social breakdown is that the poor become disgusted with the wealthy. There is a "secession of the proletariat," "a withdrawal of mimesis on the part of the majority." The people sense the impotence of their rulers and turn away from them toward new and charismatic leaders. This analysis is obviously influenced by the European experience between the two world wars, and it accounts in a rough way for much of two decades of the century.

Yet, in the post-World War II period, when the cold decadence of capitalism became more of a possibility, that development was accompanied by signs of a process exactly contrary to the one Toynbee described: that the many will imitate, rather than withdraw from, the confusion of the few.

What happens if there is an integration of the proletariat rather than a secession?

For over a hundred years, the Western poor have been the most dynamic, creative, and moral force for social justice in their culture. Some now say that their bitter struggle with the rich is at an end, resolved by a compromise. But then, what will be the political equivalent of poverty, what will replace the idealism that misery forced upon millions? Have the obscure people outside Proust's hotel at Balbec shattered the wall of glass and finally entered the aquarium, not in order to devour the marvelous beasts, but to become more and more like them?

I

In English, the factory worker was often called a "hand." Behind the term there was a theory and a contempt. The semiskilled operatives, the word implied, were no more spiritual or complex than the routine jobs they performed. They were not men and certainly not hearts or brains; they were hands. The idea was quite logical and utterly wrong.

Adam Smith reflected this attitude when he wrote, "The understandings of the greater part of men are necessarily formed by their ordinary employments. The man whose life is spent in performing a few simple operations . . . has no occasion to exert his understanding . . . He generally becomes as stupid and ignorant as it is possible for a human creature to become." At the end of the nineteenth century, Frederick Taylor, the father of "time study," was even more brutal. "One of the first requirements for a man who is fit to handle pig iron is that he shall be so stupid, so phlegmatic, that he more nearly resembles an ox than any other type."

In 1895, Gustave Le Bon, the French psychologist, was one of the first to generalize this theory into a prediction of the civilization of the future: "the era of the masses," he called it. The trade unions, he said, were a major agency of the rise of mass man. The latter was destructive, barbaric, suggestible, simple, sentimental, and credulous. The emergence of the labor movement therefore was a sign of social decline, a harbinger of the coming reign of the incompetents. This judgment and those of Smith and Taylor were the self-interested observations of the defenders of a system. Yet, they have a ring of common sense. After all, degradation should degrade.

It was Karl Marx, more than any Western thinker, who penetrated the obvious, which was false, and formulated the paradox, which was true. (The Karl Marx to whom I refer here, and throughout this book, is not the mythic figure to whom the Russians assign the honor, and the Americans the shame, of being the father of totalitarianism. He is the revolutionary and democratic humanist who reveals himself in his own writings, those books which most people with opinions about him have never read.)

For Marx, the working class was a dynamic contradiction. On the one hand, the workers suffered the concentrated horrors of industrial society "in their most inhuman form," and they were denied "even the appearance of humanity" (Smith, Taylor, and Le Bon got no further than this). Yet at the same time, this "irremediable and imperious distress" forced the proletarians to revolt out of practical necessity. And since they rebelled against inhumanity itself, their values were those of humanity itself.

Thus, Marx forged a strange, dialectical chain of reasoning. Capitalism, the wealthiest system the world has ever known, created a new kind of industrial poverty; this misery, in its specifically working-class form, becomes the driving force of a movement for human happiness.

The precision of Marx's ultimate expectations are obviously open to question. Their accuracy is the subject of much of this chapter. But in terms of understanding the dynamic and general direction of the industrial masses, his intuition has been corroborated by events. In broad compass, the "hands" acted much more as Marx said they would rather than according to the predictions of Smith, Taylor, and Le Bon. For over a century, the Western labor movement has been crucial to practically every advance in social ethics.

At times, this process produced moments of a rare idealism. Manchester mill hands supported Lincoln and the North even though they lost materially in the doing. Australian workers, in a vast outpouring, made it possible for London dockers to organize in the late nineteenth century. In the United States, perhaps the most violent nation of class conflict, history is studded with strikes and even massacres in which the workers were starved, beaten, and murdered. But in addition to the dramatic events, there was the constant, grinding social war of attrition between the poor and the rich, filled with anonymous acts of heroism on the part of the people.

These facts have been, and can be, sentimentalized. There is a "proletarian" literature which, in Empson's brilliant image, is a form of pastoral poetry. Like courtiers singing the virtues of idealized rustics, middle-class writers turned the lives of the workers into a sociological romance. Because of these mawkish odes, there are now those who would deny the practical, and utterly human, idealism that seized upon "ordinary" people. Yet a history remains, even if many of its protagonists are nameless.

Some of the causes for which the workers fought were in their immediate, obvious self-interest, like higher wages and the right to organize. But others went far beyond any calculus of personal or even narrow class gain. Throughout Europe, the trade unions and socialist parties championed democratic freedoms and universal suffrage. In

Germany, the anticlerical Social Democrats defended the Catholic victims of Bismarck's *Kulturkampf;* in France, socialist workers rallied against the anti-Semitism of the Dreyfus case, supporting an essentially conservative man who had his heroism thrust upon him; in England, the unschooled mass was a driving force for the expansion of education; and in every Western nation, the humble tutored their "betters" in some of the fundamentals of human decency.

It was an American socialist, Eugene Victor Debs, who most profoundly incarnated this libertarian aspect of the socialist ideal. Debs left no heritage of theory nor even of party leadership. But more than any of his contemporaries, he understood his movement as one of self-emancipation, its essential power deriving from free men and women rather than from any economic doctrine or plan. "I don't want you to follow me or anyone else," he said in one of his most famous statements. "If you are looking for a Moses to lead you out of this capitalist wilderness, you will stay right where you are. I would not lead you into the promised land if I could, because if I could lead you in, someone else could lead you out."

Clearly, the original party of the poor did not merely seek to make society more tolerable. It believed that the struggle could not possibly stop this side of a new way of human life. But by the mid-twentieth century, the American unions had removed most of the passionate references to the class struggle from their constitutions, and the European Social Democrats seemed to have accepted the mixed economy and the welfare state as a substitute for the Parliament of Man.

These developments raise momentous questions. Have the Western poor vanished as a social reality, or at least as a social force? And if they have, does the event mark their triumph or their decadence?

II

The paradox of defeat through victory has intrigued the West since the Greeks and their theory of *hubris*.

It has been given as an explanation of the decadence of nations and institutions. Rome declined, Gibbon once wrote, out of its own "immoderate greatness." And R. H. Tawney said of Christianity, "The Church of the third century, a minority of believers confronted with an alien civilization, might protest and criticize. But when the whole leaven was mixed with the lump, when the Church was regarded, not as *a* society, but as society itself, it was inevitably diluted by the mass it absorbed."

Now, this kind of analysis is used to explain the corruption of the party of the poor. The working-class and socialist movement, it is said, was so successful in its day-to-day battle that it accomplished something the capitalists could never have done: it gave the masses a stake in, and a consequent loyalty to, capitalism. The revolution was put down, not by the violence of the masters, but by the achievements of the former slaves.

This thesis is peculiar to the richest of the advanced nations—to Western Europe and the United States (although it now tends to merge with a theory of the decadence of the poor proved from Russian sources). In retrospect, its symbolic date is August, 1914, when the movement of the poor joined the army.

The thought that reform subverted revolution was, of course, urged before 1914. As early as 1870, a veteran of the British struggles complained, "In our old Chartist times, it is true, Lancanshire working men were in rags by the thousands and many of them lacked food. But you could see them in groups discussing the great doctrine of political justice or the teachings of socialism. Now you will see no such groups. But you will hear well-dressed working men talking of cooperative stores and their shares in building societies. And you will see others, like idiots, leading small greyhound dogs, covered with cloth. They are about to race and they are betting their money as they go."

This puritanical description of the flabbiness of the British working class was somewhat premature. It predated the New Unionism, when some of the lowliest of the "hands" came into the movement, the formation of the Labor Party, the syndicalist direct action before World War I, the 1926 General Strike, and the Labor Government of 1945. Yet the basic idea of the old Chartist became plausible to more and more people precisely because of the triumphs he did not foresee. Almost a century after he spoke, Raymond Aron restated his theme in sophisticated form: "Socialism has ceased in the West to be a myth because it has become a part of reality."

Between the Chartist's complaint and Aron's pronouncement, the Western socialist movement itself confronted their argument. There was a furious debate at the turn of the century when both the reformers and the revolutionists realized that society was not developing according to prediction. The discussion involved a massive and intricate shift in socialist theory, but a few important instances should suggest the new hope and the new fear: that the workers were being integrated rather than revolutionized.

Eduard Bernstein had been a guardian of Marxian orthodoxy but, as an exile in England, he had come under the influence of Fabian gradualism and its plan that socialism would "permeate" society from the intellectual top down rather than seize power from the bottom up. Returning to Germany, Bernstein argued that the polarization of classes into an arrogant, tiny bourgeoisie and an ever-increasing proletariat was not taking place. The middle strata were more tenacious than had been imagined, and were even recruiting new layers. Moreover, capitalism was learning to limit the severity of its cyclical crises; it was socializing itself in an evolutionary way. Consequently, Bernstein concluded, it was necessary to abandon the old revolutionary perspective (and with it, Engels' corresponding philosophical assertion of a dialectical leap inherent in all nature).

Time was to prove Bernstein spectacularly right and wrong. Two world wars and the Great Depression of the thirties refuted his prophecy that the West of 1900 was peacefully and progressively solving its internal contradictions. Yet, he had correctly understood that the stark model of a society more and more simplified into two hostile camps was inaccurate. The terrible proof came in August, 1914. After a few hesitations, the socialist parties of Europe supported their various national war efforts, the workers killed one another and showed, for a while at least, that their patriotism was more intense than their class consciousness. The willingness to die for a country is a profound index of a man's sense of being integrated within it. Ironically, Bernstein, the archrevisionist, was among the few

German socialist leaders who honored the traditional anti-war position and refused to support the Kaiser.

Georges Sorel was Bernstein turned upside down. He too realized that society was not developing as bitterly as it was supposed to, and the fact horrified him. In his *Reflections on Violence*, Sorel considered the gloomy possibility that the exploiters were becoming humane. If the rulers, he wrote, are "led astray by the *chatter* of the preachers of ethics and sociology, return to an ideal of *conservative mediocrity*, seek to correct the *abuses* of economics, and work to break with the barbarism of their predecessors, then one part of the powers which were to further the development of capitalism is employed in hindering it, an arbitrary and irrational element is introduced, and the future of the world becomes completely indeterminate."

With an eccentric brilliance, Sorel took his argument to its utterly logical and bizarre conclusion. The workers must militantly teach the rulers that there was no advantage in decency. Once business was forced by the proletarians to brutalize the proletariat, then the essential antagonisms would be reestablished, life would once more meet the requirements of theory, and it would move toward the preordained revolution.

In August, 1914, the very earth opened up under the feet of every Western social philosophy. At one and the same moment, both *status quo* and utopia were in crisis. A new and sophisticated savagery intruded upon the capitalist idyll of a peaceful evolution. The socialist dream that the worker's allegiance was to an international class rather than to a nation-state was ended. And every nineteenth-century hope, to use Sorel's phrase, became indeterminate.

When Vladimir Ilyich Lenin received a copy of the German Social Democratic newspaper announcing the Party's support for the Kaiser's war, he first thought it a forgery of the General Staff designed to deceive the revolutionary workers. When he learned that the document was genuine, he decided that the revolution would never take place in his own lifetime and turned to the study of Hegel. When the initial shock wore off, he angrily came back to political life and declared the decadence of part, but only part, of the socialist movement.

Lenin argued that society had tamed the revolution by corrupting the leaders of the party of the poor. Imperialism had provided super profits to capital—and bribes to a small group of traitors within the working-class movement. This was not done conspiratorially, by actually buying off these leaders. It was a social and economic process: "Scraps of the booty enjoyed by the privileged as a result of this oppression undoubtedly fall to the lot of certain sections of the petty bourgeoisie and the aristocracy and bureaucracy of the working class." This "labor aristocracy" in turn misleads the entire movement even though the masses remain as desperate as ever. And the millions are taken in because the leaders continue to talk the old rhetoric, using it as a cover for their betrayal.

Given this analysis, Lenin could maintain his hopes. Only a minority of the working class had been integrated with the profiteers. The majority remained poor and basically revolutionary. The problem was to emancipate the hungry masses from the deceptions of the well-fed few in their midst.

Lenin's attempt to salvage the old faith was compelling

enough to furnish the programmatic basis for the Western
Communist movement. Yet one of its more important assumptions—that only a thin stratum of the workers was
sharing in the growth of capitalism—was not true. In England, for example, the real wages of the whole working class
nearly doubled from the end of the Hungry Forties to the
turn of the century. And if there was any effect of growing
capitalist wealth, it was to reduce the differentiation within
the working class. (Between the two wars, for instance, a
plumber in industrially advanced Britain received 147 percent of the unskilled wage, and in backward Rumania,
300 percent.)

But poverty was not eliminated, and, particularly during
the Depression, life was lived day to day and not in a
statistical long run. There were the rise of fascism, World
War II, economic crisis. These explosions lent plausibility
to Lenin's thesis. And the rich did not become socially
responsible. The welfare-state reforms that are now established institutions in the West were created against the
educated will of the powerful and through the action of
the "hands" and their middle-class allies.

Yet there was a long run and it eventually was fatal to
Lenin's analysis. In fits and starts, through conflict rather
than conciliation, and with persistent inequities, the lot of
the entire Western working class gradually improved, particularly after the recovery from World War II. It was the
reality of this experience which drove the Continental Social Democrats to their revisions of doctrine, pushed the
Italian Communists into struggling within the context of
neo-capitalism, and decreased the influence of radicals
throughout the American union movement.

There were scholarly explanations of this process. One of the earliest was made by Karl Mannheim in a most influential distinction. In the first, terrible stage of industrialism, the worker's movement was utopian (or revolutionary) because the poor felt that they had literally nothing to gain from the existing order. But as their protests and struggles, carried out in the name of a total transformation, provoked partial reforms, the revolutionists themselves achieved a stake in the very society they opposed. As a result, they moved from utopian vision to practical ideology, though often keeping the old language.

Recently, some scholars—one of the most brilliant is George Lichtheim—have argued that this very pattern of change is even visible in Marx's thought. They chart a transition from the intransigence of the *Communist Manifesto*, in which the proletarians have nothing to lose but their chains, to the more modest formulations of the *Address to the International Workingmen's Organization*, where the British Ten Hour Law (limiting the working day) is described as a triumph of the political economy of the working class.

By the fifties, this idea had become a global thesis. In his *International Economy*, for instance, Gunnar Myrdal held that the internal class struggle of the advanced Western nations had become so moderate that the workers were only a pressure group. They seek modifications in the distribution of the Gross National Product but without any desire to challenge the basic mechanism of ownership and production. At the same time, Myrdal continued, an international class struggle had emerged. The developed countries, including their workers, had become a collective rich, the developing lands, including their rulers, a collective poor. In this view, social peace in the West could have serious, even disastrous, consequences for world politics.

And indeed, the Social Democratic descendants of the original European party of the poor had all revised their doctrines in the fifties. In Germany, Austria, England, and Scandinavia, the mass socialist parties seriously modified the old view of a social war between capitalist and worker. The persistence of the middle class and the increase in the number of white-collar and service employees were major factors in this decision. As a result, most of these parties followed the lead of the German Social Democrats, defining themselves as national parties "of all those who work" rather than as a class party of the proletariat.

In the United States, a formal party of the poor never developed as an independent institution in its own right. Major sections of the American labor movement contented themselves with Samuel Gompers' pragmatic nonideology, the simple slogan of "more." But the industrial unionists of the CIO had come to think of their organization as a unique social force. And in the sixties they, too, were undergoing a crisis of identity and purpose.

So it was that movements that had once thought of themselves as the cells of a new social order settled on rearranging society rather than revolutionizing it. The growth in living standards and relative social peace of the postwar years may, or may not, be a permanent development in Western society. But what is incontestable and momentous is that the West, for the first time in its history, is not fundamentally challenged from within.

III

The fate of the poor—or, some said, the ex-poor—in the advanced nations led to these theories that utopia had been either approximated or corrupted. In every version of this basic idea, the praise or blame for the fact is attached, not to the people themselves, but to a social process.

A second definition of the decadence of the poor is more poignant.

In this analysis, it is argued that the mass is incapable of ruling itself or society. The majority therefore failed, not out of immoderate greatness, but through inherent impotence. To a large extent, the spread of this notion was, ironically, a response to the fate of the Russian Revolution, an event that had raised new hopes after the collapse of international socialism in World War I.

One of the first powerful statements of the theme of the impotence of the poor was made on the eve of World War I. In his *Political Parties*, Robert Michels studied the German Social Democrats, the most numerous and model socialist party of its time. He found there the rule of bureaucrats rather than the self-emancipation of the people. Qualities and emotions that had grown out of the days of passionate, spontaneous risings—solidarity, loyalty, comradeship—had become institutionalized, Michels said. As a result, the Party leadership presided over a docile rank and file, the Party had become an end in itself, a political machine rather than a genuinely popular movement. And the oppressed remained an object of history, a pawn, rather than a new liberating force.

When the international socialist movement collapsed in

1914, its Left Wing bitterly corroborated Michels' data, but it refused to admit to his iron and inevitable law of bureaucracy. Rosa Luxemburg saw the same ossification of the utopian impulse as Michels (indeed, as a leader in the German Party she had seen it before him and denounced it with enormous vigor), but she insisted that the creative action of the mass could still break through the bureaucratic crust. In Petrograd in October of 1917, it seemed that her hope had been fulfilled. The majority of the Soviet of Workers and Peasants Deputies rallied to the demand for Peace, Bread, Land, All Power to the Soviets. The Soviets were themselves continuous parliaments of the revolution. For their leaders, Lenin and Trotsky, October was to be only the prelude to a Europe-wide insurrection of the proletariat. Germany's huge and educated working class would take up the banner raised in Russia and carry it to the industrial heart of Europe, thus rescuing history from the anomaly that the first proletarian revolution took place in an overwhelmingly peasant nation.

Even then, Luxemburg had her doubts about some of the bureaucratic practices of the Bolsheviks, but she was murdered before her worst fears were confirmed. The man who lived out the anguish of the Revolution's defeat in the most profound and personal way was Leon Trotsky. He was brutally killed in the name of the very October which he helped to make. Before the pickax drove into his skull, this extraordinary man tried to understand what had happened to its great promise.

Leon Trotsky was perhaps the one figure of twentieth-century politics who completely fit Aristotle's definition of a tragic hero. He was a towering personality, the Renaissance man of the Revolution. He was the leader of the Saint

Petersburg Soviet in 1905, the military commander of the insurrection in 1917, the organizer of the Red Army in the midst of civil war and foreign intervention. He was also the author of one of the most literate political books of his age, the monumental *History of the Russian Revolution,* and once wrote a study of poetry and aesthetics while riding an armored train into battle. And Trotsky had the classic flaw, the *hubris* too. He was supremely confident of his own brilliance, arrogant, and distant. Because Stalin was of another breed, shallow in any kind of culture, Trotsky saw him as a mediocrity. Trotsky measured Stalin by Marxist standards and found him banal; but what Stalin was doing was no less profound for being totally un-Marxist. He was creating a new form of society, neither capitalist nor socialist.

In 1940, just before his assassination, Trotsky was involved in a factional dispute that centered in the American section of the tiny Fourth International. For a man who had known debates which affected the lives of millions and the course of history, this argument within an isolated remnant must have seemed a mockery of his hopes. Yet, typically, he approached it with all the passion and intellectual energy that he once devoted to affairs of state and revolution, and he raised large and important questions.

Trotsky insisted that the Soviet Union, despite the crimes of Stalin, was still a "worker's state" in which the bureaucrats had only temporarily usurped the power of the masses. The nationalized means of production, he held, were a long-run guarantee of a humanist and progressive outcome; the Stalin period was an episode in the Revolution, not its epitaph.

Trotsky's chief adversary, Max Shachtman, was one of

the first democratic Marxists to hold that October, 1917, had been completely annulled (Trotsky's old comrade, Khristian Rakovski, had hinted at the idea in the twenties). The means of production, Shachtman replied to Trotsky, indeed belonged to the state. But the state did not belong to the people. It was "owned" by the bureaucracy through its monopoly of political power and force. This, in turn, secured economic and social privilege to the bureaucrats, raising them to the level of a new ruling class. (A decade and a half later, a similar theory emerged from within the communist movement itself in the writings of Milovan Djilas.)

Trotsky could not make the enormous spiritual leap of admitting that the Russian Revolution, his revolution, had not only been betrayed but destroyed. When he contemplated this possibility, he could not, like Shachtman, see it as the specific consequence of Russian conditions, a product of the isolation of October in a backward, peasant country. For Trotsky, if the Russian Revolution had failed fundamentally, then socialism itself was a fantasy.

In 1939, while his assassin already lurked in the shadows, Trotsky considered what it would mean if World War II did not result in a revolution of the Russian masses against the bureaucratic dictatorship. "If, however, it is conceded that the present war will provoke not revolution but further decline of the proletariat, then there remains another alternative: the further decay of monopoly capitalism, its fusion with the state. . . . The inability of the proletariat to take into its hands the leadership of society would actually lead under these conditions to the growth of a new exploiting class . . . nothing else would remain except only to recognize that the socialist program, based on the internal contradictions of capitalist society, ended as a Utopia. It is self-evident that a new 'minimum' program would be required—for the defense of the interests of the slaves of the totalitarian bureaucratic society."

It is typical of the man that his first conclusion from this analysis was that of action "for the defense of the interests of the slaves." But that cannot conceal the fact that he here considers the possibility that socialism has become a utopia (in the pejorative, otherworldly sense of the term). In terms of his own Marxist premises, Trotsky's conditional pessimism was much too absolute. The destruction of the Russian Revolution proved, not the inherent incapacity of the people to rule, but the specific result of an attempt to construct a socialist order in a backward, peasant land (a tragedy now being reenacted in China and, in various forms, in most of the developing nations).

Yet, Trotsky's dialectical lapse did correctly express the psychology of a good part of a generation. The totalitarian fate of the October Revolution was taken by many as proof that the millions cannot democratically guide society. When it happened, 1917 in Russia seemed to hold out the hope of annulling the collapse of international socialism at the outset of World War I, of putting the party of the poor back on its historic road to the socialist future. Instead, there emerged from the event a bureaucratic and totalitarian state and one more argument for the decadence, rather than the vitality, of the masses.

There was another irony in this process. The two theories of the decadence of the poor—that they are either too impotent or else too satisfied to create a new society—represent a division within the West: between the rich and poor variants of the advanced economy. History had played

a joke on Marxism. It had sundered the revolutionary will
and the revolutionary possibility. Where, as in Russia in
1917, misery drove the people actually to take power, the
economy they seized was not technologically adequate to
fulfill their aspirations. Poverty was socialized, not wealth.
The result, as Marx himself had foreseen years before, was
one more form of the domination of the many by the few.
And where, as in Western Europe and the United States,
the economic preconditions for socialism existed, the political will to utilize them did not.

Eventually, these two conceptions of the decadence of
the poor merged into a single cynicism about social change.
The increasing complexity of the capitalist economy, its
corporate collectivization, seemed to prove that the majority could not take their destiny in their own hands even if
they wanted to—which, in any case, they did not. And the
Russian experience demonstrated that, if the millions were
presumptuous enough to make a revolution, they would
succeed only in trading one class of exploiters for another.
The conclusion drawn from these contrasting examples was
the same: that socialism had ended, in Trotsky's phrase,
"as a Utopia."

And if these arguments were right, then those two con-
vulsive dates of August, 1914, and October, 1917, were,
among other things, the beginning of the decadence of the
poor.

IV

In France and in the United States, one outcome of these
developments was the proclamation of the "end of ideology."

Speaking of the great upheavals between 1930 and 1950, Daniel Bell wrote, "For the radical intellectual who had articulated the revolutionary impulses of the past century and a half, all this has meant an end to chiliastic hopes, to millenarianism, to apocalyptic thinking—and to ideology."

The end of ideology is a shorthand way of saying the end of socialism, at least as that idea was conceived of by the nineteenth-century party of the poor. In one sense, Bell rends a straw man. He defines ideology as a passionate, over-simplified program for the immediate incarnation of an abstraction, and it is not surprising that he (or anyone else) would greet the passing of such an anachronism. But there is more than a tautology at stake. For Bell must include a very substantive argument in his analysis: "The old political economic radicalism (pre-occupied with such matters as the socialization of industry) has lost its meaning. Socialism arose as an irreverent movement for the de-mystification of the capitalist ideology. But then, it in turn did not notice its own irrelevance and itself became an ideology."

In short, Bell refashions Mannheim's theory of the transition from revolutionary utopia to self-satisfied ideology. The issue is no longer that of the very structure of power (that would be "the old political economic radicalism"). The poor, the once-poor, are now fairly contented. The real problems are those of the quality of life: leisure, mass communications, and the like.

Bell is not one of the cynical detractors of the party of the poor. A convinced reformer with a sympathy for the tradition which he criticizes, he is concerned for the emergence of a new utopia, purged of the old arrogances (he even calls his hope "socialism"). But then, one must confront the basic issues he raises. First of all, is it true that the "old" radicalism is now irrelevant? Has social development so far departed from the predicted patterns that the classic analyses simply no longer apply?

Secondly, and even more basically, if not only the old ideologies, but the conflict of classes that provoked them as well, are finished and done with, where is the political equivalant of poverty that will motivate the new utopia? Where, in a time of centralizing, concentrating power in every advanced nation, is there a substitute for the creativity of misery?

The Future of Socialism, by C. A. R. Crosland, was published in 1956. It is one of the most brilliant and thoughtful books of Social Democratic rethinking to have been published in the West. In his study, Crosland makes a point quite similar to Bell's: that the traditional socialist formulations have lost their meaning through the integration of the workers' movement into a reformed society. He took the countervailing power of the unions as one of his cases in point, and the American experience as a classic demonstration. Writing about the situation in coal, steel, and automobiles, Crosland said, "Even in those industries traditionally considered the citadels of capitalist power, the Trade Union strength is now overwhelming."

Even as Crosland was theorizing, approximately half of the jobs in the American coal industry were being canceled out and the union was powerless to do anything about it (in fact, the union aided the process). The automobile workers declined in membership in the same period, and within three years of the publication of *The Future of Socialism,* the steelworkers were forced to wage a six-month strike to protect the very existence of a quarter of a million jobs. Indeed, far from being "overwhelming," labor strength in the United States consistently declined throughout the decade of the fifties and into the sixties. Organized union membership dropped, both in absolute numbers and as a percentage of the total working force.

The issue here is not a quarrel over a footnote but the underestimation of a revolution. It is in America that automation and cybernation first became a massive social force, a chaotic planner of unemployment, regional decay, and a new relation between labor and business. It proved that what technology can integrate, technology can dis-integrate. The immediate result was not a return to the generalized crisis of the 1930's and most of the nineteenth century, but a chronic, nagging, new pattern of wasted human and material resources.

One might even speculatively generalize this situation. If the first Industrial Revolution called into life that utopian movement that eventually ameliorated society sufficiently to make utopia unnecessary, what will the second industrial revolution do? An unprecedented, urbanized environment is emerging in the United States, and Europe is not far behind. Is it possible that this upheaval could once more goad people into action? Is it conceivable that the theories of the happy integration of Western society are themselves as transitory as the theories of its increasing proletarianization?

In any case, it would seem at least premature under such circumstances to declare the old radicalism utterly irrelevant. It is, as the last chapter noted, one of the most basic tendencies of the contemporary technological revolution to collectivize economic and social life. In the Megalopolis, the characteristic habitat of mid-twentieth-century man, one cannot take a drink of water or move a step without entering into a web of collective relationships. The advanced economies of Europe have recognized this interdependence by opting for one or another form of state planning.

This issue, once again, is not whether the West will be collectivized, but how and by whom. And this problem suspiciously resembles the old-fashioned questions that Friedrich Engels used to put in popular form for the socialist movement. How, he asked, can an essentially social system of production be directed by essentially private decision makers? A hundred years later, a technology not subject to conscious and democratic controls is making a minor shambles out of the integration of some of the workers.

Thus far, this second industrial revolution has mainly affected the semiskilled and the unskilled. In part, this has seemed to corroborate the various theories of the passing of the poor. More and more heavy industrial jobs have been mechanized, automated, or cybernated. There is a vast migration from secondary occupations (factory labor) to tertiary ones (the office and service trades) just as the nineteenth century saw a movement from primary occupations (agriculture, raw materials) to secondary ones. But the process will not stop at the factory. Menial office jobs are now being abolished; middle management's turn could come tomorrow.

It would be foolish to think that the mere existence of a crying need for the conscious socialization of the modern economy will create an effective movement with that end in view. In the United States, the first response of the labor movement has been more or less conservative. Some unions, classically the United Mine Workers, accepted the change as inevitable, bade farewell to a good part of the membership, and retrenched in those areas that the whim of technology and fuel consumption still allowed them. Others, like the United Automobile Workers, called for a much more effective counterattack, yet it did not materialize on a national, political scale.

There is much, then, that is indeterminate. Consider two contrasting possibilities: that this same technological revolution could produce the most decadent poor the world has known in modern times; or a new kind of internal opposition.

George Orwell's *1984* has been widely characterized as a repudiation of its author's socialist convictions. He denied the charge, but more significantly, such an interpretation cannot be demonstrated in his novel. His tyrants are not tortured Dostoevskians whose blind faith in absolute freedom led them to totalitarianism. On the contrary, they are determined, thoughtful antiutopians who detest freedom and solidarity. But Orwell was an extraordinarily candid man, and in his book he presents an image of the decadence of the poor.

The "proles" of *1984* are so impotent and helpless that they are not even subjected to totalitarian discipline. This is an important distinction between Orwell's version of the future and Huxley's. In the *Brave New World*, the mass has been reduced to a vegetable existence, but they are well fed. They are creatures of the future, a new kind of slave. In *1984*, the proletarians still exist, but more than that they have retrogressed to the brute levels of existence of early capitalism.

"And even when they became discontented, as they sometimes did," Orwell's hero writes of the proles, "their discontent led nowhere, because, being without general ideas, they could only focus on their specific grievances." "Left to themselves, like cattle turned loose upon the plains of Argentina, they had reverted to a style of life that appeared to be natural to them, a sort of ancestral pattern. They were born, they grew up in the gutters, they went to work at twelve, they passed through a brief blossoming period of beauty and sexual desire, they married at twenty, they were middle-aged at thirty, they died, for the most part at sixty."

Orwell pictured this retrogression as the outcome of totalitarianism and permanent war. But something like it could be a consequence of technology of abundance.

Already in the American mid-sixties, nearly a third of the young people were without the high-school education that the skill level of the society required as a minimum. There was widespread youth unemployment and underemployment, most particularly among Negroes who were the double victims of poverty and racism. There were those who talked of a new "underclass," of a "non-revolutionary proletariat" (both phrases are Gunnar Myrdal's). This mode of existence was not based on the solidarity of vast numbers in a single plant, but upon the disintegration of life in the streets. Its protests were not organized movements, but the urban *jacquerie,* mob violence like the Harlem riots of 1964.

If this tendency continued, it could produce a tragic,

rather than contented, definition of the decadence of the poor. At the top of the society, there would be a bureaucratic elite; beneath them, technicians and skilled, organized workers; and, at the very bottom, the class of janitors and the jobless, those who perform those functions too menial even to bother mechanizing or automating. And such a group would indeed have an Orwellian hopelessness. They would suffer a poverty that had been purged of poverty's one virtue, that of forcing men to fight against their misery.

Or, perhaps there would be another consequence of the technological revolution: the emergence of an educated opposition.

In the fifties, as noted before, blue-collar work bore the brunt of automation and cybernation. But in the sixties, the distinct possibility appeared that the machines would more and more replace clerks and even middle-level executives. If this trend were to persist, if a working-class insecurity were to intrude upon middle-class life (and, in the past, one of the most essential differences between the two existences was that the one was cyclic and unstable, the other much less so), a new stratum of society might be energized to seek basic and structural reforms. There would be an obvious danger that such a development would be technocratic and authoritarian, carried on, as in *1984*, at the expense of the "proles." But, as the teachers' union in France, and more recently in the United States, and the engineers' union in Britain demonstrate, this need not be the case.

It is, of course, impossible even to hazard a serious prediction with so many variables, technical and human, involved. Yet, just as some of the unemployed leagues of the American thirties sold "life memberships," perhaps some of

the proclaimers of the finished and unideological society
will have mistaken a passing historical moment for an entire
future. The thesis of the integration of the party of the
poor into the life of affluence and bureaucracy waits for
confirmation upon the disintegration of the rest of the
century.

But, assuming for a moment that the internal opposition
of misery has ceased to matter in the West, a huge question
remains: Where will society find the political equivalent
for poverty?

The echo of William James's quest for a moral equivalent
of war is, of course, intentional. James was not in favor of
organized slaughter. Yet he understood that war touched
something profound in men. It was an outlet for deep frus-
trations, an occasion of almost utopian fraternity behind
the lines. Similarly with poverty. It would be insane to wish
to maintain human misery in order to preserve the creativity born of despair. But, if there is no longer a militant
poor to teach the rich, where then will the West discover
its practical idealism?

Long ago, William Morris anticipated this problem,
though certainly not in its contemporary form. He asked,
"Whether the Society of Inequality might not accept the
quasi-socialist machinery . . . and work for the purposes
of upholding society in a somewhat shorn condition, maybe,
but a safe one . . ." That, after all, is one description of an
integrated society as is Huxley's *Brave New World*. In it,
who has any motive for freedom?

The answer to this question given by Bell and many other
end-of-ideology-ists is essentially that the advanced Western
societies have reached (or are reaching) such a consensus

that passionate political conflict is no longer a necessity. The big issues of freedom have been resolved, and if society settles down to a "stolid acceptance of things as they are" (Barrington Moore's phrase), that reality is good enough for all but incurable romantics. As Seymour Martin Lipset puts this mood, "the workers have achieved industrial and political citizenship; the conservatives have accepted the welfare state; and the democratic left has recognized that an increase in over-all state power carries with it more dangers to freedom than solutions for economic problems."

Or, as Bell said, "the old politico-economic radicalism (preoccupied with such matters as the socialization of industry) has lost its meaning . . ."

Within these assumptions, the poor (or, more precisely, the ex-poor, since "the workers have achieved industrial and political citizenship") surrendered their *élan* out of good common sense. Why sacrifice to create a new world when the present one is more or less satisfying? The basic material and social questions have been settled to the satisfaction, if not according to the ideal, of all major groups. After the wars, revolutions, fascisms, and depressions of the century, history has turned out to be sportsmanlike after all. All retire for the celebration, for everyone has won.

But this static assumption may be untrue. Indeed, I assert that it *is* untrue. And if this is the case, the end of ideology, if it is in fact taking place, is a catastrophe.

Some of the evidence for the accidental, and continuing, revolution of these times has already been stated. In the cold decadence of capitalism, one can see that the Western economic structures are now, and have been for some time, in process of basic modification. The fragility of the "industrial citizenship" of hundreds of thousands of American coal miners, automobile workers, and steelworkers has been remarked. The present effect and enormous future potential of automation and cybernation will be described later.

But here there is no point rehearsing, or anticipating, statistics and data. It seems clear enough that the technological revolution of this century is far from over—and therefore the social and economic revolution remains on the agenda.

Indeed, one might even suspect that the idea of the end of ideology is a product of the Indian summer of the old-fashioned Industrial Revolution, the first one. During the fifties, it was possible to look back on the accomplishments —and relative political consensus—of the last stages of the factory age without looking forward to the radical dislocations of the automating and cybernating age. From such a point of contemplation, basic change and its corresponding social conflict were the fate of the developing, but not the advanced, societies, and the West could busy itself with exporting its wisdom to those historical unfortunates.

But if the accidental revolution is a present fact, then the end of ideology would mean the beginning of decadence.

Under such conditions, there would be the most basic options to make, and no humanely oriented class or group to make them. Who will direct the concentrated economic power and with what priorities? Will planning be totalitarian, technocratic, or democratic? Will cities simply sprawl and sprawl and sprawl, abolishing the landscape? Will the new leisure take the form of the old unemployment; will it be manipulated by advertising or will it be creative? The list of momentous, fundamental, and unavoidable questions could be prolonged almost indefinitely.

Businessmen and bureaucrats are notoriously unprepared for the creation of a new, and anticapitalist, social order. Should they continue to back into one, it would almost undoubtedly combine the worst of the past and future. The ex-poor, the end-of-ideology-ists say, are so content that they have abandoned all but an occasional rhetorical reference to the Good Society. And the new poor are more like Orwell's proles than Marx's proletarians.

Who, then, will decide the shape of the new civilization? By far and large, the proclaimers of the end of ideology are men of the moderate, democratic Left. They happily assume that the passing of the simplifications of the once oppressed will open up the way for a tolerant consideration of the unfinished business of the West, the questions of the quality of life. Even granting their complacency about the way in which the advanced nations have permanently adjusted their economies, these theorists have no group, outside of a few intellectuals, that is impelled to make their cautious utopia a cause in the way that poverty provoked the old utopia.

But then, history has not granted the complacent premises. Technology bids to transform the second half of the century as vigorously as it did the first. And correcting these theories for their omission of an upheaval, a grim possibility emerges: an insistent, revolutionary situation without any revolutionists, a society urgently requiring movement but without an Archimedean point of leverage in the lives of men.

V

And those obscure people outside the hotel at Balbec: are they decadent or not?

It is possible that this is indeed the age of the decadence of the poor. If so, it is another one of history's many jokes on socialism, somewhat similar to making social revolution politically possible in a nation where it was economically impossible, and economically possible where it was politically impossible. Only this time, the black humor would mark, not the disappointment of a class, but the decline of a society.

Western technological ingenuity is now subverting Western economic, political, and social assumptions. That has been the case for the whole of the century, but in the fifties and early sixties it was not so obviously expressed in the collapse of dynasties and nations. As a result, some were able to overlook a revolution, but it continued just the same. In the fairly immediate future, this process will probably become dramatic once again.

The old-fashioned ideology of the poor predicted that the political and economic context of Western capitalism would prove incapable of containing, much less mastering, its own technological revolution. The old-fashioned movement of the poor proposed to take over the direction of this rampant technology and apply reason to its uses as well as to its inventions. There are inconclusive signs that both the ideology and movement of the Western poor have irretrievably lost their force. And there is no successor utopia with an appeal to the hearts and minds of millions.

If this trend turns out to be decisive, then machines, under the control of antisocial geniuses or dictators, will guide the revolution. The conditions of life will be as utterly changed as Marx or any prophet had ever predicted, only without the participation of the majority of the people.

The West would then stumble into an unprecedented environment, and the ideal of the autonomous and choosing man will become a memory, like Eden.

Or, it could be that the technological revolution will create new revolutionists.

The traditional movement of the oppressed could be slapped back into life. That, of course, would not mean some mystical reincarnation of nineteenth-century proletarians, a resurrection of the Communards. It would signify that chronic unemployment, the problems of automation, and the complexity of city life would provoke millions to a new ideology and action for change. The bond between these people would be deprivation, however relative that term might be in relation to the misery of the past. Or perhaps, there could be a new, unimpoverished political equivalent of the poor, a middle class (or an ex-middle class) driven into politics by the new insecurity.

These are possibilities, not answers. The one certitude is that the decadence of the poor would be so much more momentous than that of the rich. The one involves the corruption of individuals; the other, the fate of a society.

5

The Crisis of Belief
and Disbelief

After God died, Man, who was supposed to replace Him, grew sick of himself. This resulted in a crisis of belief and disbelief which made the twentieth century spiritually empty.

God died in the nineteenth century. Nietzsche announced the event as a fact, not as an argument, and his report has been taken as the starting point of most serious theology ever since. C. S. Lewis called the process the "unchurching" of the West and the result a "post-Christian" age. Another religious writer said, "We must realize that when we use the word 'God,' we are talking about something which no longer connects with anything in most people's life, except with what happens to be left over when all the vital connections have been made."

But since God did not have any heir, the funeral has been going on for over a hundred years. The nineteenth century had predicted often enough that the modern world would dispel faith. It did not, however, expect that it would subvert antifaith as well.

God, the atheistic humanists had said, was to be followed by Man. Nature had been an inexplicable fate of plagues and famines, but now the earth was going to be remade according to human specifications. The other worlds of religion had been made necessary by bitterness, ignorance, and poverty of this world. Once these miseries were abolished, man would become his own most profound value. He would choose his destiny through science and technology rather than be subjected to it by accidents of birth and catastrophe.

As it turned out, Western man revolutionized everything except himself. The fabricated environment in which he lived was consequently as perplexing as thunderstorms had once been, or rather, more so, since it was the work of his own hands. Henry Adams described the new human condition at the turn of the century, and his words remain in force to this day: "The stupendous acceleration after 1800 ended in 1900 with the appearance of a new class of supersensual forces before which the man of science stood at first as bewildered and helpless as, in the fourth century, the priest of Isis before the Cross of Christ."

The contemporary spiritual crisis is the result of this simultaneous loss of faith and antifaith (and it is a religious analogue of the capitalist expropriation of the capitalist ethic and the loss of socialist conviction). Its unique characteristic is that no one really seems to believe in anything.

I

It was in the nineteenth century that Western man felt, for the first time, the fear of his own power. Out of this mood there came one of the strangest, yet most persistent, definitions of modern society as a spiritual decline: the idea that bread for all is a decadence.

The world of democracy, science, and technology, it was and is still said, must be thin and shallow. In it, men will lose contact with their own depths. The sense of tragedy will vanish, the highest values will smother under the weight of material satisfaction. Ultimately, all this mindlessness, this ignoring of the irrepressible irrationalities of life, will lead to a disaster. Gradual progress prepares an apocalypse.

This theory has profound roots in Western culture. For thousands of years, the exile from the Garden of Eden was a basic certitude. It was written in the divine order of the theologians and the natural order of the philosophers. It was shocking when, with the development of the industrial revolution, there appeared the possibility of abolishing the sweat of the laborer's brow. The reformers and revolutionists set off in search of the New Eden. But others thundered against the blasphemy of ending economic misery.

The greatest among the latter were Nietzsche and Dostoevsky.

The intellectual convergence of the nihilist and the mystic is curious in itself. They saw the same moral rot and predicted the same disaster for opposite reasons. The one feared that the future would be hostile to antifaith, the other to faith, yet they agreed on what was wrong with the present. Basically, what their contradictions shared was the sociology of Adam and Eve, the conviction that social unhappiness is inherent in man. Dostoevsky found the suffering of the people holy unto their salvation, Nietzsche regarded it as necessary for the freedom of the few.

The wars, revolutions, and totalitarianisms since their

death have made Nietzsche and Dostoevsky prophets with
honor. The nihilist is quoted approvingly by theologians,
the impassioned antisocialist is cited in self-criticism by
reformers and revolutionists. The times seem to have confirmed the terrible dialectic each, in his utterly different
way, announced: that the quest for bread for all would end
either in spiritual banality, political slavery, bloody destruction, or all three.

Yet, if one takes Nietzsche and Dostoevsky seriously, as
thinkers rather than as fortune-tellers of history, they were
in part prophets by accident—and an accident they tragically helped to create. They were right when they saw a
potential of vacuousness and violence in the emerging industrial civilization. They were wrong in deducing this
doom from inexorable principles, and, above all, they did
not see the actual alternatives to it right in front of their
own visionary faces. As a result, they mistook a choice for
a fate and helped men make the worst decision by convincing them that it was the only one.

The nihilist and the mystic have been properly praised
for their foresight. Now it is necessary to understand the
way in which they were blind. The unacademic point of
the analysis is to learn how to make their prophecies not
come true.

It would be hard to imagine two geniuses who disagreed
more fundamentally than Dostoevsky and Nietzsche. The
novelist believed in a messianic vision of a Russian Christ;
the philosopher rejected all final causes, proclaiming the
struggle of "Dionysius against the Crucified," insisting that
reality was its own, and only, justification for being. Dos-

toevsky was antisocialist because "socialism is above all the question of atheism, its contemporary incarnation; it is the question of the Tower of Babel built without God, not in order to reach the heavens from earth, but to pull the heavens down to earth." Nietzsche was antisocialist because socialism was a disguised form of Christian sentimentality, an incomplete nihilism which did not have the courage to break from religious traditions.

So it was that the nihilist and the mystic predicted the coming of totalitarianism for almost exactly opposite reasons.

In *The Possessed*, Chigalev argues, "Starting from an unlimited liberty, I reach unlimited despotism." The theme runs throughout Dostoevsky's work. For him, the atheist, utilitarian world sets no limits on human action. It had dismantled morality in the name of freedom, but this emancipation made everything licit, including the destruction of freedom. The individual, defined by Christianity as a unique and irreducible soul, was thus transformed into a means to an end. And, Dostoevsky concluded, the holiness of life could only be guaranteed by recognizing a God who was above it.

For Nietzsche, the tragedy was that man was afraid to live without rules of any kind. Having killed God, he continues to act religiously. "The malignant powers," he wrote, "were brought together in the Middle Ages by the Church and through the brute power which it exercised they were, partially at least, assimilated to one another. As this binding broke, as the religious authority disappeared, the powers revolted against one another: . . . And now, the state in the hands of the militarists seeks . . . to organize all things out of itself . . . that is, it wants men to serve it as God, even as the Church did." The holiness of life, Nietzsche concluded, can be guaranteed only if it is recognized that there is nothing above it, neither God, nor the Prussian state, nor socialism.

And yet, Nietzsche also wrote, "Dostoevsky was the only psychologist from whom I had anything to learn." More broadly, the nihilist and the mystic agreed on practically everything but fundamentals. As Henri de Lubac summarized their strange accord (and it is typical of the contemporary crisis of belief and disbelief that a French Jesuit should sympathetically point out the similarities between a German atheist and a Russian Orthodox who hated the Roman Church): "The same criticism of rationalism and Western humanism, the same condemnation of the ideology of progress, the same impatience with the reign of science . . . the same disdain for a civilization living on the surface of things . . . the same presentiment of a catastrophe about to engulf the world."

Nietzsche despaired because the emerging society would place limits upon man, Dostoevsky because it would not. They were irreconcilably divided over the ultimate meaning of the world, yet they had the same intuition of its present meaninglessness. Why?

There is a clue to the resolution of this paradox in an important fact. Both called their completely different versions of what would be wrong with the future by the same name: socialism. Beneath their theoretical conflict, there was a practical agreement that the movements that sought to solve the problem of bread were contradicting the nature of man. Dostoevsky was against them because they violated the supernatural order of grace, Nietzsche because they flaunted the natural order of inequality. For both, the idea of a democratic abundance was an impiety, in the one case against God, in the other against the superman.

This analysis illuminated and it blinded. With their dogmatic pessimisim, Dostoevsky and Nietzsche could see through the dogmatic optimism of their opponents. As history turned out, theirs was by far the more profound and creative error to make. And yet, for all their psychological acumen, they ultimately derived their predictions from abstractions about man as much as from the men and women before them. They affirmed human unhappiness a priori, as if nothing had changed since the Gates of Eden. These visionaries looked deeply into the next generation's fate; only they ignored the possibilities of their own age.

In 1871, Nietzsche wrote of the "Alexandrian culture," of the movements that seek an earthly happiness for all. "But let us note," he said, "the Alexandrian culture requires slavery in order to keep it existing. In its optimistic view of reality, this culture denies the need for such an institution. Therefore, as the effect of its tranquilizing, bureaucratic talk about the 'worth of man' and the 'value of labor' dissipates, this culture gradually moves toward its own terrible annihilation. There is nothing more terrible than a barbarian slave class which has learned to recognize its own existence as an injustice and is ready to take vengeance, not only for itself, but for all the past generation as well."

In part, this is a brilliant attack on the liberal myth of inevitable, effortless social progress. Nietzsche knew that these bourgeois utopias were constructed by denying the actual enslavement of millions who lived at the bottom of the new industrialism. And he rightly unmasked the hypocrisy and naïveté of this attitude. Yet, obviously, he did not do so in the name of reform or revolution. The victims of the system were a "barbarian slave class" and their hunger for bread and justice was a tragedy.

For, as Nietzsche wrote in 1878, "A high culture can only develop when there are different castes in society; the workers and the leisured . . . the caste of forced work and of free work." It was not that he was against slavery, which he regarded as inevitable, but that he was outraged by the dangerous dishonesty of those slaveholders who said it did not, and need not, exist. The internal reform of the system, he argued, was impossible, for there was an "essential poverty" at the very center of technology: the fact that its "impersonal enslaving" could never be transcended. (In a relatively benign mood, he once told the workers to stop trying to build a socialist society in Europe and to emigrate instead.) Therefore, optimism, utilitarianism, and democracy, as he said in 1886, were "symptoms of declining power, of the approach of the age of psychological impotence."

In the name of the "children of tomorrow," Nietzsche announced, "We think on the necessity of a new order, and of a new slavery." God was dead, but religious sentimentality persisted in the form of socialism. The Church had been destroyed, but the state now sought the ecclesiastical power. The spiritual crisis derived from the fact that man could not take his own murder of God to its ruthless, logical conclusion.

The moral and political attitudes behind these pronounce-

ments can be debated (I will only note that the celebration
of slavery is monstrous). But over and beyond any value
judgments, it was clear that Nietzsche was mistaken about
his facts. The working-class and socialist movements of his
day had inadequacies enough and perhaps some of them
were tragic (this has been discussed in the chapter on "The
Decadence of the Poor"). Yet, at no point did they show
themselves as the expression of a "barbarian slave class" or as
an instrument of unlimited vengeance. The German Social
Democracy, which Nietzsche had before his very eyes, was
in particular a civilizing influence among the factory
workers, teaching philosophy, art, and literature as well as
the practice of the class struggle.

Similarly, Nietzsche was wrong about the "essential poverty" of technology, the eternal impersonality of the factory process which he said could not be transcended. Some
years before the philosopher wrote his first article, Marx
had understood that technology carried within itself the
possibility of abolishing all routine, repetitive, and "enslaving" work (the socialist thinker's remarkable anticipations
are analyzed in the chapter on "The Statues of Daedalus").
And indeed, since Nietzsche wrote, without a revolution or
any motive more profound than efficiency, the number of
working hours and degrading occupations have been reduced in every Western nation.

The prophet did not see deeply into his own age; he mistook a historical moment for a natural law. Nietzsche completely discounted both the human and technical capacity
for emancipation in the society which he criticized. As a
result, he simplified the future into its catastrophic component, seeing only the stultifying, destructive possibilities

in democracy, technology, and science. Most of the liberating potential that Nietzsche ignored never became reality, and this makes him seem right in his predictions. But one of the reasons it was not energized was Friedrich Nietzsche. He made deep deductions from a half-truth which, as they entered into Western history, helped to make his pessimism come true.

Dostoevsky the novelist; Dostoevsky the psychologist of the underground man; Dostoevsky the existentialist poet who understood that bugs and flies always attend moments of high human drama: the greatness of these Dostoevskys is not in question. But Dostoevsky the mystical sociologist who argued that it is what men believe that shapes their economy and society is something else again.

He said that man without God would build a tragic civilization with false idols of science and social progress. But who, then, was this God whose disappearance would be so disastrous? For Dostoevsky, He was Russian peasant society. In the holy of holies of his theological determinism there was, not divinity, but an idealized agricultural order. And in the final analysis, Dostoevsky, the passionate believer, lacked faith. His God could not survive in a modern city.

Dostoevsky set bread against freedom. Western Christianity, liberalism, and socialism, he said, had fallen into a terrible heresy, that of the third temptation of Christ, the conviction that God reveals Himself in an earthly kingdom. And yet, that is exactly the temptation to which Dostoevsky himself succumbed. The God in whose name he anathematized the earthly kingdom to come was Himself the earthly kingdom of the past.

Albert Camus said of Chigalev in *The Possessed* that he prefigured the "totalitarian theocrats of the twentieth century." Yet neither Chigalev nor any of the other tortured, deracinated revolutionists of the Dostoevskian world resemble the efficient bureaucrats of communism. More plausibly, Henri de Lubac has argued that Dostoevsky had detected the "drama of atheistic humanism" in which sincere men would be led, through moral relativism, to attack the very freedom they proclaimed. But this interpretation omits an embarrassing fact: that Dostoevsky saw modern life itself, including Father Lubac's Jesuits and every other religion, as atheist.

On the surface, to be sure, Dostoevsky gives an analysis of the political consequences of godlessness. In an atheistic world, he held, there is no grounding for ethical values ("If God does not exist, then what meaning does my rank of captain have?" one character asks). In the social order, however, it is not simply that the distinction between good and evil has been obliterated. The revolutionists are positively driven to choose evil. Having killed God, they must substitute themselves for Him (this is close to Nietzsche's assertion that the state had become a new religion). The earthly misery, which His grace alone justifies, still persists. In their tragic attempt to deny the suffering inherent in reality, to suppress the irrepressible, the atheists are driven to a frenzy of force. So it is that Chigalev's formula—"Starting from an unlimited liberty, I arrive at an unlimited despotism"—is the consequence of an inexorable dialectic.

It is this line of mystical reasoning that is at the center of the legend of the Grand Inquisitor. The Inquisitor is a Spanish Jesuit, a symbol of Roman Catholicism, and for that matter, of socialism, which Dostoevsky saw as a continuation of the Papal heresy. He has succumbed to the third temptation of Christ: the idea that God reveals Himself in an earthly kingdom. The Inquisitor rejects the grace of temporal evil; he refuses to accept misery as a means to salvation. In this, he is, for all his clerical pretension, an atheistic revolutionist. And therefore, the Inquisitor must sadly keep Christ from speaking His truth to the people. Material fulfillment is the enemy of eternal happiness (of Christ); bread (or social Christianity or socialism) is against freedom.

The Christ who listens sadly and wistfully to the Inquisitor's apologia is, as Romano Guardini has remarked, an egotist. The masses instinctively recognize Him, and love Him, yet He is utterly irrelevant to their actual lives. He is unconcerned with bread, that is, with the daily cares of the people. He regards their suffering as the best and holiest thing about them. In this context, Dostoevsky's theistic world is peculiarly godless, or rather, in it God is reduced to the role of a spectator at a human tragedy.

The source of this radical quietism, this divorce of God from the helpless world He created, can be traced in the history of theology (and particularly, in this case, in the early writings of Dostoevsky's friend, Vladimir Soloviëv). But Dostoevsky was much too passionate a thinker to derive a philosophy from commentaries and texts. And, in fact, just behind the otherworldly exaltation is a this worldly despair. Dostoevsky's essential drama is not one of atheistic humanism; it is the passing of peasant society.

In *The Possessed*, Shatov develops the theme of the third temptation of Christ in summary form. Then Stavrogin asks him, "I simply want to know if you believe in God or not?" "I believe in Russia," Shatov answers, "I believe in its orthodoxy . . . I believe in the body of Christ." The equation of Russia with the body of Christ is no accident. Any form of modern society, be it built by God-believers or not, is atheist, since its very attempt to alleviate man's suffering is a denial of God. ("Catholicism," Dostoevsky once wrote, "having ceased to be Christian is turning into pagan idolatry; Protestantism is fast approaching atheism.") But Russia, and particularly backward, immemorial Russia with its oppressed, yet Orthodox, peasants, is the very image of the divine order. When Dostoevsky speaks of man without God, he really means man torn from the land, and his condemnation of atheism is an indictment of cities.

Dostoevsky was right. The Megalopolis which came after him is inhabited by a rootless, confused people. The ancient God, the traditional wisdom, the old institutions have either shattered or vanished. Dostoevsky was also wrong, terribly wrong. His Russian God was as much identified with a specific political order as the Inquisitor's Spanish and Jesuit God. More than that, he believed that man can indeed kill God, and simply by becoming scientific and urban. (Dostoevsky was himself a 99 percent atheist and therefore a 101 percent believer, which accounts for some of these paradoxes.) He denied, in short, any possibility of a new spirituality.

So Dostoevsky was a passionate believer of little faith, who did not think his God strong enough to survive a city. His affirmations were all variations upon a despair. (Albert Camus quotes a critic who recounts that the positive chapters of *The Brothers Karamazov* were written in three months, the blasphemies in three weeks. If this was indeed the case, it is another instance of the Devil's Party in modern literature.)

And finally, taking Dostoevsky and Nietzsche together, a strange paradox is revealed. The believer exacerbated the crisis of faith, for it was a Dostoevskian defeatism and identification of God with the social order of the past which caused the churches (particularly in Europe) to lose so much of their hold upon the people, which made God so uncomfortable in the cities of the twentieth century. And the atheist abetted the crisis of antifaith, for his rejection of democratic humanism led, not to the superman, but to the pseudoreligions of barbarian elites, to the metaphysical cults of totalitarianism.

II

The fear of abundance, the conviction that bread for all is a spiritual decadence, persists to this day. Dostoevsky and Nietzsche had a vast intellectual progeny.

Yet, the mystic and the nihilist were necessarily and inevitably misinterpreted. More often than not, they became the patron saints of their enemies. They had proposed impossibilities—the rule of sensitive dictators, the reign of peasant values in the modern world. Once the crisis they announced burst out of men's minds and into the streets, their reactionary utopias were seen as the irrelevancies they were. What remained was their opposition to democracy and socialism. And this inspired both an armed and passive reading of their words.

The point here is not a scholarly critique of Dostoevsky's and Nietzsche's exegetes. Rather, it is to show how history discriminated among their ideas, choosing the negative, discarding the positive. The Russian's old faith and the German's new atheism rejected the only alternative to the catastrophe they predicted: that man, whether inspired by God or his own values, would order his world. Events took ironic vengeance upon their error.

Thomas Mann was influenced during World War I by both the mystic and the nihilist. Nietzsche had been a deep opponent of the Prussian state and of militarism, Dostoevsky of the Protestant spirit. Mann turned them into defenders of both. For in August, 1914, there was no question of going forward to the superman or backward to the peasant, but there was a threat of democracy and socialism. History had refused their hopes and confirmed their fears, and Mann made an obvious and practical choice. Zarathustra and Alyosha Karamazov had degenerated into Kaiser Wilhelm.

But then, Nietzsche's fate at the hands of later disciples was even more notorious. His philosophy was turned into a justification for a Nazi movement he would have despised. He was antireligious, fascism represented a pseudofaith; he was European, at times almost philo-Semitic, they were nationalist and the most monstrous racists the world has known. Above all, Nietzsche was an aristocrat, a man of standards and values, while Hitler incarnated a murderous vulgarity. And yet, with all the differences, Nietzsche bears a responsibility for his brilliant eulogies of war and oppression. He has been forgiven too much for the sake of his genius.

After World War I, events posed the Nietzschean problem but not the Nietzschean solution. Not only the God of religion was dying, but the God of the liberal economy as well. The Nazi theorist, Alfred Rosenberg, started from a classic Nietzschean premise: "All social, religious and physical knowledge and values are shattered. There is no fundamental principle, no ultimate idea, which dominates the life of the people."

Nietzsche had predicted that it would come exactly to this. In his perspective, the moment should have been a signal for thoughtful dictators to put down the barbarian workers. (In the Nietzschean dream, as Eric Bentley has pointed out, the hero was to be a fusion of Cesare Borgia and Buddha, of will to power and of a stoic acceptance of a world that came from nowhere going nowhere.) Nietzsche had been wrong about the actual lives of the workers in his own lifetime; he was even more wrong about the imagined lives of the supermen who would come after him.

It was not simply that the Nazis misread his philosophy, which they did. More basically, the Dionysian elite of Nietzsche's vision, the pre-Socratic dictators, could not possibly be resurrected in a technological world. The suppression of a modern, urban mass, unlike that of Greek slaves, required scientific brutes rather than sensitive aristocrats. And, insofar as there was opposition to this barbarism, it came, to a large extent, from the "slave class" of workers Nietzsche had so despised.

In addition to these militant, but understandable, misreadings of Nietzsche and Dostoevsky, the times also evoked a helpless version of their thought.

They had brilliantly expressed the notion that material abundance would inexorably smother the deep life. Since the West, like them and partly because of them, ignored the alternatives to this fate, their predictions seemed more and more to come true. But, at the same time, Nietzsche and Dostoevsky offered no way out of the impasse. One deduction from this situation was fascist desperation; another was tragic contemplation.

Their pessimism was in the very air of the age. Freud argued that the history of social progress was the record of instinctual repression. Spengler saw the modern city as the graveyard of Western culture. Novelists like Lawrence, Faulkner, and Camus chronicled the sexual, social, and individual loss of potency that accompanied the growth of collective power. In the name of a Tory Christianity, T. S. Eliot intoned,

> O wretched generation of enlightened men,
> Betrayed in the maze of your ingenuities.

Recently, a Dostoevsky scholar, George Steiner, correctly located a major source of this mood in the Russian novelist. Dostoevsky, he wrote approvingly, had opposed all "paralysis of secular reform which would lull man's soul into a sleep of comfort and material satiety, thus banishing from it the tragic sense of life." But perhaps the boldest statement of the theme was made by the American poet, Robinson Jeffers. He said,

> We must adapt our economy to the new abun-
>   dance . . .
> Of what? Toys, motors, music-boxes,
> Papers, fine clothes, leisure, diversion.
> I honestly believe (but really an alien here; trust
>   me not)
> Blind war compared to this kind of life
> Has nobility, famine has dignity.

These theories are quite often (and usually in the case of Freud) profound descriptions of contemporary feelings. Yet they are Dostoevskian in their dark faith that abundance can take only one spiritual form: a satisfied emptiness. In this, they are sociologies of Adam and Eve, the reaction of those terrified that man might no longer labor by the sweat of his brow.

The thrust of this point of view becomes particularly clear when it is placed in its Dostoevskian context. The novelist had argued on religious grounds that the suffering of society was part of the body of Christ, and social revolution therefore a blasphemy, a laying of hands upon the person of God. He identified the miseries of a given political order with the divine will and made them uniquely holy. Similarly, the theory of the spiritual disaster of abundance equates the tragic sense with one of its specific historical guises. Man's relations with his own depths, like his faith in Dostoevsky's God, needs a particular, and parochial, kind of unhappiness in order to take place.

And tragedy indeed did appear in the West as a privileged experience of the few which demanded the lowliness of the many as a backdrop. Aristotle's insistence upon the nobility and stature of the flawed hero is an admission that spiritual suffering must build upon a certain level of material existence. The mass acted out a brute, ignoble fate instead of living a life. Only an elite was comfortable enough to suffer from its humanity rather than from its animality.

Abundance and technology certainly threaten the aristocratic right to tragedy. They could level everyone down to a common denominator, sating material needs and creating a spiritual hunger. But they could also raise everyone up to the level of the tragic. It is quite possible that a decent society in which men die from death rather than plagues and famines will have a stark sense of the tragic. Under such conditions, man's finiteness could not be blamed on nature or gods; it would be essential. It is also possible that such a society could sterilize the spirit, that it would create a placid, antiseptic citizenry, devoid of any sense of awe. But which of these variants will fit the future is not, as in Dostoevsky and his followers, a question of philosophic necessity, but of as yet undetermined—and unchosen—history.

Here, and in the other instances above, Dostoevsky and Nietzsche became the household gods of the most contradictory theories, of conservatisms, fascism, various existentialisms, and pessimisms. The armed fanatics and helpless moderates whom they inspired all shared their conviction that abundance could not be humanely democratized and spiritualized. And they helped create the very doom their masters feared.

III

Nietzsche and Dostoevsky had asked if society could survive if it believed in the wrong theory. In the twentieth century, a more fearful issue was put. Could society survive if it believed in nothing?

Religion sought its answer. By far and large it took the death of God as a fact. So it was in France, once called the eldest daughter of the Church, Catholics began to speak of their land as a "mission" country. In Protestantism, there was a social gospel which tried to adapt the traditional faith to the new environment. But, more significant, there were the despairing responses. In some cases, God remained only as a symbol (Tillich said that God "is what you take seriously without any reservation," a description that would have struck most premodern Christians as atheistic). In other cases, there was a neoorthodoxy with its emphasis on original sin and the limitations of man as a reaction to the failures of liberal religion and politics. In almost every instance, the argument for the deity had become Pascalian: He is because He is not apparent, He is Deus Absconditus. As the theologian Dietrich Bonhoeffer wrote, "Man has learned to cope with all questions of importance without recourse to God as a working hypothesis."

But this crisis of religion had been anticipated. What came as a surprise was the emergence of a tragic sociology. It developed from within the tradition that held that man could order his own world and thus dispense with a need for God. Now, rationalists announced that reason was becoming irrational. They did not do so as a deduction from philosophic premises, but from an examination of historic experience.

Max Weber was one of the first to formulate this fear analytically. The modern world, he argued, was characterized by a continuous growth in "functional" rationality. In government, in industry, in every aspect of life, scientific principles of organization were becoming more and more dominant. But, at the same time, "substantive" rationality, life as a meaningful experience for individual human beings, as an explicable totality, was on the decline. Technology would progressively bureaucratize and bureaucratize, and in this context it made little difference whether a socialist order would succeed capitalism. The future, under any guise, would be more oppressive and hostile to freedom than the past.

"The fate of our times," Weber wrote, "is characterized by rationalization and intellectualism and, above all, by the 'disenchantment of the world.' Precisely the most ultimate and sublime values have retreated from public life either into the transcendental realm of mystic life or into the brotherliness of direct and personal human relations . . . today only within the smallest and most intimate circles, in personal situations, in pianissimo, that something is pulsating that corresponds to the prophetic pneuma, which in former times swept through great communities, welding them together."

Weber was a liberal democrat. Karl Mannheim, whose roots were in the socialist tradition, carried his thought to a further irony. For the first time in history, Mannheim said, man stood in danger of losing his utopian vision, his horizon. And, strangely, this was because utopia had moved so much closer to realization and thus become, not a matter of dreaming, but of practical action and compromise. As Mannheim summarized this development:

"The disappearance of utopia brings about a state of affairs in which man himself becomes no more than a thing. We could then be faced with the greatest paradox imaginable, namely, that man, who has achieved the highest degree of rational mastery of existence, left without any ideals, becomes a mere creature of impulses. Thus, after a long, tortuous, but heroic development, just at the highest stage of awareness when history is ceasing to be a blind fate, and is becoming more and more man's creation, with the relinquishment of utopia, man would lose his will to shape history and therewith his ability to understand it."

These theories are aspects of the crisis of disbelief. They do not come from the conservative or religious tradition that thought it unnatural or blasphemous for man to make himself the highest value. They reflect, rather, the liberal and socialist traditions seen from the vantage point of spirituality. They predict, not simply the political and economic consequences of the failure of the party of the poor, but the attendant moral and ethical desolation as well. In a way, they are modern, and empirical, Greek tragedies in which man's assertion of his freedom is simultaneously the working out of a terrible fate.

There were two main ways in which the first half of the century seemed to confirm these fears. In two world wars, on the one hand, the most sophisticated techniques were put to barbarous uses without ethical restraint; and, on the other, peace and prosperity appeared to many as barren, meaningless accomplishments. Albert Camus and C. Wright Mills were among those who stood in the middle of these events, fighting against them. In their own terms, they failed, but their failures were more profound than most of the successes around them.

Camus and Mills were exceptional men. That gave them a perspective to view what was typical in their times.

They were both outsiders, even to their birth. Camus was a French Algerian, Mills an American Texan. The biographical detail is not a mere literary reference: both of them remained aliens all their lives. Camus found a meaning in the antifascism of the Resistance, yet after the Liberation he broke with his former comrades-in-arms and refused to make politic lies about Russian totalitarianism. Mills was a bull in the academic china shop, a rowdy genius who scandalized his fellow scholars by alternating research with political partisanship. The Texan died of heart disease before he was fifty, torn apart by his own energies; the Frenchman was killed in an automobile accident which he might have invented as a symbol of the absurdity of life.

Camus was a man of the Left. Yet before World War II his most important experience was not that of solidarity but of an alienation in which nothing had meaning. He called this being a stranger "in a universe suddenly deprived of illusions," an "exile without recourse since it has no memory of a lost homeland and no hope of a promised land. This divorce between man and his life, between the actor and the scenery, is the sentiment of the absurd."

This is a particularly French literary echo in Camus's description of a life perched between a forgotten homeland and a promised land that is not hoped for. In the 1830's, Alfred de Musset had written his famous description of the "sickness of the century": "The people who have experienced 1793 and 1814 have two wounds. All that was is no longer; all that will be is not yet. Look no further for the secret of our ills." All that was is no longer; all that will be is not yet. That is where Camus lived, in between faiths. But then, Musset was talking only of the staleness of existence in a bourgeois monarchy which followed upon the heroic age of Napoleon. For Camus and his generation, it was not that history had become boring, but that it was meaningless.

With the Second World War, Camus found a new promise. He had felt the unforgettable experience of human solidarity and it became his central value. Men of the Resistance like Camus saw their movement as the cell of a new society and not just as an uprising against the Nazi oppressor. The talk was of the "tomorrows which will sing." Within a few short years after the Liberation, the endless compromises of the Fourth Republic had killed the dream. More than that, the Left was split on an issue which did more to undermine the secular confidence and conscience than any other in the twentieth century: the totalitarian regime of Joseph Stalin.

For Camus, Weber's prediction of the rationalization of life thus came true in its most nightmarish form: the premeditated, scientific crime. In Nazism and communism, the most advanced technological knowledge was put to primitive purpose. In the case of Communist totalitarianism, the irony was even more terrible, since the rhetoric of human emancipation was used as a justification for slave labor.

Out of his personal experience with two monstrous bureaucratic states, Camus received his particular political anguish. "The nineteenth and twentieth centuries," he wrote, "are, in their most profound tendencies, those times which have attempted to live without transcendence." " 'How can we live without grace' is the question which dominated the nineteenth century. 'By justice,' all those who rejected nihilism answered. To people who had despaired of the kingdom of God they promised the kingdom of man . . . But now that kingdom has grown more distant . . . The question of the twentieth century for which the terrorists died and which tears at the contemporary world is more and more clear: how live without grace or justice?"

Camus's bewilderment was not confined to the secular Left. At roughly the same time as he was writing these words, Jacques Maritain, the Catholic and humanist philosopher, was admitting that ethics seemed to be completely irrelevant in a concentration camp. Nazism and communism had posed Camus's question to every decent man: How live without grace and without justice?

Camus could not answer his own cry. He saw through the various totalitarian ideologies, refusing the argument that murder and repression were the way to the Good Society. The end, he said, does indeed justify the means. But what justifies the end? He replied: the means. At every moment, the means are the end, the end is the means, and there can be no separation of them. The suppression of the truth in the name of the ends of justice actually contains within it the ends of antijustice.

And surveying the century, Camus could find movements and moments when solidarity expressed itself in action, but, whenever these institutionalized themselves, they became another source of power and repression. Positively, he could find nothing more than a romantic syndicalism to counterpose against his own corrosive skepticism. He died as he lived: a victim.

Camus faced a society without transcendence in its murderous and totalitarian form. So did Mills, but he also confronted the well-fed variant of the same phenomenon.

The Modern Age has passed, Mills said. The world has entered the Fourth Epoch. The mark of this transition is that "ideas of freedom and reason have become moot; . . . increased rationality may not be assumed to make for increased freedom. The underlying trends are well known.

Great and rational organizations—in brief, bureaucracies—
have indeed increased but the substantive reason of the
individual has not. Caught in the limited milieux of their
everyday lives, ordinary men cannot reason about the great
structures—rational and irrational—of which their milieux
are subordinate parts."

In this analysis, Mills is very much in the Weberian tradition. As society becomes more complex in its activities, as
its economic and political operations become more "rational," the individual is less and less able to grasp the
totality of the world in which he lives. Thus it is that an
environment made by men becomes more puzzling to men
than nature itself.

The liberals, Mills continued, had counted upon the educated public to counterbalance the concentration of power.
But the bureaucracies of government, business, and the
military manipulate mass communications to their own ends;
the "market place of ideas" has been destroyed. The socialists, Mills contended, believed that the labor movement
would prove the source of a new life driven to idealism out
of practical necessity. But the "over-developed society" has
integrated the movements of economic protest into the
power structure; it has made them part of the system.

As a result, the really crucial decisions were made by
tiny groups of bureaucratic strategists. The arenas of debate—the press, the Congress, the unions—were reduced to
insignificance and democracy itself had become a mas-
querade for the impotent.

In such a view, the crisis of spirituality, of identity and
values, has deep social roots. Neither God's writ nor the
laws of the market are in force; the majority are increasingly

divorced from any participation in the choices that affect their lives; human action becomes more and more routinized and bureaucratized. The personal experience of such an existence is one of ignorant participation in the most knowledgeable system the world has known. (In 1964, James Reston described how this mood expressed itself in the insurgence of a radical conservatism in the United States. These people of the new Right, Reston said, had a "deep feeling of regret in American life; regret over the loss of religious faith; regret over the loss of simplicity and fidelity; regret over the loss of the frontier spirit of pugnacious individuality; regret, in short, over the loss of America's innocent and idealistic youth." Reston's specific terms of reference were American; yet, the process which he depicted could be taken as a case in point of that "disenchantment of the world" that the conditions of modern life have brought to the West as a whole.)

Like Camus, Mills had once looked for a socialist reorganization of the twentieth century. But then, he analyzed the very possibility of his own hope out of existence. Toward the end of his life, he frantically sought some Archimedean point for social change. At one time, he thought he had found it among young people, but the very candor of his own mind must have told him that youth is no match for modern power. Finally, he became more sympathetic to the Communist road to industrialization, particularly in its Cuban form. There are signs that, just before his death, he was becoming disillusioned with this commitment, understanding that it amounted to embracing his problem rather than solving it.

By far and large, Mills, Camus, and thinkers like them

tried to disprove their own theses. If they had determined that the traditional statements of atheistic humanism were inadequate to the incredible century, they nevertheless persisted in the secular hope and sought a new basis for it. Others—the end-of-ideology-ists would be a case in point—accepted the passing of the grand visions, convinced that it was all to the good that man had become essentially pragmatic.

And curiously, there was even the possibility that the problematic technology itself might exorcise its own specters of bureaucratization and rationalization. Computers and cybernation could conceivably eliminate the middle levels of executive decision. This could accommodate either an even tinier elite and a larger, alienated mass, or it could make it possible for the majority to implement their broad choices democratically without recourse to a bureaucratic caste. Which of these alternatives would triumph is not, once again, a matter of fate but of choice. If a second chance were granted by an accident of ingenuity, it would still be necessary to take it. For if one thing is clear in this age, it is that untended machines create problems for man rather than solve them. If cybernation would open up a nonbureaucratic road to the future, the issue would remain essentially as it has been for over a century: whether society can make the rationality of its productive system into a human rationality.

For now, there is the crisis of belief and disbelief. The simultaneous undermining of confidence in the two Western ideals of man was parallel to, and related to, the decline of both the capitalist and socialist ideologies. So there is a massive intersection of uncertainties, a time of interregnum, of indeterminacy.

IV

T. S. Eliot once expressed the unique aspect of the contemporary plight. He wrote:

> But it seems that something is happening that never
>   happened before . . .
> Men have left GOD not for other gods, they say, but
>   for no god; and this has never happened before.

As a Christian, Eliot was speaking of a transition from faith to atheism. But the change was even more basic than he imagined.

"God," Nietzsche had said, "is my word for the ideal." The death of the divinity was not to be simply the passing of an ancient religious hero. It was to mark the end of all metaphysics, final purposes, and higher values. Nietzsche thought that a few stoic aristocrats would rejoice in this new, and unrelieved, imminence of the world. He did not understand that the denial of all ideals demanded an intolerable idealism and that a general loss of conviction would therefore peril his antifaith along with the other faiths. He was, as usual, more adept at anticipating the future than in proposing ways to cope with it. Now, Nietzsche's theoretical error has become a problem of Western daily life. The gods and utopias have, temporarily at least, lost their practical meaning to society (faith and antifaith survive, of course, as professed ideas but less and less as cultural forces). If man's purpose is not to be found either in heaven or on earth, does it exist?

So far, this question has been posed under conditions of relative internal stability in the West. The failure of the central visions did not become apparent until after World

War II (the socialist prophecy was battered, but intact and whole, until then). It therefore coincided with a sort of prosperity, evoking personal bewilderment rather than mass desperation. But in the crises to come it is possible that the vacuum of values would drive people toward some fabricated, and fanatic, pseudofaith. This has already happened, for example, in Germany in the thirties. It could happen again.

To avoid this, one must propose a most curious convergence: the united front of atheism and religion.

Religion has lost the discipline, solidarity, and awe of primitive hunger. Short of nuclear catastrophe, it will probably never again build upon such necessities, and in a technological time it cannot possibly construct itself as a mystery cult. The inexplicable natural events which God once made supernaturally reasonable are now scientifically explicable. Either religion will constitute itself as the expression of a higher anguish or else it will have less and less relevance to the future. This, however, is more easily said than done. For if religion is Dostoevskian, if it sees a spiritual leveling down as the only consequence of abundance and is therefore hostile or indifferent to the social task of mastering technology, it has signed its death warrant. The exaltation of man is not a blasphemy against religion, it is religion's only hope. Rootless city people trapped in a sterile, routine, yet perplexing, world will lack both the motive of hunger and that of freedom. They will thus exist in between any need for God.

Atheistic humanism has much the same problem as religion.

The secular tradition has long understood that it did not simply and vindictively seek the death of God but the birth of man as well. The objection to religion was that it mystified the natural. But if the natural, or more precisely the man-made, turns into a mystery, the line of succession is broken. Man can hardly make himself his highest value when he feels himself problematic. He will vegetate as long as that is permitted; he will turn to new irrationalities in time of crisis.

If Weber's deepest pessimism is right—if there is to be an utterly naturalistic world, engineered by man but inexplicable to him as any kind of a meaningful whole—there will probably be an end to faith and antifaith, at least as the West has defined them. There could be bureaucratic cults, as under Stalin, but that would still mean the death of the Western tradition in all of its variants. The problem of both religion and atheistic humanism is the same: that a puzzled society without hunger or freedom has no need for higher values of any kind. So, in this crisis of belief and disbelief, the antagonism between faith and antifaith is less important than their common challenge: the construction of a world in which the debate between them will be meaningful, in which man chooses between God or himself—and chooses freely.

6

The Magnificent
Decadence

A few men in the twentieth century were the beneficiaries of decadence.

Toward the end of his fearsome life, Friedrich Nietzsche (who must run like a red thread through a book like this) wrote, "Let it be known that I am decadent—and the opposite of decadence." Nietzsche's paradoxical self-identification was not a play on words. He believed that nihilism was a sign of weakness in that it tokened an inability to affirm new values, and a sign of strength in that it meant that the spirit had broken with old values. Decadence as a denial of the past was a necessary act of cultural destruction; decadence as a denial of the future, a refusal of the superman, was an act of social cowardice.

Nietzsche's idea ramifies in many directions. One of them is toward the geniuses who were enriched by the general disintegration, the artists who made in this century a magnificent decadence.

For the overwhelming majority of Westerners in these times, social breakdown was, and is, the failure of the present and future. There was the fiery decadence of war and revolution that produced none of the new orders that had been predicted; there was the cold decadence that through the bureaucratization of life was, and is, creating an uncertain, unpredicted order. Countless millions lived their lives in terror, and even more millions passed them in bewilderment. It was impossible to say that any of these had gained from the turmoil.

But for a handful of great men, the upheavals of these times were a liberation. They allowed them to see more freely and deeply than anyone had done in some centuries of Western history.

This idea of a magnificent decadence is hardly new. In the nineteenth century, the conservative Jacob Burkhardt wrote that Augustine's *City of God* would not have been such a great book were it not for the collapse of the Roman Empire. "Great and tragic events," Burkhardt said, "fill the spirit and give it a new measure of things." More recently, Ortega y Gasset noted that "Periods of desperation open a wide field for all personal fictions," and Arnold Toynbee intoned, "The painfully perturbing dissolution of familiar forms, which suggests to weaker spirits that the ultimate reality is nothing but chaos, may reveal to a steadier and more spiritual vision the truth that the flickering film of the phenomenal world is an illusion which cannot obscure the eternal unity that lies behind it."

But unquestionably the most beautiful statement of the theme of the magnificent decadence was made by W. B. Yeats in his poem, "Lapis Lazuli."

One day, Yeats received a piece of lapis lazuli carved with the figure of an ascetic and a student about to climb a mountain. He wrote to Dorothy Wellesley, "Ascetic, pupil, hard stone, eternal theme of the sensual east. The heroic cry in the midst of despair. But no, I am wrong, the East has its solutions always and therefore knows nothing of tragedy. It is we, not the East, that must raise the heroic cry." Yeats's prose definition of tragedy, "the heroic cry in the midst of despair," was the starting point of a much more complex poetic statement.

One issue in the poem which the gift of lapis lazuli evoked is that of the relevance of beauty to social catastrophe (Adrian Leverkühn's question):

> I have heard that hysterical women say
> They are sick of the palette and fiddle-bow,
> Of poets that are always gay,
> For everybody knows or else should know
> That if nothing drastic is done
> Aeroplane and zeplin will come out,
> Pitch like King Billy bomb-balls in
> Until the town lie beaten flat.

And, under one important aspect (for obviously these comments are sketchy and seen from only one of the poem's many angles), the rest of the work is a defense of art and its meaningfulness even in times when "aeroplane and zeplin . . . pitch like King Billy bomb-balls in" (King Billy is William of Orange, the phrase echoes an Irish folk song and puns on Kaiser Wilhelm).

The first response Yeats gives is in terms of the perennial Western conviction that tragedy, as distinguished from the tragic event itself, is affirmative. As Ernst Bloch, that strange, heterodox Marxist has noted in the same mode,

Requiems are in Western music a locus of the utopian impulse, of transcendent hope more than of lamentation.

> All perform their tragic play,
> There struts Hamlet, there is Lear,
> That's Ophelia, that Cordelia;
> Yet they, should the last scene be there,
> The great stage-curtain about to drop,
> If worthy their prominent part in the play,
> Do not break up their lines to weep.
> They know that Hamlet and Lear are gay,
> Gaiety transfiguring all that dread.

As will be seen, Yeats's belief that the artistic articulation of chaos and dread is not chaotic or dreadful, a thesis going back to Aristotle, is one of the fundamental rationales of the magnificent decadence. Then, Yeats moves on toward the Eastern source of his meditation. His subject is now even more specifically the ruin of cultures:

> On their own feet they came, or on shipboard,
> Camel-back, horse-back, ass-back, mule-back,
> Old civilizations put to the sword.
> Then they and their wisdom went to rack.

The lapis lazuli with an ascetic and student which Yeats had been given is now poetically transformed. It depicts

> Two Chinamen, behind them a third . . .
> The third, doubtless a serving man,
> Carries a musical instrument . . .

And finally, Yeats sees the three figures at a little halfway house:

> and I
> Delight to imagine them seated there;
> There, on the mountain and the sky,
> On all the tragic scene they stare.
> One asks for mournful melodies;
> Accomplished fingers begin to play.
> Their eyes mid many wrinkles, their eyes,
> Their ancient, glittering eyes, are gay.

This, in incomparable imagery, is the fundamental notion of the magnificent decadence. The artist can find in breakdown and the passing of societies not hysteria but beauty. Chaos given form, no matter how twisted that form may be, is no longer chaos. And, perhaps one step beyond Yeats in this poem, the collapse of the traditional meanings offers confusion to the many and new truths to the few who are geniuses.

W. H. Auden significantly ended his lovely eulogy to Yeats, "In Memory of W. B. Yeats," on precisely this theme. In a sense, his lyrics sum up both "Lapis Lazuli" and the idea of the magnificent decadence:

> Follow, poet, follow right
> To the bottom of the night,
> With your unconstraining voice
> Still persuade us to rejoice;
>
> With the farming of a verse
> Make a vineyard of the curse,
> Sing of human unsuccess
> In a rapture of distress;

In the deserts of the heart
Let the healing fountain start,
In the prison of his days
Teach the free man how to praise.

What follows are some thoughts on the ancient, glittering, and gay eyes of some modern geniuses, and the rapture of distress that is the magnificent decadence.

I

The first problem in the definition of the magnificent decadence is semantic, but there is living history just behind the debate over a name.

Conventionally, the literary term, decadence, applies to a French school, more or less begun by Baudelaire and Gautier, carried forward by Verlaine and Huysmans, and imported into England by Wilde, Beardsley, and Swinburne. In this version, the word applies to a group containing only one artist of the first rank, Charles Baudelaire, and conjures up the scent of both the precious and the perverse.

Yet if one takes the basic image of the term "decadence" with seriousness—the fate of art and artists in a decaying society—it deserves a deeper content. Those whom we call the Decadents were but a first anticipation of a process that continues to this day. For modern art, the most decisive fact has been that of breakdown. The interrelations of artist and downgoing values which the decadence proper exemplifies in a minor way are much more profoundly expressed by the artists who came after it. This is the basic reason for giving the term "decadence" a much wider literary range.

In the process of extending the word, it is also deepened. The narrow, traditional definition, given the men whom it encompassed, implied that the Decadents were themselves decadent in the popular (Oscar Wilde with a lily in his hand) sense of the word. This was not true even for them, but when the term is given its rightful scope, taking in Joyce as well as Wilde, this fact becomes unmistakable. An artist of the time of social decay may, or may not, be personally corrupted and deformed. His art, even as it is marked by the general decadence, is precisely not decadent since it is an attempt to affirm value, to respond to the crisis, not by sinking into it, but by making it the stuff of a vision. Like Nietzsche, these geniuses can say that they are decadent—and the very opposite of decadent. This important concept was debated at an international literary meeting in Leningrad in August, 1963. During his remarks, Jean-Paul Sartre attacked the casual Communist use of the word "decadent." "Either one adopts a naive and simple Marxism," Sartre said, "and one argues that when a society is decadent then the artists who write of this society are decadent. Example: the great decadent of Tsarist feudalism is obviously Gorki! Or else one says: a decadent society poses new problems for a writer, torments him in his conscience and in his creative activities." It is, of course, the latter meaning of the term which is intended in this chapter. Most communist definitions of decadence as an artistic fact are aesthetic curses and without intellectual value.

These statements are general and theoretical. History will give them more substance.

The term "decadence" first appeared in its modern sense in a French literary polemic. In 1834, Désiré Nisard wrote his *Études sur les Poètes Latins de la Décadence*, and analogized the Romantics of his own day with the artists of the late

Roman Empire. Even in this first appearance, the sexual connotations of the term were present. Both Nisard's Rome and his Paris were decadent by virtue of "the fume of festivals, the promiscuity of the public baths, Greek wine, banal women . . ."

But the historic definition of decadence was given some years later in Théophile Gautier's introduction to *Fleurs du Mal*. "The style of decadence," he wrote, ". . . is nothing else but art arrived at that extreme point of maturity produced by those civilizations which are growing old with their oblique sins—a style that is ingenious, complicated, learned, full of shades of meaning and research, always pushing further the limits of language, borrowing from all technical vocabularies, taking colors from all palettes, notes from all keyboards . . . We may remind ourselves in connection with it of the language of the late Roman Empire . . . and of the complicated refinements of the Byzantine school."

This was the time of the Second Empire, of Napoleon III, a period whose corruption was to usher in the debacle of the Franco-Prussian War. Baudelaire, who had been briefly at the barricades in 1848, had turned his back on all hopes of reform or revolution. The intellectual atmosphere was described by the brothers Goncourt: "Hence no cause is worth dying for, any government can be lived with, nothing but art may be believed in and literature is the only confession."

For some, the military collapse of 1870 reinforced this mood. By the French 1880's, "decadentism" was a fully fledged cult. There was a magazine, *Le Décadent* (Paul Verlaine wrote for it), and the real-life figure of Count

Robert de Montesquiou-Fezensac, the man who was possibly the model for both Huysmans' Des Esseintes and Proust's Charlus. And the precious, semihomosexual connotation of decadence flourished and was imported into England. In a study of Aubrey Beardsley, Arthur Symons described a new British hero, Pierrot: "Simplicity, in him, becomes learned, perverse, intellectualizing his pleasures, brutalizing his intellect; his mournful contemplation of things becomes a kind of grotesque joy which he expresses in the only symbols at his command, tracing his Giotto's O with the elegance of his pirouette."

Yet, even in this narrow, literary history of the term "decadence," there is the hint of more profound meanings. In his *Romantic Agony*, Mario Praz brilliantly charted the transition from Romanticism to decadence in terms of a change in subject·matter from the Fatal Man to the Fatal Woman. Taking Praz a step beyond his own analysis, one can note how this sexual shift in theme is the reflection of a social upheaval. And understanding this, it is possible to see the Decadents proper as simply the advance guard of all those artists and writers whose lives and works were to be marked by the shattering of the Western social order.

The artist of the nineteenth century was, more often than not, a foe of capitalism, or rather of the bourgeois. But the very society and class he hated determined, to a large degree, how he hated them. In the heroic period of capitalism, the aesthetic opposition to it was virile; in the mature period, resigned. The transition from the Fatal Man to the Fatal Woman expresses this social shift.

The Fatal Man, as Praz locates him in the literature of the early nineteenth century, was a powerful, Satanic hero. In one of the most influential versions of him, that of Byron, he embodied a mood that pervaded the entire Romantic movement: a sense of the isolation of the artist in the bourgeois world. In the Balzacian image of Vautrin, the social dimension is even more explicit, and the Fatal Man is a bitter, moral comment upon the new order itself, identified with it through the persistent metaphor of both businessman and police chief as archcriminals.

The Fatal Man was a figure of energy and action. Paradoxically, the Romantic movement, for all of its hostility to the new bourgeois society, shared its dynamism and *élan*. Some of the Romantics might dream of a return to feudalism (which they defined as a kind of medieval anarchism), but they were still political men and not just dreamers. In England, one need only mention the names of Blake, Keats, Shelley, Wordsworth, and Byron to make the point. In France, Balzac (and it was Baudelaire who was among the first to realize what a Romantic that great Realist was) supplies an even richer illustration of the way in which Romanticism was simultaneously a reaction against, and a child of, a social revolution. Balzac was a Legitimist, a fervent Catholic, a champion of the *ancien régime*—and the unrivaled chronicler of the world he despised. His talent was as revolutionary as the revolution he hated.

The Fatal Woman appears after the mid-century ("Baudelaire and Flaubert," Praz writes, "are like the two faces of a Herm planted firmly in the middle of the century, marking the division between Romanticism and Decadence, between the period of Delacroix and that of Moreau"). She comes after the failures of 1848 in France, Germany, and Hungary, the end of the Hungry Forties in England.

Baudelaire's tigress-like Negro women, Mallarmé's Hérodiade, Wilde's Salome are separated from Byron's and Balzac's men by history. For the new generation of artists, capitalism was no longer a vigorous abomination. It had become cloying.

The mood of the Fatal Woman and the images of the Decadents are thus related to major changes in Western society. In 1884, Henry Adams wrote that the "tone of European thought has been distinctly despondent among classes which were formerly most hopeful." In 1885, Paul Bourget was to note that "from one end of Europe to another, contemporary society presents the same symptoms, with national nuances, of melancholy and dissatisfaction," a "universal nausea." France went from the threat of Boulanger to the Dreyfus case and the Panama scandal. In England, the depression of 1875 was followed by a revival of the socialist movement, the New Unionism, the London dock strike. Max Nordau, the author of a strange and widely read book, *Degeneration*, wrote in the 1890's, "Interregnum in all its terror prevails."

In 1897, Émile Durkheim, the great French sociologist, caught the mood of the turn of the century in a striking phrase: there was, he said, a marked increase in the "collective sadness" of Western society. "It is necessary to take count of all those who, under different names, proceed from the same spirit. The anarchist, the aesthete, the mystic, the revolutionary socialist, if they do not despair of the future, agree with the pessimist at least in sharing the same sentiment of hate and disgust for what is, and a common need to destroy the real or to escape from it."

The Decadents, narrowly defined, were one expression

of the "collective sadness." In the twentieth century, the
uncertainties and doubts which assailed them became the
experience of millions of daily lives. The decadence of
Western values which the Decadents had only glimpsed became more intense. And when this crisis met up with a man
of profundity, the art which it then evoked was a magnificent decadence.

II

The anarchist and the aesthete, the mystic and the socialist, Durkheim had observed, shared in the same collective
sadness at century's end. They had a "common need to destroy the real or to escape from it."

So it was that Naturalism and Symbolism flourished side
by side. Rimbaud was writing the *Illuminations* while Zola
was working on the first volumes of his determinist saga.
And indeed, as Martin Turnell points out, Mallarmé sent
Zola congratulations when *L'Assommoir* was published.
The Naturalists scorned the official, and antiseptic, version
of the times in the name of the subreal, the Symbolists in
that of the surreal. They both, as Durkheim understood,
detested the present.

In the twentieth century, there is a similar convergence.
On the surface, it seems that *avant-garde* and the disciples
of the Naturalist tradition were at odds. Yet, they were like
the patterns of crazy cracking which depart from the impact of a single blow upon a pane of glass: they shared a
common catastrophe, theirs is the unity of a disintegration.
Avant-garde fled toward the subjective and the halluci-
nated, yet it could not escape the social world which smug-

gled itself into their dreams; realism, even when it sought to be activist and political, was constantly hounded into the inner self.

The intersection of these opposites, of *avant-garde* and realism, can only be understood in terms of their common matrix, the contemporary decadence. And the same is true of their profundity. The great artists of the century were liberated by breakdown, they were driven into freedom. With so much flux and transformation, society would no longer sit still as an artist's model. The flouting of aesthetic precedent became a practical necessity.

Viewing twentieth-century Western art in these terms, it is upheaval which is the unifying experience, and decadence is the setting in which a considerable magnificence took place.

In attempting to explain a curious similarity in the personal psychology and actions of the French royal house in 1789 and the Russian in 1917, Leon Trotsky remarked that men react in many ways to being tickled but in the same way to a hot poker. The twentieth century was a red-hot poker which seared the artistic imagination. What follows is a few cases in point.

James Joyce and Marcel Proust were two of the greatest *avant-garde* geniuses of the age. At first glance, they seem to represent that modern tendency to fall out of the social world and into the private self. The Irishman was an actual exile, the Frenchman in his cork-lined room an internal alien. They were the artist as Jonah (the metaphor is George Orwell's). Or, in more scholarly terms, they exhibit the modern characteristics that Erich Auerbach has described:

"multi-personal representation of consciousness, time states, disintegration of the continuity of exterior events . . ."

And yet, as the critical literature has more and more realized, this is only a half-truth. Joyce, it has been said, celebrated the shotgun wedding of Symbolism and Naturalism. In the midst of Proust's delicate Impressionism, there sits a Balzac.

Both writers were obviously involved in the breakup of the ninteenth-century value system. In Proust, nothing is what it seems to be (much as in another work written at the time of the crumbling of established verities: *Hamlet*). Aristocracy is not aristocracy: the middle-class Madame Verdurin, a scheming social climber, winds up as a noble Guermantes. Men are not men and women are not women: a good half of the characters in the *Remembrance* are homosexual. Even the individual is not himself twice in a row, since the Balzacian structure in which unity was achieved through the entry and reentry of a mob of relatively fixed personalities has given way to a Bergsonian flux in which everyone is new at each successive appearance.

Joyce dissolved the Newtonian world even more radically. *Finnegans Wake* begins on the last page, ends on the first, and theoretically can be begun anyplace and read around.

In a brilliant essay, Joseph Frank analyzed these kinds of innovations as part of a basic trend in Western letters. The novel, he suggested, has been moving from linear to spatial form. In the classic tradition, the narrative had a beginning, middle, and end. In the new technique, the plot is encircled by the author's consciousness. This method, Frank continues, first appeared in the scene at the Fair in *Madame*

Bovary. There, a single moment is viewed simultaneously from three different points of view.

In part, such a development is the outcome of the formal evolution of the novel; in part, it is a response to history. Reality was no longer one thing, and *Finnegans Wake* and the *Remembrance* are thus necessarily as fluid as the times they depict. In this, they are part of the same process that led the Cubist painter to see a guitar or a woman's face from several contradictory angles. When Proust wrote, "The human face is truly like the God of oriental theology, a cluster of faces in different planes which one cannot see at the same time," he might have been stating a program for his contemporary painter-revolutionists. Both he and Picasso and Joyce were attempting to penetrate the straightforward deceptions of nature and society which the nineteenth century had assumed as truth and in which the twentieth century could no longer believe.

The gaiety of these writers, their "heroic cry in the midst of despair," is that they were able to affirm at all, that they found a magnificence in decadence.

A plausible case can be made out for the proposition that *Ulysses* is a bitter book, an angry illustration of Hegel's remark that events repeat themselves, first as tragedy, then as farce. The symbolic naturalism of the novel seems derisive. Dublin on a day in June, 1904, is a tawdry analogue of Greek saga. The exile-author, one might think, is playing a cruel joke on his native city by discovering its Ulysses in the cuckolded, frustrated fantasy maker, Leopold Bloom. Even the yea-saying of Molly at the end of the masterpiece is ironic. Her "yeses" come at the conclusion of an interior monologue on infidelity, and her remembered sexual surrender is preceded by the unromantic thought, "as well him as another." The elaborate parallels with Homer, it can be argued, are the invidious assertion of a decadence.

This theory of the novel is corroborated by Joyce's own concern with the historical philosophy of Vico. In Vico's law of "ricorsi," of return, events proceed from the age of the gods through that of the heroes to the age of men and the cycle is completed by a second barbarism. Thus, the contrast between the original, godlike hero, Ulysses, and the all-too-human Leopold Bloom can be seen as an instance of time repeating itself, but on an inferior scale, and preparing the descent toward a new barbarism.

Joyce's joke on Dublin is unquestionably there. But so is something else. As Richard Ellman, among others, has pointed out, the very existence of the novel is a tribute to Bloom, Stephen, Molly, and the rest: they are deemed worthy of great art. If they suffer by comparison with their prototypes, their lives are still proclaimed as universals and not just as banal particulars. As Ellman brilliantly put the case, "The first aim [of the Homeric parallels in *Ulysses*] is the mock-heroic, the mighty spear juxtaposed with the two-penny cigar. The second, a more subtle one, is what might be called the ennoblement of the mock-heroic. This demonstrates that the world of cigars is devoid of heroism only to those who don't understand that Ulysses' spear was merely a sharpened stick. . . ."

Joyce himself understood that upheaval was his vantage point. In 1918, he wrote to George Borach, "As an artist I attach no importance to political conformity. Consider: Renaissance Italy gave us the greatest artists. The Talmud says at one point, 'We Jews are like the olive: we give our best when we are being crushed, when we are collapsing under the burden of our foliage.' Material victory is the death of spiritual pre-eminence. Today we see in the Greeks of antiquity the most cultured nation. Had the Greek state not perished, what would have become of the Greeks? Colonizers and merchants."

Then Joyce went on to make his own statement of Durkheim's insight into the unity of the revolutionists and aesthetes. "As an artist I am against every state. Of course I must recognize it, since indeed in all my dealings I come into contact with its institutions. The state is concentric, man is eccentric. Thence arises an eternal struggle. The monk, the bachelor and the anarchist are in the same category. Naturally I can't approve of the act of a revolutionary who tosses a bomb in a theatre to destroy the king and his children. On the other hand, have those states behaved any better which would have drowned the world in a blood-bath?"

In short, breakdown was for Joyce the liberation of eccentric man from the concentric state, a moment of truth. In times of surging transformation, like the Renaissance, great art was peculiarly possible. Here, as in Yeats, there is a consciousness of the gaiety of the tragic, the opportunities of decadence.

Proust provides many echoes of the Joycean tension between Naturalism and Symbolism. In terms of the literary debate within his own country, he aggressively put himself on the side of the anti-Naturalists, but in the doing, he paid his respects to his foe.

This disenchantment with Naturalism is part of the turn-of-the-century critique of all the old determinisms. In the *Remembrance*, for instance, Proust meditates on the fact that, after Swann's death, his wife and daughter finally achieve the long-desired entrée to the world of the Guermantes—but only when that world no longer supported the significance which Swann attached to it. "The work of causality," Marcel thinks, "in the end produces practically all possible effects, and consequently, even those which one never thought would come to pass. But this work is slow, it is made even slower by our desire (which seeking to hasten it, impedes it) and even by our existence, and its end is not accomplished until we have ceased to desire it, or even ceased to be."

This ironic indeterminacy is clearly at odds with the whole Naturalist tradition and part of the sea change at the turn of the century. And yet, in the end Proust's objection is not directed against the Zolaesque attention to detail but with its superficiality. "The literature which contents itself in 'describing things,' rendering them in a miserable sketch of lines and surfaces is, even while calling itself realist, most distant from reality . . ." Like the Impressionist painters, Proust departed from the obviousness of reality and violated the traditional canons of nature in order to be more precise.

This attitude is, of course, a reflection of the tremendous social flux in which Proust lived. One of the most striking ways in which it is expressed is in the theme of homosexuality. In part, Proust's handling of the subject flaws the novel. He transposes sexes, his heterosexual affairs, like the one between Marcel and Albertine, are actually the descriptions of homosexual relations. This literary transvestism falsifies in many ways—for example, it magnifies the element of jealousy between men and women by projecting upon them the importance that that emotion assumes in love affairs between men.

And yet, Proust's assertion of an almost universal homosexuality plays an important symbolic role in his thought. The homosexual's view of social life, like that of the revolutionist (and Proust makes this Durkheim-like equation on many occasions), is fixed upon its hypocrisy and sham. So, for example, when Marcel thinks of how Albertine lied in denying Lesbian relations with Andrée, he remembers how Swann believed Charlus' friendship with Morel to be Platonic. Then he generalizes, "I should have realized that there are two worlds, the one behind the other, the first composed of the things said by the best and most sincere people, and the second made up of what these people actually do."

At times, this sad, homosexual knowledge of the fraudulence of society becomes angry, almost political. When Swann comes to tell the Guermantes that he is dying, Proust gives a bitter description of Oriane's evasion: "Placed for the first time in her life in the presence of two duties as different as whether to leave by car and dine in town, or to show pity to a man who was going to die, she saw nothing in her code which told her which choice to make, and not knowing where her preference should be directed, she decided to pretend that the second option had not been presented to her, which would allow her to follow the first course of action and demanded less effort, thinking that the best way of resolving the conflict was to deny it. 'You want to joke,' she said to Swann."

One would be hard put to imagine a more brilliant, and anguished, depiction of social breakdown than the one found in the *Remembrance*. Aristocracy is seen as the breeding ground of the monstrous and the perverse; the old values and measures have lost their meaning. Indeed, as Harry Levin has pointed out, there were those who accused Proust of sponsoring the vices which he described, of thereby corrupting the French nation and thus becoming an accomplice in the defeat of 1940.

And yet, the point of the *Remembrance* is not simply that of contrasting the nobles and parvenus with their legendary forebears any more than *Ulysses* is merely a joke on Dublin. For in the midst of the flux of time, Proust seeks a solid place to stand, and he finds it in memory. In this context, the whole point of the book is an affirmation.

In the last volume, three concurrent accidents—a paving stone is uneven, a servant strikes a spoon against a plate, Marcel tastes cake—summon up similar events in the past. Why, Proust asks, does this experience render him "indifferent to death"? He replies that such incidents—"these identities between the present and the past"—place one in "the only milieu where one can live, enjoying the essence of things, outside of time." This is because that part of one's self which is suddenly, and accidentally, called up out of the past into the present is "extra-temporal, and consequently careless of the vicissitudes of the future." When the past is recalled into the present, the present becomes that past and loses all of its indeterminacy, for there is no threat of the future or of death.

Art, for Proust, performs the same liberating function as memory. It is a quest for remembrance (*A la Recherche* is much more active, and *temps perdu* much more poignant, than their translation as the *Remembrance of Things Past*).

Like Mann's Adrian Leverkühn, Proust achieves a vision of permanence and a release from flux by giving chaos a form. His novel is thus an exorcism of all that it portrays.

In Proust and Joyce, then, one can see two important aspects of the magnificent decadence. The more obvious is that their art is signed with their times, that the breakdown of determinisms and values allowed them to investigate realms of experience denied to the nineteenth-century genius. In this context, one can say that upheaval was an advantage for them.

More subtly, Proust and Joyce (and their confreres in greatness) were not simply the objects of a decadence, the products of an era. They responded actively and positively to their experience of social disintegration, and this is the sense in which the great art of the period of decadence is not itself decadent. In Joyce's joke on Dublin, there is love and warmth; in Proust's chronicle of a decaying aristocracy, there is the knowledge that a man and artist can still stand back and find personal and aesthetic meaning.

The triumph of each is that they found a way to affirm, discovering a magnificence in the decadence.

III

The concept of the magnificent decadence can be read both in the life and in the theories of André Malraux. In analyzing it there, the idea becomes more contemporary and relates itself to the European political writers of the century who, even as they attempted to remake their times, fell out of history.

If the failure of the past was a liberation for *avant-garde*, the failure of the future was the decisive experience for these novelists who continued to try to confront the social world. Joyce and Proust journeyed inward, but, as has been seen, their private psychologies were also public sociologies. Malraux—and Camus, Koestler, Silone, the representatives of a generation—reversed the paradox. They set out for the class struggle, and in it they discovered their own subjectivity as least as much as the clash of historic forces. Disillusionment with the next century was as shocking a process as the disintegration of the last century.

André Malraux began his legendary career (and he has fostered his own myth by refusing to affirm or deny its most outrageous assertions) as a revolutionary Faustian. With little formal education, he suddenly appeared in the Indo-Chinese jungle. Through the international scandal which he created when he was charged with taking ancient *objets d'art* out of that country, he burst into the middle of the Parisian intellectual world. In his earliest books, he was already criticizing Western culture from the point of view of the Asiatic East.

In the twenties and thirties, Malraux's search for values became explicitly political. He played a role in the Chinese Revolution (typically, the details are utterly imprecise), moved on to become a chief of the Spanish Loyalist air force, and emerged from a fantastic Resistance experience (he escaped capture twice, and once argued theology with a Nazi officer while wondering if his disguise was going to be penetrated) as one of the few men in France who commanded the personal admiration of Charles de Gaulle.

Malraux's novels in this period tended toward revolutionary heroes. In *Man's Fate*, his Communists suffer the terrible consequences of their Party's cooperation with the Kuomintang. Indeed, the book could be taken as a none-too-subtle attack on Joseph Stalin's Comintern policies in China, the Russian dictator's insistence that his followers disarm themselves in an alliance with Chiang. Its point of view, for instance, is exactly the opposite of Brecht's play, *Die Massnahme*, which takes up the same events but in the name of Communist (or more precisely, Stalinist) orthodoxy. Ostensibly, then, *Man's Fate* is a continuation of the classic Zola tradition which married the formal techniques of realism to the conscience of the political Left. In the particular case of this novel, one would have thought that Leon Trotsky would have welcomed the book since, on one level, it is the fictional analogue of his Left Opposition's denunciation of Stalin's China strategy.

Yet Trotsky wrote that Malraux was not at all political, a judgment which did credit to the Russian revolutionist's ability to read a book's true meaning and to dismiss its apparent congruence with his own thought. For, as William Empson noted of *Man's Fate*, ". . . the heroes are Communists, but they are frankly out of touch with the proletariat; it is from this that they get their pathos and dignity. . . ." The politicals confront, not so much imperialism, as the problem of evil. The revolution, as Trotsky understood, is only decor, the setting in which a metaphysical drama is played. The solidarity of the heroes is incidentally an act of social consciousness and profoundly the establishment of a community that seeks to rise above death. So it is that the crucial moments of *Man's Fate* turn upon individual choice (a revolutionist surrenders his poison pill to a comrade and voluntarily accepts the agony of being burned alive) rather than upon class action.

The problem which Malraux defined in those early books

is clearly stated in *The Conquerors*: "All Asia is entering a phase of individualism and discovering death." The heroes find themselves in a culture that once had accepted history as a fate, as an inexorable wheel, in which there was neither individuality nor personal death, but only an endless, circular process. Now that quietism is breaking up and the challenge is to find a way of coping with death. Thus, the significance of the revolution is not so much social as it is philosophical, the opportunity for a few Communist aristocrats of the spirit to respond to ultimate questions.

This is why *Man's Fate* in its French title was *La Condition Humaine*," a phrase that owes its origin to Pascal rather than to Marx. The "human condition" of which Malraux (and Pascal) speaks is that every man is born sentenced to death. Christianity had once given a rationale for this huge fact, but now it is losing its hold upon the West. For the younger Malraux, revolution and communism were an attempt to develop a secular answer to the human condition. As he became disillusioned with politics, Malraux's hero changed from the revolutionist to the painter.

Malraux's artists share with his revolutionists the desire to transcend their own death. They are seen from the point of view of immortality. His Goya is as aristocratic as his Communists (and it is Malraux's Goya: not the portraitist but the savage chronicler of men facing execution, a distinction that puzzled literary Paris several years back when an exhibition of the non-Malraux Goya was held). He is the rare individual who lifts himself above the endless cycle of death. In this thought, the activist Malraux and the withdrawn Proust are brothers.

The Walnut Trees of Altenburg is Malraux's last (and incomplete) novel. Its pessimism marks the transition in the

author's life from revolution and creative writing to De
Gaulle and art criticism. But the basic issue remains as it
had been defined all along: "If the world has any meaning,
death should find a place in it, as it did in the Christian
world; if humanity's fate is a story with a point, then death
is a part of life; but if not, life is a part of death."

Significantly, what there is of the positive in *The Walnut
Trees* derives from two images: of gnarled, indomitable
trees; of peasants, timeless in the midst of battle. These peasants are familiar figures in the twentieth-century political
novel and they symbolize a disenchantment. The worker,
say as Gorki or Zola presented him, stood for urban hope
and social change. He was restless, in opposition to established order. His present misery was seen as containing the
seed of future happiness. The peasant, on the other hand,
incarnates time passing without any transformation; today
his existence is as it was a century ago and as it will be a
century hence.

The appearance of peasant-figures in the political fiction
of the Left is a sign of despair. It happens in Silone's turning
back from the Communist Party to the traditional wisdom
of his native province, from proletarian revolution to *jacquerie*. It is present in Arthur Koestler's continued dream
of a "new Franciscanism" that will rise out of a Europe in
ruins. Although Faulkner was not a man of the Left, this
same point of view inspires his contrast between the heroic
early generations of Yoknapatawpha County, the hunters
and farmers, and their urbanized descendants. And on a
different, but related, plane, the Oran of Albert Camus's
Plague is a place without an economy or social classes, a sort
of metaphysical city.

To return to Malraux, his association with De Gaulle

after World War II, his abandonment of the novel, and his concentration on art history and criticism came as a shock to many of his readers. Yet, these seemingly radical departures concealed a deep continuity. Politically, De Gaulle was an aristocratic hero much like Malraux's Communists or his Goya. Malraux was maintaining his search for an answer to death with a new, and living, symbol.

Obviously, André Malraux's achievement is fundamentally implicated in the upheavals of the century. His vantage points, his very personality, are a consequence of a time of disintegration and breakdown. In this aspect, as with Proust and Joyce, his brilliance issues out of the general decadence. But in addition to living and portraying this basic experience, Malraux theorized it. In his discussions of art, one finds one of the most sweeping statements of a specific elucidation of the magnificent decadence, all but called by this name. And though Malraux's scholarship has been attacked, the issue here is not the accuracy of his dating of painterly trends, but rather the framework of his ideas.

For Malraux, the most basic explanation of modern art is that it occurs during the "twilight of the gods," that it is the product of an agnostic civilization. In this, he is stating a variant of the theme put forward by Tönnies, Durkheim, Spengler, Mann, and so many others, that the disappearance of community, of *Gemeinschaft*, is the great fact about this century. What makes Malraux fascinating is how he relates this thesis to contemporary painting and sculpture; how he presents the catastrophe as a kind of aesthetic advantage.

"In civilizations whose unity is based on a supreme Truth," Malraux wrote in *The Voices of Silence*, "art nourished the best in man by the loftiest type of fictions.

But once a collective faith is shattered, fiction has for its province not an ideal world but a world of untrammeled imagination." As a result of the fact that civilization "had ceased being under the sway of the gods," art emerges as an autonomous activity in its own right.

It is this historical setting, according to Malraux, which gives the modern painter his unique personality: "The outcast artist had taken his place in history; haunted henceforth by visions of his own absolute, while confronted by a culture growing ever less sure of itself, the modern painter came to find in his very ostracism the source of an amazing fertility." (Along the same lines, Harry Levin has remarked that the modern movement in literature began with that supreme technician, Flaubert, who was characterized by a " 'need for metamorphoses,' for exhausting subjects, experimenting with forms, and outdoing himself along with his predecessors . . ." This could also stand as an outline biography of Malraux's life.)

Malraux attempts to fill in these general propositions with history. He particularly emphasizes the relation of the artist to the bourgeois. The precapitalist middle class— Dutch sea rovers, Medicean and Flemish bankers—had belonged to a coherent world and thus inspired an art. But "the world of the Nineteenth century bourgeois was a disrupted world . . . in the Nineteenth century, for the first time, the artists and the ruling class ceased to have the same values." The previous rulers had all recognized some absolute and expected art to transcend reality in its name; "the bourgeois . . . wanted a world made to his measure, devoid of intimations and owing allegiance to nothing that transcended it."

As a result of this fissure in the very core of culture, two arts developed. In Paris between 1870 and 1914, Malraux remarks, it would seem that there were "two antagonistic civilizations in water-tight compartments." There were the official painters and the exile painters, and the former were not less talented versions of the latter but inhabitants of a different planet.

With this breakdown in values, the very theme of art changed along with the personality of the artist. "The truth was that the 'subject' [of painting] was bound to disappear, because a new subject was coming to the fore to the exclusion of all others, and this new subject was the presence of the artist himself upon the canvas. To realize his portrait of Clemenceau, Manet, greatly daring, had to be everything in the portrait and Clemenceau next to nothing." This, in turn, led to the secularized art appropriating some of the mysticism of the religious painting which it displaced: "That is why our modern masters paint their pictures as the artists of ancient civilizations carved or painted gods."

It seems logical to Malraux that this process would sponsor paintings which diverge from representational reality. All of the great religious art of the past was in a sense surreal, even when it depicted the world realistically, since it was based on the faiths that the saints and gods were transcendent (Erich Auerbach called this latter phenomenon "figural realism"). The modern artist retained this basic attitude—indeed, he ransacked the past and, as an agnostic, was able to note how all the masters assumed a world beyond actuality as the primordial subject of their genius. But now, the unreligious painter found these values in his personal absolutes, in his consciousness and imagination.

And because society no longer really believed in anything, it changed its very definition of art and of decadence.
"A great Egyptian work of art," Malraux writes in describing nineteenth-century reactions, "was admired in proportion to its congruity, subtle as that might be, with the
Mediterranean tradition; we, on the contrary, admire it the
more it diverges from that tradition. Traditional works
were composed, classified and reproduced, while the others
were relegated to an obscurity from which but a few
emerged, as fortunate exceptions, or as examples of an
alleged decadence. That is why the connoisseur of this
period was so ready with the charge of 'decadence' and to
define it primarily in terms of what it lacked." No longer
believing in the absolute truth of its own classic tradition,
the West was suddenly able to absorb all traditions, to
consider painting as painting independent of the subject
matter, to appreciate an Aztec mask and a Baroque ca-
thedral.

Here, Malraux is describing another one of the positive
aspects of the contemporary upheaval and uncertainty.
When the present was considered vital and meaningful, as it
still was during most of the nineteenth century, much of
the past seemed to be a "decadence." But when the present
has itself become problematic and decadent, then previously
"crude" works reveal their power and coherence.

In particular, the art once considered primitive came
more and more into its own: "The more ground the new
devils gain in Europe, the more her art tends to draw on
earlier cultures which, too, were plagued by their contemporary demons." And yet, these ancient forms are
changed in their rebirth: "a Picasso steps into the place of

a Cézanne and the sense of conquest, of man triumphant, is replaced by a spirit of questioning, sometimes serene, but usually anxious and perplexed. And thus it is that the negative values which bulk so large in our civilization as well as in our art come to the fore and the fetishes force their way into the culture. For the men who made them, fetishes were not necessarily disturbing elements, but for us, when we discover them, they are."

So there is the paradox that the most advanced of the great twentieth-century painters were those who turned most resolutely to the past. Cézanne "applied to landscapes the planes of Gothic statues," Gauguin sought inspiration in the art of the South Seas, Derain and Picasso "recalled to life the Fayum paintings and the Sumerian idols."

In short, for Malraux the contemporary breakdown affected every aspect of art. It created a new kind of exile-artist and secular holy man who painted a new subject, himself, which was all that was left when the established values disintegrated. It provoked a new taste, for once the current standards of the West were no longer exclusive truth, the outlandish idols and fetishes suddenly became meaningful, and there was in particular a rediscovery of the dark gods. This development created a new public, or rather two publics. On the one hand, there were those who contented themselves with the official optimism, that painting in which all was right with a serene, familiar world; and on the other, the small but growing group that not only accepted, but promoted, the liberating aspects of cultural despair.

These are only some of the applications that Malraux made of his theory of the "twilight of the gods," of the emergence of an agnostic civilization as the decisive experience of the century. In most of them, one sees cultural collapse as having its aesthetic advantages. But in Malraux's argument, perhaps the most fascinating consequence of disbelief is in the way in which it reasserted the fundamental Western conviction that tragedy is not tragic. What Mann asserted in the fictive music of Adrian Leverkühn and Proust in the remembered taste of cake, Malraux puts as art criticism and history.

He writes: ". . . the Aztec social order is now regarded not as mere savagery but as a cruel culture, and its art is not seen as a gloating over human sacrifice, but as a communion with the Saturnian underworld. The mosaics of Byzantium do not portray tortures, nor the best Aztec sculptures massacres. The ghastliness of even the most violent Spanish Crucifixion is fundamentally different from wanton cruelty. *Always, however brutal an age may actually have been, its style transmits its music only;* our own Museum without Walls is the song of history, not its newsreel" (emphasis added). Norman Brown, one of the socialist interpeters of Freud, has located Malraux's insight in the theory of the Viennese analyst. "Animals let death be a part of life and use the death instinct to die"; Brown wrote, "man aggressively builds immortal cultures and makes history in order to fight death." Therefore, Brown would say, art is, by its nature, on the side of life.

Malraux's final image suggests Yeats's "Lapis Lazuli" once again. The mournful melodies are gay, the art of a brutal age is nevertheless a song. In this paradox is recorded the one really positive aspect of decadence. The present uncertainty is a marvelous vantage point for the viewing of the past, a liberating agnosticism. It can justifiably be called, from the point of view of literature and art, a magnificent decadence.

And yet, it would be wrong to end this chapter on such a note, for it falsifies. The magnificent decadence is a fact, and it must be described as such. Yet, even though it has broadened and deepened the perceptions of a few geniuses, even though it transmits a considerable aesthetic heritage, no decent man would choose it if there were alternatives. A monstrous aesthete might welcome the carnage and upheavals of the century because it has set such a marvelous stage for the play of the creative spirit. He would be inhumanly wrong. Even in recognizing this curious and positive by-product of these times of trouble, there can be no implication of wishing the deaths and bewilderments of tens and millions to provide poignance to that handful whose anguish makes beauty.

The magnificent decadence happened because the twentieth century failed to master the environment it made for itself. Its art will transmit the song and gaiety of this travail. But, ethically, humanly, the only position is to seek a future in which there will not be a magnificent decadence for the few, but a magnificent birth for the many. History is ultimately more important than its singers.

7

The Masses

Who is destroying Western culture? One of the most ubiquitous answers of the century was and is: the masses.

In the magnificent decadence of contemporary art, the most divergent aesthetic points of departure, like Proust's and Malraux's, passed by way of the same trackless history and often led to surprising similarities. So also with political theory. The fear of the masses affected every faction in the age, moving from the Right to the Center and Left.

The conservative denounced the millions who no longer deferred to an aristocratic elite. The religious existentialists were horrified by the hollow men of the secular metropolis. The liberal (and the term is used here in its American, social-reform sense) often sadly concluded that the people had been taught to read just well enough to drag the standards of literacy down. And disillusioned revolutionists mourned the transformation of the conscious working class into the lemming-like mass. Indeed, so many versions of the mass man have been nominated to explain the contemporary crisis that one theory's mass is another theory's aspiring class which then fails and itself becomes yet a new kind of mass.

Yet these contradictory dooms with the same name do have something in common. All of them are conceived in defeat. They are sociological postmortems. And since the revolution of these times has so far taken place without the victory of revolutionists (and sometimes in the absence of revolutionists), there was ample room for speculation about what went wrong.

Each of these reverse utopias about the insidious mass is presented as a generality about the very nature of social life. Yet, when they are examined carefully, each of them is actually a sad retrospect upon a disastrous (from the point of view of the author) decade or two. Since all of them describe a failure, no matter how divergent their descriptions of the mass they tell of the same kind of process. It is said that a class (a conscious, self-organized group of people deriving common values from common experience) has been replaced by, or dissolved into, a mass (unconscious, manipulated by demagogues rather than self-organizing, a lonely crowd in the place of a community).

For the Right, the downgoing class is aristocratic or bourgeois; for the liberal, the educated; for the disenchanted socialist, the workers. For all of them, the tragic victor is the mass.

The methodology of these prophecies is abstract existentialism.

Every one of the theories of mass society departs from a nostalgia for the existential past. There was a time, they say, when there were real and personal relations among people or within a social class. This golden age varies according to the prejudices of its celebrant, ranging from feudalism through nineteenth-century liberalism to the early, revolutionary days of the labor movement. But now, the theories go on, one must recognize in the name of this vanishing and human past that the people have become faceless, depersonalized, empty: a mass.

Yet, when these existentialist reverences to the dear, dead days confront the present, they often become as undiscriminating as the masses they claim to describe. Human beings are crowded into the sociological abstraction of mass, and their differences, their conflicts, and eccentricities are suppressed in order to make them fit the theory. In the case of two major definitions of the mass, the mass men have already refused to accept the fate assigned them and broken through the categories in which they were placed.

But perhaps the most surprising single thing about the masses is that those who deplore them promote them. In the normal theory, the good writer tells of how the bad masses are about to overwhelm decency and dignity or have already done so. Yet the threnodist is almost always in league with the enemy masses, demoralizing them by wrongly explaining how innately stupid they are, creating them by systematically miseducating them for the society in which they live. The real villain of mass society is the non-mass man.

There remains the real possibility that the future will indeed be the era of the masses. Joyless and human robots could indeed pull Western culture down. For now, though, it is clear that the decadence of the mass has at least been prematurely announced—and perhaps there is even still hope for the whole person.

I

In the conservative vision of mass society, the unkempt and incompetent millions have usurped the political, economic, and, above all, social power of that elite that is the true keeper of norms and standards.

The decisive flaw in this analysis is that its central, traumatic event—the revolt of the masses—never took place.

One of the first expressions of this view was Taine's *Origins of Contemporary France*. It was a reaction, not against socialism, but against the French Revolution itself. Since the people played a role in that event, they were seen as its cause. It mattered little that the plebeian power was expropriated quickly and the triumph accorded to the bourgeois. The old order had been overturned, the masses were there dancing at its demise, and they were to blame. Indeed, in an Italian statement of the theme by Lombroso, the psychology of the masses was treated as an aspect of "criminal anthropology."

Since these conservative fears were basically unhistorical, since the masses never did conquer political power, the theories had to bypass governments and institutions that were obviously not under the sway of the millions. Instead, they railed against the mass emotion, the mass spirit, which was said to have prevailed even though the popular revolution had been defeated. After all, from the real or fancied vantage point of a landowner or entrepreneur, all possible outcomes of the late nineteenth and twentieth centuries were catastrophic because none of them led back to the eighteenth century.

As a result, the conservative outsiders not only called down a plague upon all contemporary houses but refused to see the differences between them. In reactionary Catholic theory, for instance, the "three R's" of Renaissance, Reformation, and Revolution were seen as a single undifferentiated conspiracy against the religious nature of man. For Thomas Mann, writing his epitaph for the merchant oligarchs in *Buddenbrooks,* the modernizing capitalist was more of a threat than the revolutionary worker. And Spengler announced "the new nomad, a parasite, the citizen of the great city, the fluctuating, traditionless mass," a definition that encompassed just about everybody in the twentieth-century West.

In 1930, Ortega y Gasset published a book which gave this tradition its current catch phrase: *The Revolt of the Masses.*

Ortega spoke as one who watched with horror the growth of population, the gathering power of the multitudes who thoughtlessly enjoyed higher and higher levels of life. He wrote as a nineteenth-century European liberal who remembered when the state was a night watchman for Property, the populace deferential, and science an aristocratic pursuit of the upper classes. Ortega was not a classical conservative—he was, for example, an early champion of the European Common Market. Yet, his book is a classic statement of the conservative confusion about the masses.

In Ortega's case, it is particularly easy to see the failure of his analysis because he hazarded a prediction. Since the masses had taken over, he thought—and it was a logical deduction from his premises—that the immediate future held forth a decline in science and industrial technology. Had his revolt occurred, that would have been true. But it did not exist and never had, science did not decline, the seams of his abstraction burst.

There is, to begin with, the curious vulgarity of Ortega's denunciation of the vulgar.

In *The Revolt of the Masses*, the fundamental determinant of the mass is not economic function or social position. The conservative theory cannot afford to focus on the
centers of political and economic power, as noted earlier,
for they then would come up against the embarrassing fact
that the masses do not occupy them. Instead, the masses
express a vague mode of thought and feeling: "The mass is
all that which sets no value on itself—good or ill—based on
specific grounds, but which feels 'just like everybody,' and
nevertheless is not concerned about it . . ."

Such a definition allows Ortega to find the mass man
everywhere. He invades the upperclasses: ". . . a characteristic of our times is the *predominance*, even in groups
traditionally selective, of the mass and vulgar" (emphasis
added). This is true even in the most intellectual circles
and, as a matter of fact, "the scientific man is the prototype
of mass man." In this regard, "the most immediate result of
this unbalanced specialization has been that today, when
there are more 'scientists' than ever, there are much less
'cultured men' than, for example, around 1750."

In 1930, of course, it was simply not true that the pre-
dominant sentiment among the European upper classes was
that they were "just like everybody." In most countries,
they were carrying out the bitterest class war, and even
turning to fascism, in order to preserve their privileged position. But then, from a conservative point of view, neither
the bourgeois nor the worker really had anything in common with the cultured men of 1750, and that meant they
must be the same. (In the United States in 1933, an Ortegan
fear was expressed by Bernard Baruch when Roosevelt went
off the gold standard. "It can't be defended except as mob

rule. . . . The crowd has seized the seat of Government and is trying to seize the wealth. Respect for law and order is gone." This, too, was a somewhat excessive judgment.)

However, Ortega does reserve a particular scorn for the proletarians. He gives a "trivial example" of the way in which the lower orders had taken over refinements once regarded as the "patrimony of the few." In 1820, he notes nostalgically, there were no more than ten bathrooms in the private houses of Paris. Now they are everywhere. This is part of a process in which the workers, from 1900 on, felt life as "*exempt from restrictions*" (emphasis in the original). Even at first glance, these are novel judgments: that civilization has declined as bathrooms increased in number, and that the Western workers, who went through World War I and were in the midst of a depression when Ortega's book appeared, were more and more "exempt from restrictions."

In fact, when Ortega is required to define the actual process of the "revolt of the masses," he omits the aristocratic and scientific mass men and concentrates upon the workers. The "recognized method" of the mass is syndicalism of the French type (a tactic which, with an exception or two, was confined to the Latin labor movement). And, "Today we are witnessing the triumphs of hyperdemocracy in which the mass acts directly, outside the law, imposing its aspirations and its desire by means of material presence."

The idea of the barbarism of the workers has already been dealt with in this book. Ortega, however, provides an ironic footnote to the theme. A few years after his analysis appeared, civil war broke out in Spain. The workers of Barcelona, anarchists and syndicalists for the most part, briefly held power in their city. As the event was movingly described by George Orwell in *Homage to Catalonia*, it was beyond any of Ortega's imaginings. The revolutionists established a remarkably tranquil order within the city. The waiters and barbers, far from thinking themselves "just like everybody," placed a high enough value on their personal dignity to abolish the tip as a survival of bourgeois servility. (A similar revolutionary tranquility ruled Budapest for four days in 1956.)

In any case, one need not argue the specifics of Ortega's definition at too great length. He presents a mass style which is said to have the scientist as prototype, the majority of the rich as participants, the proletariat as shock troops, and direct, syndicalist action as its "recognized method." Such a synthesis explains everything and nothing, but it is more than a bizarre sociology. For the conservative, the word "mass" is a synonym for "modern." It is not an indictment of any particular group, but of the whole trend of society for almost a century. The revolt of the masses is thus not a serious assertion that the millions have taken power, which did not happen, but a lament that the aristocrats have been dispossessed, which did.

Basing himself on this indiscriminate definition of the mass, Ortega developed his remarkably unpredictive prophecy.

When Ortega talks of mass action, he writes of workers and not of the vulgar rich or specialized scientists. Given this angle of vision, the mass man has two decisive qualities: "free expansion of his vital desires, and therefore of his personality; and a radical ingratitude toward all that has made possible his ease of existence." In a striking metaphor, no less inaccurate for all its drama, Ortega analogizes the masses to the mob which goes in search of food and destroys the bakery. This is a consequence of unfettering appetites without instilling in people a respect for the means of satisfying them.

This combination of limitless demands upon industrial civilization and a complete lack of understanding of the scientific and intellectual process that makes civilization possible points straight to a retrogression of technology. That, in 1930, was precisely Ortega's prophecy, and it has been abused by subsequent events. The problem for him is "a caste of men—the mass men in revolt—who are placing in imminent danger those very principles to which they owe their existence." (In *The Future of an Illusion*, Freud shared Ortega's basic premise, writing that "the masses are lazy and unintelligent" and "the individuals composing them support one another in giving free rein to their indiscipline." But Freud was shrewd enough to say this in the context of arguing for the necessity of the continuing coercion of the masses and not as a sign of their triumph. His ideas on this subject are treated at greater length in the next chapter.)

Ortega then went on to the specifics of his prophecy. "If that human type [the mass man] continues to be master in Europe, thirty years will suffice to send our continent back to barbarism. Legislative and industrial technique will disappear with the same facility with which so many trade secrets have disappeared. The whole of life will be contracted. The actual abundance of possibilities will change into practical scarcity, a pitiful impotence, a real decadence. For the rebellion of the masses is one and the same thing with what Rathenau called the 'vertical invasion of the barbarians.' "

The United States is singled out for special treatment in this thesis, for it represents the "paradise of the masses." Physics and chemistry, Ortega believed, required intellectual preconditions for their development which were only available in the "small quadrilateral enclosed by London, Berlin, Vienna and Paris and that only in the nineteenth century." The conclusion: "Blissful the man who believes that, were Europe to disappear, the North Americans could *continue* science!" (emphasis in the original).

But the causes that produced Ortega's mass man have doubled and tripled since 1930, and, thirty years later in 1960, his announcements of scientific decadence looked a bit preposterous.

In the intervening years, and even with World War II, population increased in the West, living standards continued to move up, the state became more and more of a factor in the daily lives of the citizenry. The scientists were more specialized, the appetite of the Europeans for consumer goods had become more American by Ortega's 1930 standards. In short, history conspired to create more mass men as Ortega defined them, and it should have simultaneously fostered that "radical ingratitude" that would plunge industrial civilization into decadence.

At the same time, there was an unprecedented growth in both pure and applied science. This phenomenon was perhaps most unmistakable in the "paradise of the masses," America. It was possible, thirty years after *The Revolt of the Masses*, to declare the West decadent, and not a few writers did. But then, the accusation was, and is, leveled on the grounds of the overdevelopment of technology, not its decline.

So in Ortega's theory, the masses are composed of everyone who is not an aristocrat. Such a definition is revealing of the author's feelings but weak as sociology. It is part of that conservative opposition to the modern world per se, that nostalgia for a time when great estates and venerable oaks were the expression of society.

And in some ways, Ortega's social science is like Dostoevsky's theology. The Russian believed in a God who could not survive city life; the Spaniard in the impossibility of the intellectual life in the same environment. As God was Dostoevsky's name for nineteenth-century Russian peasant society, science was Ortega's term for an empirical humanism under the liberal state. Both thinkers were right, but not in the way they imagined themselves to be. Peasant religiosity and aristocratic science were most certainly decadent by the middle of the Western twentieth century, at least in the sense of being the dynamic principles of society. But Dostoevsky and Ortega had assumed that civilization could not continue without their particular God or science. And they were wrong.

The Revolt of the Masses, and the conservative theory of the mass which it typifies, is existential in the memory of the past and abstract in its analysis of the present and future. It is more a lament than a prophecy.

II

"If revolutionary propaganda recruits many adherents in diverse lands today, it is not because of the theories which it puts forward, but because of the general indiscipline of spirits."

It is a measure of the shock of the rise of totalitarian movements that this thesis, put forth by Gustave Le Bon in 1923 in the defense of established order, would reappear as a theme of disillusioned revolutionists. The masses, the latter would say in their hour of defeat, are not the source of a rational and democratic utopia but of a mindless totalitarianism. They are the revolutionary conformists of their time, not the inventors of a new age, an enraged horde whose loyalty is pledged to the blind value of loyalty itself.

Ortega's sadness derived from the nostalgia of an old and defeated ruling class; this new version of the revolt of the masses was a funeral oration of disappointed futurists. In the anticipation of the Left, the workers were to take power from the bourgeoisie and build a new, humane civilization. Now, it was suggested, the workers had ceased being a class, had been dissolved into a mass, and, under conditions of general social collapse, had become the agency of their own enslavement (this is a radical variant of the theme of the integration of the "hands" discussed in the chapter "The Decadence of the Poor").

The setting for this vision was Europe between the two wars, and most particularly Germany.

There were fascist movements of consequence in Italy, Spain, and the Balkans, but the fall of the Weimar Republic and the rise of Nazism were the events that suggested the existence of the new, totalitarian mass. In the German twenties, there had been a ruinous inflation, striking especially at the middle class. As the economic crisis intensified, there were more and more "doctors without patients and lawyers without clients" and bankrupt shopkeepers. As unemployment became massive, the working class was split between the socialists and the Communists on the one hand, and the employed and the jobless on the other.

In this context, the vote of the various parties shifted erratically in a series of elections. The old ideological lines could not contain the new catastrophe. The Nazis appeared, somewhat like the mob which supported Napoleon III, "armed Bohemians" as one writer put it, but more dangerous and fanatic than any political formation in Europe's history. Finally, in 1933, all of this culminated in Hitler's seizure of power, an act accomplished under the fictions of legality (power had been in the streets for some time). German heavy industry had turned power over to paramilitary brawlers in an attempt to maintain its rule. There followed the most barbarous retrogression of civilized values the world has ever known.

After World War II, it seemed to some observers that this experience was to be repeated, but this time on the Communist pseudo-Left. In Italy and in France, huge Communist parties emerged out of the Resistance and the ruins.

In Czechoslovakia, a *coup d'état* succeeded because of the proximity of the Russian Army, but it was carried out with the support of a significant minority of the population.

Probably the most sustained theoretical effort to comprehend this new kind of mass was made by Hannah Arendt in *The Origins of Totalitarianism*. Human loneliness, she argued, had become politically explosive.

"What prepares men for totalitarian domination in the non-totalitarian world is that loneliness, once a border-line experience usually suffered in certain marginal conditions like old age, had become an everyday experience of the ever-growing masses of our century." As she attempted to detail this insight in terms of recent history:

"The fall of protecting class walls transformed the slumbering majorities behind all parties into one great unorganized, structureless mass of furious individuals who had nothing in common except their vague apprehension that the hopes of party members were doomed, that consequently, the most articulate, and representative members of the community were fools and that all the powers that be were not so much evil as they were equally stupid and fraudulent. It was of no great consequence for the birth of this new terrifyingly negative solidarity that the unemployed worker hated the status quo and the powers that be in the form of the Social Democratic Party, the expropriated small property owner in the form of a centrist or rightist party, and former members of the middle and upper class in the form of the traditional extreme right."

Out of this collective loneliness, Arendt concluded, the mass men develop a single common value: the demand "for total, unrestricted, unconditional and unalterable loyalty of the individual member." This was the only escape from the "uprootedness and superfluousness" of the mass state.

As a description of the specific conditions, social and psychological, which led to the rise of Hitler, there is clearly much that is valuable in this analysis. But Arendt went far beyond the single case of Nazism. In Russia, she said, Stalin consciously fabricated a mass society to be the basis of his totalitarian rule. First he liquidated the power of the Soviets, then he destroyed the peasant class. Writing in the last, insane years of that dictator's rule, Arendt sees this development culminating in the creation of a monolithic society in which, for a good time at least, all principles of internal opposition had been overwhelmed. There was a ruler with his weapon of absolute terror; there was the mass; and nothing in between.

Finally, in order to make it clear that *The Origins of Totalitarianism* applied across the twentieth century, Arendt extended her generalization to the French Communist movement after World War II. In that country, she said, the class system broke down after Liberation. And quite on schedule, the collectively lonely appeared and provided the Communists with the largest following they ever had.

In short, Arendt's thesis was fundamentally pessimistic. The totalitarianism the lonely mass contains within itself "threatens to ravage the world as we know it—a world which everywhere seems to have come to an end—before a new beginning rising from this end has had the time to assert itself." And here, as events have demonstrated, abstraction took over from existential psychology. Arendt's mass was not, like Ortega's, an artificial construct. It had existed, approximately at least, in Germany in the early thirties. But like *The Revolt of the Masses*, *The Origins of Totalitarianism* overlooked the conflicts and differences within the mass, a potential that existed even at the terrible moment when Hitler seized power or Stalin ruled Russia.

Shortly after the publication of Arendt's book, the East German general strike took place in June, 1953. It was a classic case of working-class protest carried out by workers who had spent twenty consecutive years under two totalitarianisms. They did not behave as a mass, blindly seeking a leader, but as a class. There were even more profound upheavals in Poland and Hungary in 1956, and, throughout the years of thaw, stirrings occurred in almost every one of the East European satellites.

In Russia itself, the totalitarian system remained basically intact. Yet, Khrushchev was forced to the revelations about Stalin at the Twentieth Party Congress in 1956, and he removed his predecessor from his mumified tomb at the Twenty-second Party Congress. A struggle broke out between the generations, and writers like Yevtushenko and Voznesenski attracted thousands of young people to poetry readings in Moscow. By the mid-sixties, these transformations had become so marked that the Chinese, still in the classic, Stalinist phase of capital accumulation, charged the Russians with doctrinal heresy and a fat, complacent refusal to fulfill their obligations to the rest of the Bloc. And even when Khrushchev was deposed in 1964, his hostile successors proclaimed that they would not return to the Stalin era.

The difficulties of squaring Arendt's original abstraction with the events that came after it were revealed in her 1957 epilogue to *The Origins*. The fundamental thrust of her ideas had become, by that time, an argument for a conservative foreign policy in the West. (Any theory that describes the millions as a "mass" is conservative; it implies that the author is part of a superior elite—and the notion applies to nations.) If there was no internal dynamic in the Communist system, if the people had been turned into so many sheep, then there was no hope from within Communism for change or for *détente*. If, as George Kennan and others held, an evolution was taking place within the Communist system, then a policy of playing for time made sense, particularly if the direction of the transformations was benign.

Arendt, however, maintained her original bias in the 1957 retrospect. Though the masses and their loneliness were peculiarly absent from her account of what happened in Russia, Poland, and Hungary, she kept her static version of the Communist system. Whatever had happened in the post-Stalin years, it was "certain" that pressures from below had nothing to do with it. Khrushchev's revelations in 1956 were a "tactical retreat, and there are indications that [he] quite deliberately has left the door open for the re-establishment of full-fledged terror as well as the resurgence of the super purges." At the same time, Arendt argued that the Twentieth Party Congress marked the end of the thaw.

These deductions from the theory looked rather feeble when they were made and have become even more so in the intervening years. The Hungarian workers, who were supposed to be a fabricated, alienated, isolated mass, created revolutionary councils in 1956, i.e. institutions of conscious and democratic solidarity. As an anti-Communist, Arendt celebrated the fact; as an interpreter of the mass she could not really explain it. And the Russian events since 1956–57 have belied the thesis that the thaw has ended or was a mere tactic. Indeed, to understand the distance traveled by the Russian rulers since Stalin's death requires—if one rejects the notion that the Kremlin is motivated by benevolence—the inference of a pressure from below.

In West Germany, there was also a break with the patterns of the past. Under the pressure of the Cold War and the rigid rule of Adenauer, there were more than a few survivals of the authoritarian tradition and even careers for Nazis. But there was also a two-party system that was probably the most stable democracy the nation had ever known. Similarly, in both France and Italy, once prosperity took over, the mass communist parties either declined in membership and influence (France) or attempted to appeal to the electorate as a "normal" parliamentary formation (Italy).

Indeed, in Western Europe an American theory, which Arendt had contemptuously dismissed, seemed to explain more than *The Origins of Totalitarianism*. She had written, "The masses, contrary to predictions, did not result from growing equality of condition, from the spread of general education and its inevitable lowering of standards, of popularization of content." And, she added parenthetically in a jibe at the American sociologists who put much stock in such an explanation, "America, the classical land of equality of condition and general education with all of its shortcomings, knows less of the modern psychology of the masses than any country in the world." But by the sixties, as will be seen, the French, Italians, and Germans were using precisely this despised thesis to describe the "Americanization" of their lives.

In Russia and Western Europe, the most powerful single factor involved in abolishing, or modulating, the kind of mass conduct which Adrendt described was remarkably old-fashioned, somatic rather than psychic: the impact of economic progress, of technological change. And conversely, the kinds of mass movements which Arendt had located in an alienated, urban milieu appeared in the new nations of Asia, Africa, and Latin America. In these cases, peasants and tribesmen, rather than atomized city-dwellers, were the basis of totalitarian tendencies.

As Lenin once remarked, there are centuries that pass as if they were days—and days that pass as if they were centuries. The latter calendar clearly rules in these times. When a day passes like a century, when all of the accumulated historical and established institutions crumble in a moment, it is understandable that there are those who will interpret that day as if it *were* the century. But that is to forget that there may be a tomorrow that will pass like a century, that revolutionary truths age with incredible speed in these times. So tumultuous and concentrated has twentieth-century experience been that it has run through intellectual systems, sociologies, and metaphysics with cruel brusqueness. In this context, *The Origins of Totalitarianism* is a work which brilliantly understood the shattering changes of a given few years, but at the price of predicting an unnatural (for this country) stasis that would follow.

Even more pertinent to the analysis of the theories of the decadence of the masses, *The Origins of Totalitarianism* recapitulates the characteristic error of this type of thought in all of its variants. The horrified chronicler of mass man is, in a very real sense, the ally of those who would make mass men. He, or she, becomes sensitive to common denominators rather than to differences. The variety and vitality whose existence is celebrated in the happy past are systematically excluded from the terrible present. And since the writer of such books is, by definition, not a member of the mass (the masses are other people, Raymond Williams said in one of the best epigrams on the subject), he, or she, formulates policies and attitudes of pity and *noblesse oblige* that encourage everyone in the society to keep the masses where they are—and where they belong.

In Arendt's case as in Ortega's, the masses broke out of the categories in which they had been placed and made different Western Europes, Eastern Europes, and even Russias than they were supposed to do.

III

Enter the third, and currently fashionable, mass: neither aggressive rebels nor desperate followers, but a sluggish, passive multitude of semiliterates pulling culture down.

Arendt published *The Origins* in the early fifties, but her evidence was taken from the twenties and thirties for the most part. At almost the same time as her work appeared, another analysis was put forward. *The Lonely Crowd* by David Riesman took much the same point of departure as Arendt: the alienation and isolation of contemporary man. But significantly, in Riesman's theory the consequence of this mood was not to motivate totalitarians but to explain the mentality of consumers. The convergence of the premises of these two books and the utter disparity of their conclusions are one more example of how the times cannot be fit into neat abstractions.

Essentially, the passive mass is a disenchanted vision of the post-World War II prosperity in the United States and the economic recovery in Europe. Its chroniclers are usually ex-subscribers to the notion that education progressively raises the political and cultural level of a nation. They are often confused in their own mind as to whether the disappointment of their hopes is the work of the students or the teachers, of the mass or the exploiters of the mass.

Quite often, this theory concentrates on questions of the style of life, on advertising, television, and the other means of mass communications. But even such an approach has the most basic political implications, and sometimes they are drawn. If the mass can be manipulated in the name of soap, cigarettes, or sex, it can be similarly used for voting and the establishment of economic and social attitudes. Consequently, there can be no real hope that the numerical majority in this century can ever assert itself in the name of positive values. The elite corrupts the mass and receives profits and power for its trouble; but the elite is also corrupted by the mass, for the precondition of its rule is that it create an inferior culture. The resulting dialectic is the decadence of an entire society.

One can say of Ortega's mass that it never existed and of Arendt's that it existed much more momentarily than she thought. But this third mass is not so easily dismissed since it is presently in existence. More than that, insofar as it exists, it is the result of a relatively conscious decision rather than of historical trends. If it is to be abolished, an act of the political will is required. And the first step in this direction is to realize that the passive mass is not the fatal outcome of the inability of the millions to cope with the twentieth century, but the result of a choice imposed upon the mass men by the non-masses.

Dwight Macdonald has made one of the best summary descriptions of the passive mass.

In the twentieth century, Macdonald says, political democracy and popular education broke down the old upper-class monopoly of culture. At the same time, business realized that it was possible to make money in producing mass culture products. Communications technology—the movies, radio, and television—gave this development an unprecedented scope and tempo. The commodities of the new cultural assembly line flooded the society. Serious art fled to the margin, folk art was all but abolished by the city, an entire way of life became committed to machine-tooled mediocrity.

And finally, Macdonald theorizes, this process took on the aspect of a vicious circle: "The masses, debauched by several generations of this sort of thing, in turn came to demand trivial and comfortable cultural products." The people were no longer the helpless victims of their exploiters; they were cooperators in their own degradation.

Why did this happen? Most of those who share Macdonald's approach do not attribute mass culture to the workings of the Western capitalist system alone. There is, they often point out, a mass culture in the Soviet Union as well as in the United States (here, there is sometimes an echo of Arendt's thesis about the totalitarian prefabrication of the masses). When this point is emphasized, it leads to the conclusion that mass culture and society are not the outcome of a given way of organizing modern life, but of that very life itself. As Bernard Rosenberg put it, "If one can hazard a single positive formulation . . . it would be that modern technology is the necessary and sufficient cause of mass culture."

If this judgment is right, it would confirm the fear that functional rationality shall increasingly produce irrational lives in this century. The very mind and culture of man is to be calculated along with everything else, and there is no alternative to the fact. The vision of a people becoming more and more autonomous through the collective control of nature would be replaced with the vision of a mass that becomes more and more malleable with every advance in technology. Under such conditions all utopias would, of course, be impossible, and even reforms could only be sought from the elite in the control of mass communications.

C. Wright Mills also drew just about this conclusion toward the end of his life. The old middle class, serious about ideas and committed to politics, had been transformed into a swarm of dependent white-collar employees, he said. The small communities have declined, the city increasingly segregates its citizens into narrow milieus and routines. At the same time, economic, social, and political power is being concentrated in the hands of a bureaucratic minority. The helpless, brainwashed people of the democracies are actually without the ability to make significant decisions, but they are so mesmerized that they do not even notice the fact. In such a massified society, the countervailing capacity of the voluntary organizations has been either diminished or reduced to zero. With all of the paraphernalia of elections, discussion, and debate, a *de facto* totalitarian system has come into existence.

In the United States, these theories were primarily the concern of the intellectuals. In postwar Europe, the issue of mass culture became practical and political. Once again, the theme crossed party lines. It appeared Left, Right, and Center.

The fear of the "Americanization" of French society goes well back into the nineteenth century. Baudelaire spoke of the average French believer in progress: "The poor man is so Americanized by the zoocratic industrial philosophers that he has lost his notion of the differences which characterize the phenomena of the physical and moral world, of natural and supernatural." Significantly enough, Baudelaire made his point in the course of an aristocratic and conservative critque of nineteenth-century democracy, technology, and social vision. After his repudiation of the barricades on which he stood in 1848, he sadly saw himself as the Dandy asserting values in a time of transition when "democracy is not yet all powerful and aristocracy is tottering but only partially debased." And the terrible future of all-powerful democracy was America.

When that future came after World War II, another great French stylist and traditionalist, Charles de Gaulle, made the issue of "Americanization" political. There was more than a little ambiguity in De Gaulle's stance, since he himself was, in many ways, the chief agent of mass society in France.

On the one hand, De Gaulle was an aggressive modernizer. He embraced the idea of national planning when he took power in 1958, routed the forces of modified *laissez faire* in his cabinet, and developed a system of efficient, technocratic administration. In his view, the nation was now a single economic and political whole, since all sectors participated in the elaboration of the Plan. (Of course, this is more fancy than fact.)

The implications of this approach made De Gaulle one of the first conscious and theoretical politicians of mass culture. He sought to transcend the political parties, which he held to be the expression of the old and outlived class conflict. Democracy became plebiscitarian and television was its chosen instrument. The President at the center lectured, exhorted, defined the choices; the passive populace, whose political involvement was reduced to televiewing, had the right to say yes or no to the figure on the screen. The opposition was given a few minutes of time on the state-owned television, for that medium was no longer a means for discussion but a technique for the execution of policy.

If Lenin had been alive in the 1960's, De Gaulle's associate André Malraux remarked, the revolution would have begun when he seized the television station.

It was in this context that the considerable modernization of the French economy took place. The new industrial tempo of the society, its competition with the efficient Americans, pointed to the abolition of the two-hour leisurely and ritualistic midday lunch. The French language itself reflected this change. Americanisms appeared in part because the United States had pioneered in various innovations, and they were adopted with their original names (le Kleenex, le Coca-Cola, le missile gap).

De Gaulle spoke in the name of the old culture which he was helping to destroy. His anti-Americanism was to a degree opposition to mass culture, but he himself was the most articulate advocate for making the mass passive. And so, the issue was raised once again: Is it possible to utilize mass means of production and avoid the mass corruption of spirituality?

In England, this issue became political on the Left.

After the Second World War, the Labor Party realized that the character of its class base was shifting. To a certain extent, this was a function of economic integration—but it also involved a change in the very culture of the workers. In a brilliant study by Richard Hoggart, *The Uses of Literacy*, the decline of the old working-class way of life was described in detail. During the old miseries, there had been a vital conception of solidarity and cooperation among the people, an alternate philosophy to the Darwinian ethic of the rich. Now, with a rise in the standard of living (itself partly a consequence of the reforms of the 1945 Labor Government that established a new English consensus), this tradition seemed to be on the way out. Mass communications played an important role in the process. They tended to standardize reactions, to root out the particular world view of the neighborhood or the plant and to impose a tame, "nationalized" way of thinking and feeling upon the people.

Such a development was not new. Early in the Industrial Revolution, local working-class newspapers had appeared across England. They had been an indigenous expression of solidarity and radicalism. The new rulers quickly realized that they could accomplish two purposes with a single stroke: they could make money out of the press and put down anticapitalist sentiment at the same time, two profits for the price of one. Yet a jobless or a hungry man could be told that he was happy with only limited results. And in recent times, two important trends intersected. The severities of the system were ameliorated by Labor reform; mass communications became much more ubiquitous and scientific than the old newspapers and magazines.

A good number of Labor Party intellectuals responded to this situation by urging their Party to assert the old tradition in new ways. But within the Party, the issue of mass culture has been handled more pragmatically. Harold Wilson placed his emphasis upon television and the "scientific revolution," a fundamental change from the hymn-singing days of the old comradeship. The Party, which had denounced the use of advertising agencies in political campaigns when the Conservatives first introduced the tactic, began to look for its own agency. From the point of view of the Left, and with a democratic and social content, the Laborites seemed to be following De Gaulle's accommodation to the new realities of the mass society.

But then, does the British and French experience confirm the American pessimism about the inevitability of the passive mass and debased culture in the modern world?

One of the first thinkers to realize that the answer to this question is not fated was, curiously enough, Friedrich Nietzsche. Nietzsche, of course, would not be in the least surprised to hear the news that the democratic movements of his time had eventually created, not utopia, but a society dangerously close to the common denominator. He had, after all, loudly proclaimed that the majority of men were fit only for slavery and that culture was ruthlessly aristocratic. He even had his own theory of mass culture: "Victor Hugo and Wagner," he wrote, "mean one and the same thing: that in declining cultures where the mass takes desions into its hands, the genuine becomes superfluous, wrong, pushed back. Only the theatrical type wakens great enthusiasm." (Most present-day critics of mass culture would probably be delighted if the millions debased themselves with Victor Hugo and Wagner.)

But Nietzsche, for all his bitterness against the mass, was a brilliant and dialectical man. He could not content himself with a self-serving, conservative analysis which simply looked backward. So, in his contempt of those nineteenth-century liberals whom Ortega dreamed of restoring to their rightful power, he also wrote, "Man is permitted only that amount of culture which serves the interest of profit." The nihilist believed the people to be inferior, but he recognized the role of a specific society in promoting that inferiority, marketing it, manufacturing it. And this is the heart of the matter. It allows one to see mass culture as a historical creation of the sensitive elite rather than as the inevitable desire of the mass itself.

As Raymond Williams put it in *Culture and Society*, "What in fact do we mean by 'mass'? Do we mean democracy dependent on universal suffrage, or a culture dependent on universal education, or a reading public dependent on universal literacy? If we find the product of mass civilization so repugnant, are we to identify the suffrage or the literacy as agents of decay?" The conservative would clearly answer yes to both questions (and so, with his dialectical qualifications, would Nietzsche).

Then Williams continues, "Or alternately, do we mean by mass civilization an industrial civilization dependent on machine production and the factory system? Do we find institutions like the popular press and advertising to be the necessary consequences of such a system of production?" At this point the disenchanted radical and the saddened liberal would say yes.

Finally, Williams puts his own position: "It is clear that the highest standards of literacy in contemporary society depend on a level of instruction and training far above that which is commonly available. For this reason, it is still much too early to conclude that a majority culture is necessarily low in taste." And, the same idea in the form of a paradox, "The old democrat is too sure of man's nobility to concern himself with the means of its common assurance. The new skeptic believes what happens when such means are not assured and seeks an explanation in man's natural baseness."

What is involved here is the conception of a social choice.

It is possible that passive masses will provide the human material for a debased culture and some form or another ("democratic" or totalitarian) of political authoritarianism. This will unquestionably happen if the people are systematically tutored in the arts of being mass men by their "betters." If the educational systems of housing, school, and mass media continue to do their work as well as in the past, if the complicated society is carefully staffed with people who are not given the opportunity to rise above a vulgar simplicity, then the outcome of contemporary technology is hardly in doubt. But the responsibility for such a disaster cannot be passed off to machines. It belongs to the makers of machines —to the sophisticated and educated.

The evidence of this callousness abounds throughout the West. Some of the best cases in point might be taken from the United States in the early sixties. There, it was more and more understood that slum children are intellectually maimed before they arrive in the first grade, that is, before they are six years old. Retarded before they begin to learn, these young people are regularly assigned to the most inferior schools and largest classes. The school itself thus becomes a major institution for teaching how not to read, write, and count, and the teacher is made into a custodian and police officer. At sixteen, the adolescent "graduates" from this experience, utterly bored for not really having understood the last six or seven years of education, completely unprepared for society and ready to take a position in the masses.

By 1964, nearly a third of American youth were dropping

out of school as soon as that was legally possible. With less than a high-school education, most of these children were without an economic future or the ability to respond to any but the lowest forms of mass culture. And yet, as the Office of Education reported in 1964, the majority of the "drop-outs" were intellectually capable of completing high school, and a significant minority of them had the innate ability to complete college studies. The reasons they left ranged from the simple economic—they were forced into the labor market by the poverty of their parents—to the complex psychological. Yet, there was little question that a social investment in their plight (it would have to begin in the very early years of education) could have saved them from their present misery.

When these young people walk down the street with a transistor radio at their ear, when they consume the music, television, and films directed to their level of taste, there are those who see them as masses. They, one is told, threaten culture and standards and norms; "we," the sensitive (and it should be added, the economically secure, the educated, the physically healthy), must guard against their cultural intrusion.

Such a mass there is. It exists by virtue of society's choice. It is not inevitable, for it comes from a repression of natural abilities and talents as the Office of Education study demonstrates. And, in a very real sense, the true agents of the "revolt of the masses," the real partisans of mass society, are the elite.

In a modern society it is, after all, the economic and political elite that now determines the resources that will be provided to the people for raising their cultural level. And such a choice is not simply a matter of the funds given to formal education but those granted to, or withheld from, the informal educators like the slum and the advertising industry. And it is, alas, the intellectual elite that too often explains the result of an utterly inadequate investment in people as an expression of the innate stupidity of the majority. Once, the labor and socialist movements broke through this vicious circle dramatically. Millions educated themselves through political struggle (and not simply in politics) and thus established a popular countervalence to all of the elites. But, as was seen in the chapter "The Decadence of the Poor," this enterprise has now become problematic. So if these various trends continue, then the "best" people, after manufacturing mass men for profit, will commission studies on the incompetence of the men and women they have created.

The "masses" are perhaps the most dramatic illustration of what can happen when a world-historical revolution is accidental.

The West has revolutionized its economy, its social structure, its very life. Technology has literally been creating a new civilization. But since this process has taken place without revolutionists, without conscious direction, thought has not kept pace with technology. Millions of people are thrust, unprepared, into this unprecedented environment, and then those who systematically did not prepare them excoriate them as "masses," as vulgar, as lowly, and deplore the way in which they are pulling the high and noble values down.

In such a situation, who is it that technology has stupefied? The masses? Or those who make the masses and do not even recognize the work of their own hands?

8

The Statues
of Daedalus

There is only one condition in which we can imagine managers not needing subordinates, and masters not needing slaves. This condition would be that each (inanimate) instrument could do its own work, at the word of command or by intelligent anticipation, like the statues of Daedalus or the tripods made by Hephaestus, of which Homer relates that

> Of their own motion they entered the conclave of
> Gods on Olympus

as if a shuttle should weave of itself, and a plectrum should do its own harp playing.

Aristotle, *The Politics*, 1253b

In the middle of the twentieth century, the statues of Daedalus, that "cunning craftsman" of Greek legend, are beginning to dance in the West.

Automation (i.e., self-correcting machines that feed back information and adjust themselves) and cybernation (i.e., making the automated machines capable of responding to a near infinity of contingencies by hooking them up to computers) possess the scientific capacity to accomplish the ancient myth.

As a result, the abolition of work, as Western man has defined the term, has become a technological possibility.

Aristotle understood that such a development would have the most profound consequences. His reference to the statues of Daedalus comes in the course of a defense of slavery. He realized that their discovery would shatter his own "natural" law: Managers would no longer need subordinates, masters could dispense with slaves. This is, happily, one of the options now open to technological man. But there are other, more complex and disturbing, possibilities if the statues of Daedalus are indeed coming to life in the twentieth century.

The modern West distinguished itself from other cultures by its Faustian assault upon reality, its relentless ambition to remake the very world. In the matter of a few hundred years, this drive created an industrial civilization and a standard of living that became the envy, and model, of the entire globe. It also deeply marked the ethic, the religious values, the psychology, and social system of Europe and America. If the statues of Daedalus have indeed been found, it is clear that the moment signals the decadence of much that passed as wisdom and morality for hundreds of years. Ironically, the triumph of Faustian man could mean his suicide. For what will Faust do if, as Paul Valéry once suggested, the world is to become "finished"? Or, to put the issue in American terms, if there are no more frontiers?

Such a happening is clearly in the far distance, though not so far as to be out of historical eyesight. Closer to the present, there are even now less ultimate, but extremely profound, results of the fact that work in the West is already being redefined.

The certitude that man must labor by the sweat of his brow was a weary, but consoling, knowledge. The machines are now lifting this burden from human shoulders and, in the doing, corrupting the central Western ethic of work. The stern necessities that drove Europe and America to secular greatness are disappearing. In their place, there is a bewildering freedom. Thus, the machines are not simply a technological fact but the stuff of a spiritual crisis as well.

Then, there is another effect upon the inner man of the West. As Sigmund Freud understood it, work was essential both to society and to the self. At his most pessimistic, in *The Future of an Illusion* and *Civilization and Its Discontents*, Freud argued that civilization itself was based upon the repression of instinctual gratification, demanding that the individual sacrifice himself to the discipline and needs of the collective, to a large extent through hard labor. The majority, Freud said, were lazy and indolent. Without work and its attendant coercion, society would fall apart.

More positively, Freud believed that work was a means of linking man to reality and thus therapeutic. But taking either his dark or his optimistic theory, the disappearance of work could be a social and individual catastrophe, a psychological revolution.

Finally, that other recent Western giant, Karl Marx, argued that the coming of automation would destroy the very rationality of the Western capitalist system itself. Only, he said, in a society in which the exploitation of labor was the essential element in creating commodities could economic rewards and values be measured in terms of how much productive work a man did. Once machines and the practical application of science become the true source of wealth, he concluded, capitalism is a dangerous, unworkable anachronism.

In each of these cases, and in many others, the same irony appears. The West, which more than any other part of the globe learned to cope with starvation and gradually to conquer it, faces the distinct possibility that abundance—its long-dreamed utopia, its Cockaigne—will be the decadence of some of its most cherished values and that it will take more ingenuity to live with freedom than it did to subsist under necessity.

I

The contemporary statues of Daedalus can be described quite prosaically. With so many apocalypses depending on their dance, it is well to start *sotto voce*, empirically, statistically.

In a series of American Government documents in 1964, and most particularly in the Report of the Senate Subcommittee on Employment and Manpower, some trends of automation and cybernation were noted. Among them were changes in the increase of productivity per man-hour, an important shift in the quality of manpower needs, and chronic, high levels of unemployment.

Taken by themselves, these transformations were regarded as serious enough by the Senate Subcommittee to merit the title of a "manpower revolution." They demonstrate that at this very moment, without too many people noticing, the nature of work is being redefined. The figures do not yet show that work as it has been known is actually being abolished, but they certainly suggest this possibility in the middle historical distance.

The evidence presented here is exclusively American. There are considerable differences between Europe and the United States in this regard, most notably in the widespread acceptance of national planning on the Continent. Yet, there is every reason to believe that the Old World will soon experience the troubles of the New. The consumer boom that took place in the United States right after the war did not occur in Europe until the mid-fifties and is still in progress. That has provided a favorable context for the new technology. Once this trend plays itself out, there is no reason to believe that Europe can avoid the revolutionary consequences of its technology. These figures suggest, then, not simply the American, but the European, future and, as industrialization proceeds around the globe, the fate of the world.

The American statues of Daedalus are visible in the prosaic statistics on the increase in output per man-hour in the private economy.

Between 1909 and 1962, American industry increased the worker's output by 2.4 percent a year. But then, this five-decade trend conceals a most significant shift. From 1909 to 1947, the productivity gain was only 2 percent a year. But between 1958 and 1963, productivity per man-hour went up 3.1 percent a year, and between 1960 and 1963, 3.6 percent a year. And it was, of course, in this period of accelerated productivity growth in the fifties and early sixties that automation and cybernation began to emerge as an important factor in the American economy.

Translate these gross quantities into some of their significant details. In 1964, ten men could produce as many automobile motor blocks as 400 men in 1954; two workers could make a thousand radios a day, a job that required 200 a few years before; 14 operators were tending the glass-blowing machines that manufactured 90 percent of all the glass bulbs in the United States of America. During the fifties, Bell Telephone increased its volume by 50 percent and its work force by only 10 percent.

This same trend also illumines an economic paradox: the coexistence, in the late fifties and early sixties, of prosperity and chronic unemployment. More unskilled and semiskilled jobs in private manufacture were destroyed than created, and joblessness persisted at over 5 percent of the work force despite the prosperity (this 5-percent figure is an understatement; it does not count those driven out of the labor market, possibly a million and a half workers, nor the underemployed; a "true" estimate of involuntary idleness would be in the neighborhood of 9 percent). At the same time, the machines were the source of enormous profit, and thus there was a deformed "prosperity," benign for corporations, malignant for millions of workers.

Curiously enough, this process stands out in even starker relief in American agriculture. There, productivity increases have recently hit a prodigious 6 percent a year. One result has been to cut the postwar farming population from 14 percent of the population to 7 percent. And even this statistic conceals the radical character of the change. Farming supports a tremendous amount of underemployment and hidden unemployment. A third of the American agricultural producers do not market crops but merely eke out an impoverished, miserable subsistence for themselves.

In short, less than 5 percent of the American people are

able to produce more food than they can profitably sell to the other 95 percent under the present system. In order to satisfy these politically powerful farmers, the Government now pays them between $4 and $5 billion a year in subsidies. Here, then, is an anticipation of one of the strange logics of abundance: that American agriculture is so capable of plenty that nonproduction must be publicly supported. (The extreme irrationality of rewarding the rich farmer and penalizing the poor is not a deduction from technology but a conscious, and reactionary, political choice; yet the fundamental problem is there in any context.)

In private manufacturing, the decline in jobs has not been as spectacular as on the farm, but the trend is clearly present. Between 1957 and 1963, for instance, wage and salary employment in the nonagricultural, goods-producing sector dropped by 300,000 jobs—despite substantial increases in output, new products, and even new industries. In the ten years before this period, from 1947 to 1957, employment in the same sector had gone up at the rate of 250,000 new jobs a year.

In short, American industry broke through a technological barrier somewhere in the mid-fifties. Cybernation made it possible to expand production and contract the work force. Less labor produced more goods. Even so, the president of a corporation making automated equipment, John Snyder, remarked that his equipment was only at a "primitive" level, that an accentuation of the process was imminent.

At first, the new technology was most dramatically successful in reducing unskilled and semiskilled industrial jobs.

But as time went on, other occupations began to be affected
In the financial services industry, machines took over more
and more office work; transporation employment dropped;
the increase in retail sales work slowed down (the automated department store will soon appear in the United
States: machines will take orders, package goods, notify
inventory of the sale, and keep instantaneous financial accounts).

But employment did grow in this period. And the areas
where growth did take place indicate a significant change
in the quality and meaning of work.

The largest single increase in jobs took place on the public
payrolls, mainly through the hiring of teachers to handle
the postwar baby boom. This category alone accounted for
one-third of the new jobs in wage and salary employment,
or 300,000 new places annually. Close behind was the personal service industry—hospitals, private schools, colleges
and private social welfare organizations, hostelries—with
250,000 additional jobs each year. As *The Wall Street Journal* noted in October, 1964, during the previous year there
had been more new jobs for schoolteachers than for production workers.

So it was that in this time the most easily cybernated posi-
tions, routine, repetitive factory functions, declined; that
the simpler office tasks declined or leveled off; that retail
employment slowed down; and that real increases were
achieved in those areas, such as teaching and hospitals, which
required the human care of human beings. Given the revolutionary character of American technology, this pattern is
likely to become even more accelerated in the immediate
future. Even menial, miserably paid work, like much of

that of migrant field hands, can be taken over by machines (and, with savage irony, probably will, not out of compassion for those who bend and stoop in the fields, but because those workers will finally enforce minimal standards of decency for themselves and thus make it cheaper to enslave a machine than a man).

The striking aspect of this new pattern is that the job increases are in areas that are not "productive" in the lay sense of the term. Teaching and nursing do not make manufactured goods, or even help distribute them. The idea that the human care of human beings is an *economically* significant undertaking is a fairly new one. It was this significant change in American working life that led the Senate Subcommittee to speak of a "manpower revolution."

All of this takes place as a process, not as a sudden, definitive transformation. Million of Americans still labor in fields and on assembly lines. But, as one scholarly vocabulary puts it, the trend is clearly away from primary employments like agriculture, to the secondary functions of industry, to the tertiary of services, and now to a fourth level of training and human care. At each point, work is receding from the direct confrontation of man and nature. And, as time goes on, it is possible to conceive the abolition of entire sectors of economic activity, most obviously that of the factory worker.

Without even looking into the middle distance, however, these new patterns have already posed some massive social problems in American society.

One of the effects of automation and cybernation is to increase the skill "mix" in manufacturing. An airplane plant organized by the United Automobile Workers during

World War II had 85 percent of its work force in organizable (blue-collar, generally speaking) occupations. By the sixties, that figure had been reduced to 35 percent, and the rest of the plant was filled with highly trained engineers and other management personnel. In a 1964 Department of Labor study of 3,440 plants, 11 percent had progressed to advanced stages of automation, and, of these, 84.1 percent had reported that their skill requirements had risen.

Left to itself, this trend could create a large increase in involuntary joblessness as a by-product of abundance.

In the decade of the 1960's, according to the Government, 26 million new workers were entering the labor market. Of these, 7.6 million would be without high-school diplomas, 2.3 million without a grade-school education. At the same time, as Secretary of Labor Wirtz remarked, machines were being built with automated skills beyond the human reach of a high-school graduate. As a result, there were 730,000 youthful unemployed by October, 1963 (the figures neared a million in 1964), 350,000 young people were neither at school or work (and thus not "in the labor market" and not certified in the unemployment figures), and one million in the same age group were in what the Administration called "dead-end" jobs. Indeed, in the Selective Service examinations, fully a quarter of the young American males were declared unfit for military service by virtue of not being able to read up to seventh-grade levels.

For these young people—perhaps a third of their generation—the advance of American ingenuity is a catastrophe. Given their lack of skill and training, they are systematically misfitted for the economy which they are entering. Their future holds out chronic unemployment at worst, or at best laboring at tasks that are so menial they are beneath the dignity and education of machines. Part of their plight is already expressed in the explosive social conditions in the slums, the rise of juvenile delinquency, adult crime, and aimless violence.

Yet, under the American corporate system there are limits to this process. On the one hand, business can eliminate jobs in order to cheapen cost and maximize profit; on the other hand, it cannot abolish the consumer buying power needed to purchase the goods it produces, and this is still largely guaranteed through employment. Such a contradiction can, as will be seen, be resolved in many ways, not the least of them the transformation of the system itself. At this point, a few of the immediate American responses are relevant.

One answer, that of the Democratic Administrations of the sixties (theoretically stated by the Council of Economic Advisers), was to hold that technological unemployment was simply a temporary phenomenon. If money could be pumped into the economy by a cut in taxes, that would increase aggregate effective demand and make it profitable to put people to work (the same tax cut, however, included a corporate bonus that could well be utilized to cybernate). In addition, the patchwork of American social insurance, welfare, and relief schemes was seen as adequate to handle those who fell out of the economy altogether. As the preceding analysis should make clear, this view simply does not meet the radical character of contemporary technological change.

A second response was somewhat more profound, involving redefinitions of work. In the discussion of the Senate Subcommittee on Employment and Manpower, there were demands for an expansion of the public sector in fulfilling the nation's unmet needs for housing, hospitals, schools, and transportation systems. While clearly leaving the corporate basis of the economy intact, this would amount to a modest political allocation of economic resources on the basis of social need. In addition, the Subcommittee urged the extension of universal free public education to two years beyond high school and Government support for those workers who were retired from the economy some years before they were eligible for Social Security.

Behind these suggestions were the beginnings of new ideas. First, they recognize that the public sector—where social personal services must be provided—takes on a new significance. Secondly, there is the emphasis on education and the recognition that it is probably no longer possible to train a young person for a lifetime skill, but necessary to give him a liberal education that would prepare him to change his skill several times according to the demands of technology. Thirdly, there is the advocacy of curtailing the working life of the citizen: through a later entry into the work force after prolonged education, and through an earlier exit by retirement. All of these ideas involve the intimation of new social principles: the importance of the public service sector of the economy; the recognition that going to school is an economically productive function; the realization that not working, for the young and the old, is becoming a social necessity.

These are only some of the changes which the reality of American life in the sixties has made into questions for discussion (there are also, of course, proposals to shorten the workweek itself to thirty hours). They indicate that a profound transformation in the character of work is taking place even now. But more than that, they point in the not-too-distant future to the appearance of the statues of Daedalus. The almost totally cybernated production of commodities and routine office services is not merely technologically possible; it is now probable.

In all of this, traditional wisdoms are being turned topsy-turvy. In a statement which would have been incomprehensible to the starving man of the past, John R. Bunting, a vice-president of the Federal Reserve Bank of Philadelphia, said in 1964, "I think on balance that the American economic system is threatened more by abundance than by scarcity."

And, well to the Left of Bunting on the political spectrum, the British scholar, Richard M. Titmuss, an important adviser to the Labor Party, wrote in the same year, "If the first phase of the so-called (industrial) revolution was to force men to work, the phase we are now entering may be to force many men not to work."

To a mankind which has been engaged in a grim struggle with hunger since the beginning of time, the idea that men would be forced not to work would, at first glance, seem a salvation. That could well be the case—so long as it is understood that this salvation would simultaneously portend the decadence of some of the most fundamental economic, ethical, and even religious assumptions of Western life. It would therefore require a tremendous burst of freedom and imagination to fill up the void left by the disappearance of starvation.

II

The capitalist West was built, in R. H. Tawney's phrase, by "practical ascetics."

This is to say that the West made hard labor into an ethical dictate, a guarantee of personal worth and even a path to God. In 1900, as remarked earlier, Henry Adams contrasted the Virgin, as the spiritual principle of the medieval age, and the dynamo, the god of force presiding over the new industrialism. Forty years later, in keeping with Adams' own law of the acceleration of history, the dynamo, a source of energy, was ceding its Olympian position to the computer and its "intelligent anticipation." And just as the dynamo counterposed its social philosophy to the Virgin's theology, so the statues of Daedalus, the cybernated machines, mark the end of the practicality of asceticism.

The thesis that work took on a metaphysical and even theological significance under Western capitalism is, of course, most identified with Max Weber's provocative study of the Protestant ethic. In Puritanism, Weber wrote, "The premiums were placed upon 'proving' oneself before God in the sense of attaining salvation—which is found in *all* Puritan denominations—and 'proving' oneself before men in the sense of socially holding one's own within the Puritan sects. Both aspects were mutually supplementary and operated in the same direction: they helped to deliver the 'spirit' of modern capitalism, its specific *ethos*: the ethos of the modern *bourgeois middle classes*."

Weber's analysis of the importance of the Calvinist idea of a "calling" to the rise of capitalism has been widely disputed. Some economic historians like Henri Pirenne have claimed to trace the capitalist spirit well back into the Middle Ages before the Reformation (and Marx once admitted in a letter to being puzzled as to why capitalism had not developed in Rome at the time of Christ, all of its preconditions having been fulfilled). Yet whatever the specific weight of the Protestant ethic in *determining* the rise of capitalism, there is little doubt that its distinctive spirit was part of the event. If Puritanism was not godfather to capitalism, then it was godson. As cause or effect, the ethical and religious importance of hard work became a constituent principle of the capitalist West.

Indeed, in the past four or five centuries, it was precisely this practical asceticism that drove the West to the most extraordinary material achievement history has known. Where Eastern philosophy, for instance, would accept reality as an illusion or a fate, and the cycles of suffering and starvation as events to be ignored or endured, the West was remaking the world. (Yeats understood this point when he limited tragedy, "the heroic cry," to the West.) In the mid-twentieth century, one of the great problems of the developing nations, with their feudal and tribal heritages, is to find a cultural basis for this Western attitude.

R. H. Tawney was a friendly critic of Weber's (some of their ideas converged). He stated the theological aspect of the work ethic this way: "For since conduct and action, though availing nothing to attain the free gift of salvation, are a proof that the gift has been accorded, what is rejected as means is resumed as a consequence and the Puritan flings himself into practical activities with the daemonic energy of one who, all doubts allayed, is conscious that he is a sealed and chosen vessel. Called by God to labor in his vineyard, he has within himself a principle at once of energy and order, which makes him irresistible both in war and in the struggle of commerce."

Tawney was writing of the origins of capitalism. Over time, the spirit which he described became less mystical, more secular, yet it persisted. Thorstein Veblen's *Theory of the Leisure Class* is primarily a description of the American *nouveau riche* of the late nineteenth century. It chronicles an ethic of conspicuous consumption that is almost the exact opposite of the Protestant spirit. Yet even in this setting, he told of the continuing thrust of the earlier idea.

"The substantial canons of the leisure class scheme of life," Veblen wrote, "are conspicuous waste of time and substance and a withdrawal from the industrial process; while the particular aptitudes here in question [essentially the Protestant ethic] assert themselves, on the economic side, in a deprecation of waste and of a futile manner of life, and in an impulse to participation or in identification with the life process, whether it be on the economic side or in any other of its phases or aspects."

Veblen's leisure class did exist (even if more complexly than he imagined). In Europe, the aristocratic tradition of regarding work and commerce as degrading persisted even under capitalism. And those who actually did the back-breaking toil hardly regarded their daily toil as a spiritual value. "Certainly the workers in Hogarth's Gin Alley," Daniel Bell has written, "or the people whom Melville's Redburn saw in the Liverpool slums, were little concerned with the scourging hand of God. What drove them to work was hunger, and much of the early movements of social protest can only be understood with that fact in mind."

But then, Western capitalism has not been aristocratic, proletarian, or leisured. It has been the bourgeois economic order. Without reducing all of its complexity to a single historic strand, one can say that it was dominated by the ethic, and even religion, of work. To this day, the West believes that a man establishes his worth in the eyes of his neighbor, and even before God, through industry and drudgery and saving. In its most acutely American form, as the poet William Carlos Williams once observed, this attitude asserts itself in the conversational opening, "What do you do?" This question follows immediately upon an exchange of names between strangers, it establishes much of the substance of their talk, it is the quickest means of identification. One is, it implies, what one does. One is one's work.

What, then, would happen if technology rendered work and the work ethic decadent?

Bread and circuses are an obvious, but hardly affirmative, substitute. In a series of Italian films of Antonioni and Fellini, there is a depiction of the empty, orgiastic lives of the leisure and celebrity class. They are tormented by their free time. Significantly, each of these movies contains a scene in which an anguished protagonist looks longingly upon the vitality of working-class or peasant life, admiring its muscularity or simplicity. These particular cases are examples of what Empson defined as the "pastoral" theme in literature and art (the romantic courtier sings of the rustic swain; the middle-class novelist or movie director celebrates the noble proletarian). But they could also be the intimation of a possible nostalgia in the technological future. Will people then turn back to yearn for the working present and the even more hardworking past?

Were it possible to build a society on the principles of bread and circuses, the event would signify the decadence of central Western values. But it is doubtful whether such a society could exist at all. Here, Ortega's inaccurate charge against the twentieth century might apply to the twenty-first. The very existence of technological abundance pre-supposes a high level of science and skill, at least on the part of the minority. A social order based upon orgy would destroy its own effortless prosperity by failing to reproduce its technological genius. (In terms of myth, Cockaigne, where there is only consumption, is impossible; utopia, which recognizes some form of work, is still conceivable.)

There is another possible principle of the society that has eliminated work as it is now known: totalitarianism. In the past, hunger has been at least as important for the main-tenance of order as for the fomenting of revolution. Out of necessity, millions "voluntarily" chose brutal toil in order to survive. If this indirect discipline were abolished, it might be replaced by the dictatorship of the programmers, of those who decide what decisions the machines will make. Indeed, a society split between the highly educated and sophisticated few on the one side, and the passive, consum-ing mass on the other, could hardly be democratic, since dialogue between the rulers and ruled would be impossible. Were this to happen, it would confirm the worst fears of sociologists like Weber and Mills that the functional ration-alization of life necessarily leads to the loss of substantive rationality for the majority of individuals.

Some of the postive options of a cybernated culture will be discussed shortly, others in the next chapter. For now, it is clear that the West is already approaching the decadence of the work ethic. Thomas Malthus said, "If our benevolence be indiscriminate . . . we shall raise the worthless above the worthy; we shall encourage indolence and check industry; and in the most marked manner subtract from the sum of human happiness. . . . The laws of nature say with Saint Paul, 'If a man will not work, neither shall he eat.'"

That law of nature, so basic to the recent history of the West, is now being abolished by machines. In 1964, the President of the United States intimated the new era when, in announcing the enactment of a cut in taxes, he urged Americans to spend and consume as a patriotic duty. Paradoxically, this decadence of the Protestant ethic comes at the very moment when it has finally conquered the world. As Sebastian de Grazia has pointed out, the UNESCO Declaration of Human Rights announces, "Everyone has the right to work."

So it is that at that point in history at which the Western work ethic is finally in sight of subverting almost every remnant of tribalism, feudalism, and aristocracy on the globe, it ceases to be a practical guide for the culture that gave it birth.

III

Sigmund Freud made two basic arguments for the necessity of work. With the coming of abundance, one of them will become obsolete and the other will constitute the most fundamental challenge of the future.

Freud's first analysis of the need for work rests upon a conservative view of the industrial masses and the assumption of scarcity as a fundamental condition of human life. "The masses," he wrote in *The Future of an Illusion*, "are lazy and unintelligent; they have no love for instinctual renunciation and they are not to be convinced by argument of its inevitability; and the individuals composing them support one another in giving free rein to their indiscipline. It is only through the influence of individuals who can set an example and whom the masses recognize as their leaders that they can be induced to perform the work and undergo the renunciations on which the existence of civilization depends. . . .

"To put it briefly," Freud continues, "there are two widespread characteristics which are responsible for the fact that the regulation of civilization can only be maintained by a certain degree of coercion—namely, that men are not spontaneously fond of work and that arguments are of no avail against their passions."

Thus coercion, Freud makes clear, is essentially conservative in character. It aims "not only at affecting a certain distribution of wealth but at maintaining that distribution; indeed [it has] to protect everything that contributes to the conquest of nature and the production of wealth against men's hostile impulses." At the same time, this fact revolutionizes the majority. "In such conditions, an internalization of the cultural prohibitions among the suppressed people is not to be expected. On the contrary, they are not prepared to acknowledge their prohibitions, they are bent on destroying the culture itself, and possibly even on doing away with the postulates on which it is based."

In part, this analysis is that of a conservative mind, and was wrong on the day it was made. For Freud, it was the very nature of the masses to shirk work. Yet, as he himself was to recognize in *Civilization and Its Discontents*, the work to which these people were driven was degrading and unfree. Under such circumstances, it is realism, and not laziness, to detest work. When those same masses saw real choices, they were anything but indolent. At great personal sacrifice, even of life itself, they organized a mighty and disciplined labor and socialist movement and contributed to the very reshaping of Western society.

With all his marvelous depth and a candor that shook a culture, Freud never fully escaped from the prejudices of a Viennese bourgeois.

The second element in Freud's analysis is much less capricious. He understood that culture had "not got beyond a point at which the satisfaction of one portion of its participants depends upon the suppression of another, and perhaps larger, portion . . ." Here, his social psychology is based on understanding that economic scarcity is a massive determinant of societal structure and the individual self. His point is historical, and not rooted in any assumptions about the "natural" habits of the mass.

But events are now destroying the historical conditions that gave Freud his context. As noted before, there are already Government proposals in the United States for contracting the individual's working life through a late entry into, and early withdrawal from, the labor force. And in a time of cybernating technology, the coercive power of the Government under the neo-Keynesian ethic insists that the masses gratify their desires. The consequences of such developments for the Freudian perspective are momentous.

Insofar as Freud's deep pessimism (most poignantly put in *Civilization and Its Discontents*) rests upon the assumption of economic scarcity, then abundance makes a psychic liberation possible. Freud had said that man becomes more neurotic as society becomes more complex. The more sophisticated the collective life, he argued, the more pervasive is the denial of instinctual gratification, for increasing renunciation is required to maintain such a vast community. In this tragic thesis, there is something pathological about progress.

But if onerous work would no longer be necessary to the collective, then what function is there for coercion and repression? Under such conditions, the recent socialist interpretations of Freud by Herbert Marcuse and Norman Brown would become orthodox deductions from the master's premises. However, the matter is complicated because Freud, living through one world war, the rise of fascism, and the coming of the Second World War, also located an aggressive instinct in man's deepest self. If such a destructiveness is a "natural" human condition, then the elimination of scarcity would not mean the end of coercion but its irrational persistence. Then repression, having lost its economic function, would not express historical necessity but a basic human depravity. One hopes that Freud's dark thesis was an overgeneralization of post-1914 Europe in all of its violence. The possibility remains that it was not.

In any case, Freud's social psychology of work will be rendered obsolete if abundance, as threatened, does indeed come. Given the decadence of some of the basic assumptions of the Western psyche, the question will then be, what forms of repression or liberation will follow upon the event?

And it is here that Freud's second, and positive, argument on work becomes extremely relevant. "Laying stress upon the importance of work," he wrote in *Civilization and Its Discontents,* "has a greater effect than any other technique of living in the direction of binding the individual more closely to reality; in his work, he is at least attached to a part of reality, the human community. Work is no less valuable for the opportunity it and the human relations connected with it provide for a very considerable discharge of libidinal component impulses, narcissistic, aggressive and even erotic, than because it is indispensable for subsistence and justifies existence in society. The daily work of earning a livelihood affords particular satisfaction when it has been selected by free choice, i.e. when through sublimation it enables use to be made of existing inclinations, of instinctual impulses that have retained their strength, or are more intense than usual for constitutional reasons. And yet as a path to happiness, work is not valued very highly by men. They do not run after it as they do after other opportunities of gratification. The great majority work only when forced by necessity, and this natural human aversion to work gives rise to the most difficult social problems."

In the last few sentences on the "natural human aversion to work," Freud is once again the Viennese bourgeois. His own definition of therapeutic, i.e., freely chosen, work has been denied the overwhelming majority of men in history. The only kind of work they have known is that imposed upon them in a struggle for survival. Abundance could completely change this situation. If all routine and repetitive chores can be done by machines, man can be freed for activity of his own choosing.

Freud's really profound point here is that such activity would still be necessary, even if not for subsistence. Work, he says, does not merely discharge narcissistic and aggressive impulses; it can, when freely chosen, even be erotic, a "path to happiness." There is, Freud would say with scientific rigor, a labor of love. In it, man is united with reality and his fellowman, thus discovering some of his deepest satisfactions. And conversely, a man without any work at all would be shallow and sick and his narcissism, aggressiveness, and erotic energy could express themselves in subhuman and antisocial form.

In this psychological analysis of the meaning of work, one glimpses the extraordinary ambiguity of the present moment. Abundance could be the prelude to bread and circuses. A degrading leisure would be society's substitute for a degrading work. Some of these possibilities have already been outlined. On the other hand, there could be a new kind of leisure and a new kind of work, or more precisely, a range of activities that would partake of the nature of both leisure and work.

This latter development will not simply happen. If the decision is left to technology in its present context, then the first, and grim, possibility is more likely. A society with a cybernated revolution and a conservative mentality is not going to make new definitions of leisure and work. It is much simpler, and in keeping with the current wisdom, to vulgarize the neo-Keynesian ethic and to provide a market for the products of machines by simply injecting quantities of money into the economy, without any planning for the use of this productivity. Such a course would be defended in the name of allowing the individual freedom of choice. In reality, it would tend to constrict that freedom to its basest and most commercial options.

But on the other side there are enormous possibilities. Activities which are now regarded as hobbies, like photography, gardening, and fishing, could be seen as important human occupations in a society where machines did all the drudgery. So could the practice of the arts, of scientific research, of politics and education. To the Athenians, these latter employments were indeed the truly human work of man. But the Greek ideal rested, as Aristotle made so clear in the *Politics*, upon the degradation of the slaves. That fatal immorality of the Aristotelian scheme is no longer necessary—as Aristotle himself realized when he said that the appearance of the statues of Daedalus would obviate the need for slaves. The machine slaves, the modern statues of Daedalus, are now coming into existence. Their appearance makes the Freudian notion of the labor of love a possible choice, not simply for an elite, but for all mankind.

This varient requires the active and conscious intervention of man. Such a radical departure from present certitudes will take an act of the social imagination as fundamental as the one which, in the Neolithic Revolution, established the basis for society itself. But here again, in either case, some of the most obvious assumptions of the contemporary psychology are turned into illusions.

And the ambiguity is, one does not yet know whether these developments simply portend a decadence—or both a decadence and a marvelous birth.

IV

In some notes which he never fully expanded, Karl Marx predicted that automation and cybernation would destroy the very basis of the capitalist system itself.

The analysis appears in *The Outline of the Critique of Political Economy* (*Grundrisse Der Kritik Der Politischen Oekonomie*), some "rough notes" dating from the late 1850's which have never been translated into English. In later years, Marx refined the vocabulary and argument of his outline but, to my knowledge, never returned to his remarkable anticipation of the statues of Daedalus. The intimations of 1857 and 1858 became the more prosaic theories of the change in the organic composition of capital (the substitution of machines for men) and the consequent tendency for the rate of profit to fall. Neither of these ideas is relevant here. The insights of the original notes, however, are utterly contemporary in the age of cybernation which began approximately one hundred years after Marx wrote.

These references are not made to document a historical curiosity, nor even to vindicate Marx as a seer. They are put forth because his words contain so much present truth.

Marx did not, of course, use terms like automation or cybernation, both of recent coinage. Yet he was unmistakably talking about these phenomena. "As large scale industry develops," he wrote, "the creation of real wealth depends less and less upon labor time and the quantity of labor expended, and more upon the might of the machines [Agentien] set in motion during labor time. The powerful effectiveness of these machines bears no relationship to the labor time which it cost to produce them. Their power, rather, derives from the general level of science and the progress of technology . . ."

Then Marx, in some remarkably prophetic phrases, notes how this changes the very character of work. "Man's labor no longer appears as incorporated in [eingeschlossen] the production process. Rather, the worker relates himself to production as a supervisor and regulator [Wachter und Regulator] . . . He watches over the production process rather than being its chief agent." Clearly, Marx did not have mystical, advance knowledge of inventions that were to take place after his death. But just as he derived the tendency of capital to concentrate in larger and larger units from the limited evidence on hand in the mid-nineteenth century, so also did he understand the direction of large-scale production, science, and technology.

Actually, the factory in which the worker became "supervisor and regulator" was not built until 1939, when Standard Oil of New Jersey and the M. W. Kellogg Company erected the first fluid-catalytic crackers. Today, in such plants, the work cycle is leisurely (a man repeats his routine only four times a day in one typical case, as compared to the assembly line on which he might perform the same task several times in the course of a minute). Since the complex system does most of the work by itself, management is content to have the workers "watch over the production process" and even loaf openly. In such factories, the main function of the work force is to be ready when the costly machines break down.

This development, Marx continues, means that the very basis of wealth has been transformed. Now, "neither the actual labor expended by man, nor the length of time during which he works, is the great pillar of production and wealth. That pillar is now the appropriation of man's own universal productivity." And, a little later Marx comments that this demonstrates "the degree to which society's general store of knowledge has become the main factor in increasing productivity."

For Marx, this eventuality does not simply transform the character of work and the source of wealth. It reveals a basic contradiction of the capitalist system itself.

In its earlier stages, Marx argues, capitalism was based upon the fact that riches were derived from poverty. The labor—and suffering—of the great mass was the source of surplus production (that is to say, after the capitalist deducted from his output the cost of paying his workers, that output, produced by those workers, was still much larger than what they received, directly or indirectly, in pay). This surplus constituted the profit of the few, and it was either reinvested to begin the process anew or consumed in luxuries for the few. There was thus a conflict between the demands of the people for more consumer's goods and the money to buy them and those of the entrepreneur for more producer's goods and profits (in another form, this contradiction is constantly plaguing the developing countries of the world today). But as production became more and more sophisticated, as it depended less and less upon the exploitation of brute labor and more upon the application of science to technology, this conflict no longer was necessary. An ever larger part of production can be devoted to new machines without sacrificing the immediate enjoyment of the producers.

Up to this point, Marx's argument resembles Freud's analysis of the way in which the collective represses the instinctual gratification of the many in order to forward the common good as defined, and enjoyed, by the few. It might even win the support of some of the more educated celebrants of the corporation who would be willing to admit that capitalism vastly increased the productive basis of society while simultaneously raising the standard of living. But Marx, of course, went well beyond this point.

"On the one hand," he says, "capital uses every power of science and nature . . . to make the creation of riches independent of the labor time spent in production." The great stimulus to replacing men with machines is to cheapen the cost of production and to maximize profit. "But on the other hand," he continues, "capital measures this growing and achieved social power of production in terms of labor time . . ." As a producer, the capitalist wishes to reduce the number of workers to cheapen costs; but as a seller, he looks to an expanding work force as the source of a growing market able to buy his goods. But once technology demonstrates itself capable of restricting employment while creating abundance, the system breaks down.

In simplified terms, Marx's insight could be illustrated by a (probably imaginary) conversation of the 1950's in America. Henry Ford III was said to have shown Walter Reuther of the United Automobile Workers a completely automated engine block plant. Pointing to the assembly line, on which there were no workers, the corporate chief taunted the trade unionist, "How will you organize workers here?" To which Reuther is said to have replied, "And what workers here will buy your cars?"

In a more complex case, Daniel Bell (who is a sympathetic, but determined, critic of Marx) tells of how the new technology has perhaps already outmoded the old labor-time system of production accounting. "Most important perhaps, there may be an end, too, to the measurement of work. Modern industry began not with the factory but with the measurement of work. *When the worth of the product was defined in production units, the worth of the worker was similarly gauged.* Under the unit concept, the time-study engineers calculated that a worker could produce more units for more money. This was the assumption of the wage-incentive schemes (which actually are output-incentive schemes) and the engineering morality of a 'fair day's pay for a fair day's work.'

"But under automation, with continuous flow, *a worker's worth can no longer be evaluted in production units.* Hence, output-incentive plans, with their involved measurement techniques, may vanish. In their place, as Adam Arbuzzi foretells, may arise a new work morality. Work will be defined not in terms of a 'one best way,' not by the slide rule and the stop-watch, not in terms of fractioned time or units of production, but on the basis of planning and organizing and the continuously smooth functioning of the operation" (emphasis added).

Bell has an important point. In the cybernated factory where the machine, whose production- and tending-cost stands in little relation to its ability to produce goods, is the main source of wealth, how can the worker's worth be evaluated in production units? When the amount of human muscle expended in making an item was an essential element of its value, both the muscle and the product could be computed in terms of labor time (the wages of the muscle and the price of the product). But if that is no longer the case, how can income, the right to consume, be tied to a labor time that is less and less relevant?

As a result of this contradiction, Marx held, "the laboring mass must consume its own surplus product." This consumption is not a grudging necessity of diverting scarce resources to keeping the body and soul of the work force together. It is a precondition of the functioning of the economy, for the people must have the capacity to consume what is made or else there will be overproduction and the crisis of glut. In a moderate form, this notion has become a basic principle of neo-Keynesian economics, recognized by the Western labor movement and the welfare state governments of most of the advanced countries. But it does not stop there.

Under such conditions, Marx concluded, "It is then no longer labor time but disposable time which is the measure of wealth." Now, precisely in order to expand productivity, there must be a vast expansion of consumption. Leisure, which robbed society of resources in a time of scarcity, goads society into activity in a time of abundance.

In short, from Marx's point of view, the decadence of the old principles of scarcity would mark a decisive moment in the liberation of man. Production would no longer rest upon the hard, sweaty labor of the mass but rather upon free time and enjoyment. Where Malthus feared that raising up the poor would degrade the worth and dignity of the few, the modern technological economy of abundance must be frightened of the exact opposite: that not abolishing poverty will destroy prosperity.

Marx's description of the change in the nature of work is now beginning to take place in the West. In the automated factory, the worker is indeed one who "watches over" the production process rather than being its chief agent. His theory that increasing consumption would become an economic necessity has been modestly recognized within the welfare state as a practical reform but not as a revolutionary principle of a new life. As technology takes over more and more occupations, as the working day, week, year, and life are contracted, his ultimate prophecy could come true: that it is the economic responsibility of the citizen to be free, leisured, to develop his own individual bents and proclivities, to consume, not simply manufactured goods, but freedom itself.

And yet, paradoxically, Marx did not realize one possible consequence of his own vision of cybernation and automation. He had assumed that a working-class revolution would transform the ownership of large-scale industry before the process which he described had reached its ultimate limits. The decadence of capitalism under conditions of abundance was not simply a decadence, since the system had created the historical agency for resolving its contradictions in a new way: the proletariat. The humane possibilities of the new development would be made practical by a social class, by those who had learned how to live joyously in the future out of the sufferings and miseries of the past.

But what if the working class in the Marxist sense is abolished before, or simultaneously with, the emergence of the fatal capitalist contradictions of abundance? That now seems quite possible.

V

When Aristotle imagined the statues of Daedalus, he drew one main conclusion from their discovery: that there would no longer be any necessity for slavery and subordination.

Here I suggest that the situation is more complex than the Greek philosopher imagined. Abundance has not really yet arrived in the West, but its possibility—and the abolition of work as it has traditionally been defined in Europe and America—is within the range of commonsensible speculation. Even within the most prosaic Government statistics, one can note that the statues of Daedalus have begun to dance in our midst.

The coming of abundance will unquestionably mean a decadence. Much of the social wisdom of scarcity, that is to say much of man's history, will become irrelevant to the future.

What will replace the conviction that it is through arduous, unfree labor that man realizes himself? A void? Bread and circuses? The dictatorship of the programmers? Or new definitions of freely chosen work, work as creativity, the labor of love?

Will the ending of the economic compulsion to work allow each individual to discover reality in his own way and thus obviate the whole system of social discipline required by the struggle against scarcity? Or will it simply strip away all the extraneous historical guises from the innate destructiveness of man?

Will cybernation force the West to some kind of social humanity, providing practical reasons for making social and personal development the end of collective life? Or will the infinitely capable machines create surplus products and surplus people?

The options are of an extreme range, more so than Aristotle thought. Abundance could actually produce new slaveries, new subordinations. Or, as John Maynard Keynes once said, under such conditions, ". . . we shall be able to rid ourselves of many of the pseudo-moral principles which have hag-ridden us for 200 years, by which we have exalted some of the most distasteful of human qualities into the position of the highest virtues."

9

A Hope

Either Western man is going to choose a new society—or a new society will choose, and abolish, him.

It is clear that the contemporary revolution will continue to reshape the human environment in the most radical way. If anything, time will speed up even more, for the cybernated technology of today proceeds by geometric leaps and bounds rather than by arithmetic progression. Short of an atomic holocaust, which would simply write an end to the whole process, there is no reason to think that it will slow down. And, as this book has shown, the consequences of this development are not merely material and scientific. They invade the spirit, the psychology, politics, and every other aspect of life.

In this context, America has for some time been engaged in the wrong argument. It has been debating as to whether or not the future should be collective and social, and ignoring the fact that the present is already becoming so. The real issue is not whether, but how, this future will arrive—unwittingly or consciously chosen.

If the new society imposes itself upon a people who do not notice a revolution, the moment will constitute the decadence of the Western ideal.

The West has marked itself off from other cultures precisely by its confidence in the future. The religious form of this faith is most identified with St. Augustine, who, breaking with the cyclic theories in which time was a great wheel turning around itself, asserted the pilgrimage of history toward the City of God. The secular version of the same hope dates at least from the Renaissance and culminates in the capitalist and socialist visions of progress. It was this Faustian restlessness that drove the Western powers to remake the world during the last several centuries.

Along with this futurism there was the affirmation of the power of reason. The importance of this commitment cannot be evaded by recourse to a fashionable irrationalism. Of course, the absolute, unquestioned faith in reason has been disproved; yes, there were excesses of the Enlightenment tradition like Comte. But it was the theoretical and practical intelligence which lifted Western man out of the mire and made him, for a while, lord of the earth. Now, if reason has turned out tragically, so has the West. And if men cannot control the products of their own brain, there will be no place to hide, for mystics or for anyone else. Without rational human direction, the accidental revolution is not moving toward a rebirth of poetry but toward an inhuman collectivism.

In short, if the new society is blundered into, then all of the decadences described in this book will come roughly true. Baudelaire will have been right, for the vast, uncomprehended social structure will have little place for beauty. Nietzsche will have been right, and the dream that men can order their own destiny will have come to naught. Max

Weber will have been right, for the age of bureaucratic, antispiritual rule will come to pass. Freud will have been right, for the growth in technological competence will be repressive of man's deep, instinctual life. And so on and so on.

And yet, there is the possibility that the West will freely choose a new society.

No option which can be taken will solve all human problems. The most happy outcome could even be, as Norman Mailer has suggested, only that suffering will be raised from the level of fate to that of tragedy. For when there are no longer plagues, famines, and natural catastrophes to blame death and evil on, the essential finitude of men could become all the more stark and stripped of its accidental qualities. And, contrary to Marx, in a society where men die from death because they have been born, there could be a religious renaissance as well as a heroic atheism.

The claim put here is minimal. The free choice of the future will not abrogate the human condition. But it will provide the context in which autonomous human beings can grow in depth and understanding, which is all the West has really ever asked.

In order to choose the new society rather than being chosen by it, the West must make this accidental century conscious and truly democratic. And this goal I would call socialism.

There are many arguments against using the word "socialism." Most Americans do not understand it. Communism uses the term as a rhetorical mask for a bureaucratic minority that imposes its private desires upon a social technology. Worse yet, the Communists have attempted to identify socialism with totalitarianism. In the emergent nations, the word "socialism" is used to describe the socialization of poverty for the purposes of accumulating capital. These societies, as the great socialist theorists would have predicted, are far distant from the ideal of the free development of the individual which is of the socialist essence. And even in Western Europe where the Social Democratic parties have maintained the democratic content of socialism, they have often equated their vision with a welfare state more than with a new civilization.

Despite all these semantic and historic drawbacks, the term must be used. With the exception of the United States, socialism is what the most democratic forces in the West call their dream. And even more basically, the nineteenth-century socialists, for all their failures of prediction, were the first to anticipate the present plight and to attempt to resolve it. They were right when they said that the way in which men produce their worldly goods is becoming more and more social. They were right in asserting that this complex, interdependent technology could not be contained within a system of private decision-making. And if there is to be a humane outcome to the contemporary Western adventure, they will have to be made right in their faith that the people can freely and democratically take control of their own lives and society.

And this last idea is the heart of the socialist hope as I define it in this book. From the very beginning, the socialists knew that modern technology could not be made just by dividing it up into tiny parcels of individual ownership. It is of the very nature of that technology to be concentrated and collective. Therefore, the socialists assigned a new and radical meaning to democracy. The people's title to the social means of production would be guaranteed, they said, not through stock certificates, but through votes. The basic economic decisions would be made democratically.

In this context, the nationalization of industry is a technique of socialism, not its definition. It is one extremely important way of abolishing the political and social power that results from concentrated private ownership. It also facilitates directing economic resources to the satisfaction of human needs. When the people "own" the state through political democracy, then public corporations are truly theirs, and nationalization is an instrument of freedom. But there are other ways to forward the democratization of economic and social power. Fiscal and monetary policy, a cooperative sector, and taxes are among them.

In these terms, the one set and undeviating aspect of socialism is its commitment to making the democratic and free choice of the citizens the principle of social and economic life. All other issues—the extent of nationalization, the mode of planning, and the like—have to be empirically tested and measured in the light of how they serve that end. For certainly the old popular definition of socialism as the simple and wholesale nationalization of the economy has not survived the experience of this century, and particularly the Communist experience. At the same time, it has become abundantly clear that the commanding heights of the economy—where decisions affect more of life than most laws of Congresses and Parliaments—cannot be left to private motives.

But it is better to leave this plane of socialist generality and move to the definition of specific examples. In what follows, I am suggesting that the only way the accidental revolution can become socially conscious of itself is through a profound economic and social deepening of democracy. This I call socialism.

Education provides an excellent case in point.

Many of the contemporary arguments against democracy, and particularly those grouped around the idea of mass society, charge that the educational hopes of the nineteenth-century humanists have been utterly disappointed. The disappearance of illiteracy and the spread of universal public education have not, it is said, raised the levels of culture and of thought. On the contrary, this very process threatens to inundate the most serious works of the spirit in a vast flood of written and visual material prepared for the marketplace of mediocrity and semiliteracy. If this is an inevitable result of the combination of communications technology and political democracy, it is a frightening indictment of free institutions. For then, if one were to make the conscious choice of the people the principle of society, that would turn banality—and worse—into the official ideology.

And yet the educational and cultural level of the mass in the advanced societies is a fabricated, not a natural, fact. In the United States in 1964, once again, the Manpower Report, the conclusions of the Senate Subcommittee on Employment and Manpower, and just about every other Government report touching on the subject, told how somewhere between a quarter and a third of the young people had not received sufficient training for the lowest of the decently paying jobs. (To put it roughly, almost a third of the youth were high-school dropouts in an economy that was demanding fourteen years of education for the hope of a serious occupational future.)

At this point, two broad possibilities emerge. On the one hand, the present revolution can continue along on its accidental and creative course. This would divide the society in two: on the one side the janitors, the menials, the underemployed, and the unemployed, numbering in the millions; on the other, all those fortunate enough to have an education. Under such circumstances, there would unquestionably be theorists who would point out the low levels of aesthetic taste to be found in the underclass. The propensity to surly and illogical violence at the bottom of the society would be condemned by the best people. The activity of agitators and the role of extremist political philosophies would be deplored.

All this is, of course, a simplification. Among other things, it conceals the way in which at least some of the educated would themselves be the products of a narrow, technical formation that would fit them for their specific function and not much more. And, on a somewhat higher level than the underclass, this group could then be excoriated for the vacuity and sentimentality of its culture. Meanwhile, an advertising industry with approximately the same budget as the educational system would be reinforcing all possible spiritual deficiencies in order to turn them into a profit.

Having manufactured the ignorance of some tens of millions of people in this way, the powerful could then point out that such inferiors are not fit to rule and perhaps do not even deserve the franchise.

But there is another possibility. Instead of freeing the

people for various, and degrading, forms of underemployment or idleness, the same technology could support the channeling of their energies into education. Indeed, with society liberated from routine and repetitive tasks through cybernation, there will be resources that could make of education a basic industry, a replacement for the automobile assembly line and a most welcome one. (The phrase "basic industry" does not suggest that a school is analogous to a factory. It simply insists that education must become as central to the political economy of the future as mass production was to the past.)

Why not, for example, pay people for going to school? There is already convincing evidence in the United States that such a social investment pays enormous dividends, not simply in the happiness of the participating individual but in the growth of society as a whole. Under the G.I. Bill of Rights, veterans were paid for going to school. This was a bonus in social form (a direct cash payment to individuals would not have had the same effect at all), compensation for having faced death. It also had a pump-priming function in the postwar economy and helped to avoid a return to the Depression thirties.

As a result of the G.I. Bill, the entire United States became more productive. And, if one one wants to put it in the parsimonious terms of the conventional wisdom, the increase in tax revenue from this general upgrading far outweighed the expenditure of taxes required to bring it about. But most important of all, the G.I. Bill led to a general cultural gain for society and to the personal growth of those who benefited from it.

It does not require a war to justify such social intelligence.

On another level, the concept of education as a basic industry provides a new definition of work. If, as the coming of the statues of Daedalus promises, the old, traditional occupations are being abolished or transformed, this is an important gain. If the school system is seen as a fundamental investment, then teaching will become a much more important function. And it is relatively automation-proof, like the human care of human beings generally. Moreover, there is no need to restrict teaching to the old categories. There are those who are competent in classics or languages or higher mathematics; and those who can enrich the society with their knowledge of gardening, fishing, photography.

In such a context, older people, whom modern life increasingly segregates as surely as racial minorities, could discover new meanings for their lives. The slums, for example, desperately need nurseries so that the deprivations of poverty which are institutionalized in the tenement home can be combated at an early age. Such a program demands trained teachers, psychologists, doctors, and the like. But it also can make marvelous use of women whose only qualification is their genius with children. Such people can be found in the slums, and part of their liberation from misery can be accomplished through their helping others.

If such an approach were taken, it is absolutely certain that the cultural and educational level of the society can be raised. In 1964, as was remarked earlier, a United States Office of Education study documented the fact that the majority of dropouts were intelligent enough to finish high school and that a significant minority of them could qualify for a college education. This was true even though these young people already had been subjected to the massive miseducation system of the slums, of poverty, and of advertising. Were these terrible disabilities removed, there is no way of estimating how much more talent, and even genius, would be uncovered in the doing.

But in order to embark on such a program requires a vast expansion of the democratic and social principle.

Despite all of the complaints of the fortunate, Western society does not presently grant education the kind of priority it needs. In countries still dominated by the anachronistic search for profit, such a huge allocation of resources to an apparently "unproductive" sector seems unconscionable. The market mechanism, insofar as it works at all, will deliver to the schools just enough funds to train the people actually needed for available work. To understand education as an area for social investment is to realize that the old-fashioned criteria of efficiency no longer apply and that society is now both free and driven to devote itself to higher things. In short, one would have to break with the premises and practices which in 1964 gave General Motors, a planned economy for private profit, more than twice as much income as the federal government allocated for the abolition of poverty.

Such an undertaking would require national planning. It is impossible to structure an educational system without knowing what kind of world the young who are being trained will live in. The absence of such knowledge is unquestionably one of the elements that has made so much of the American vocational education system a waste of time and resources. The intelligent anticipation of occupational needs in the future—and of its leisure possibilities—is a necessity in a modern society. Here again, the old faith in the market, or the new faith in the conscientious corporation, is of little help.

All this points to another important fact: that education is a good (and I use the term in its ethical as well as its economic sense) which is consumed socially. Even where, as in the United States, there is a significant sector of private schooling, it is increasingly dependent upon Government subsidy. The size of the educational plant, the cost of educational technology are more and more of such a dimension that even rich individuals do not, and cannot, pay for value received during the time of training. In fact, the educational system, public and private, is part of the social wealth. Only now, access to that system remains severely limited on the basis of private fortune. Predictably, those with the greatest need—the slum children who are so carefully trained to the standards of ignorance—have the least opportunity, while those with the greatest cultural advantages receive the greatest attention.

However, when one points to the social character of education, that does not imply a uniform, utterly nationalized system of schooling. On the contrary. The G.I. Bill itself operated without any Federal intervention into curriculum and policy. And in the period of cybernation, precisely what is needed is a vast diversity in education: nursery schools; traditional schools; continuing adult education; discussion centers (these are already being provided by the American elite through the public tax subsidy of private foundations, another form of relief for the middle class and the rich).

The necessity of broadening the very concept of education has already been recognized by the Senate Subcommittee on Employment and Manpower. The Committee's report argued that it was no longer possible to train a young person for a lifetime skill. The technology is changing so fast that the old concept of vocational education is losing its relevance. Even the professionals are facing this problem. In the winter of 1964, *The Wall Street Journal* reported that engineers laid off in defense cutbacks were forced to return to school in order to catch up with new developments in their field.

The Senate Committee rightly pointed out that this accelerating technology demanded liberal education. Since the young can no longer be trained for a single occupation, they must be educated in the broadest sense of the word. In this context, the idea of a continuing and liberal education is no longer a special utopia of the intellectuals. It is a necessity of the society.

But it would be an error to put the issue simply in terms of the job future of the student. For another contemporary trend is pointing toward the reduction of the working life. This has made it apparent to more and more people that leisure will be a problem of the future. In the past, free time was so restricted that it could be left up to chance and the minimal planning involved in a park and recreational program. Now, this is no longer the case. Yet the structuring of leisure is still largely left up to the corporations and the criterion of profit.

Thus, an increasingly important educational function will be preparation for leisure and not just for work. And this new role will be more difficult to fill than the traditional one. The skill level of a job is quantifiable, and the school system can be measured in terms of how it meets these set requirements. But what are the leisure skills? Here, because the free choice, and even the whim, of the individual is an important element, it is much harder to be specific. Yet answering this challenge could provide some of the most important work of the cybernated age.

To come back to the starting point, all these changes are impossible unless there is a conscious and democratic allocation of resources within the context of national planning. The market will not accomplish such a transformation and neither will the corporation. To achieve it, society has to opt for a conscious social criterion in an area of life already social in fact. The present material eminence of the West more and more derives from the appropriation of the general level of knowledge rather than from the exploitation of the individual's labor. If there is to be a spiritual eminence, it will emerge out of that most revolutionary of the modern means of production, the human mind.

Housing is another important example of this thought.

In all the Western nations, the private housing sector has utterly failed the needs of the poorest people and thereby penalized the entire society. The paradox of simultaneous rot and dynamism is present in almost every urban center of the advanced countries. Generally, the chaos has been accomplished in part through collective subsidy. Governments have favored the housing needs of the middle class and rich at the expense of the dispossessed. In a city like New York, for instance, it has been the official public rhetoric for thirty years that the slums are to be abolished. Only they have grown.

At the same time, it is clear that public housing has been a partial failure. In the United States, where this is most strikingly true, this fact is directly related to profit speculation in the use of land. The well-to-do have generally fled to the suburbs, and enforced zoning and housing codes will exclude the typical public housing units from their retreats. Within the central city, public housing has had to compete for land with profitable slums and office buildings. The result has been the segregation of the poor in impersonal steel and concrete warrens or in the suppurating units of the ancient neighborhoods.

This situation is an agony for those who are forced to remain in the slums and an anguish to many of those who are isolated in the housing projects. But more than that, it has corrupted the quality of life of the entire society. It accounts for the class and racial segregation in the American educational system and the principle that those who most need training shall have the least chance to get it. It has been a factor in the institutionalization of racism and in the promotion of riots. It has reduced the function and sociability of parks and of the streets themselves. (The same middle-class people who complain bitterly about taxes also mourn the passing of the old urban amenities and talk of the danger in the streets, without particularly realizing how their own miserliness has contributed to the conditions they deplore.)

There is not the slightest evidence that these conditions can be dealt with by private firms. It is not simply that business prefers the profitable upgrading of the middle-class and wealthy housing stock, although that is an element in the equation. More basically, an assault upon the slums would require a social standard in valuing the use of land and could take place only within the context of a broad plan. When the United States in 1964 had still not fulfilled its 1953 target for low-cost housing, something is obviously wrong and radically wrong.

But the question of design—of public housing itself, and

of its integration with private housing—is a qualitative issue at least as important as the quantitative. Megalopolis is probably the most glaring single example of the growth of the new collectivism and one from which hardly anyone in the West can flee. And the question is, as with all the collectives of this century, can the city be humanized and made responsive to people? The market clearly will not allow a decent answer, as has been demonstrated in every advanced nation. The intervention of a social imagination is essential.

Housing and education, then, are two specific illustrations of how it might be possible to make the accidental revolution conscious of itself. These cases do not lend themselves to the old simplifications about socialism (and to be fair, many of these vulgarizations were the work of socialists themselves). Neither do they give aid and comfort to the current Western complacency that the modified welfare state has put an end to all the old problems. Democratic planning for work and leisure, an increasingly social allocation of resources, a practical attack on the power of money in all its forms: these are the present necessities.

Most of the arguments usually advanced in the United States against what has just been said are fairly weak. One is most definitely not. Before turning to that serious criticism, it is worthwhile to take up two earnestly held, but not very substantial, antisocialisms: the peculiarly American obsession that national economic planning is inherently totalitarian; the more general fear that any attempt to embark upon a socialist course necessarily involves the creation of a dull-witted, unresponsive, and powerful bureaucracy.

It is beyond the scope of this analysis to locate the antiplanning trauma in American history. It will simply be taken as a strange fact. In the mid-sixties, when Tory businessmen in England, bankers in France, and social Catholics in Italy and Belgium had all recognized the necessity of planning, a good number of Americans still thought the term meant Red Revolution. They did not realize that planning can be used for totalitarian purposes, as in Russia; for corporate ends, as in the huge American firms; for social goals as defined by corporate executives, as in France. As a result, they also did not know that planning could be used to extend and deepen the freedom of the individual.

In the first decade of the century, some big businessmen, fearful of the trust-busters, had talked of planning but what they really dreamed of was the Americanization of the German cartels. This notion persisted in one form or another, and at the beginning of the Depression even the Chamber of Commerce was speaking of a "planned economy." However, this business concept of planning never got beyond price fixing and limiting the play of competition. When the early New Deal began to take some of these theories seriously, as in the NRA, the businessmen began attacking Roosevelt as a traitor to his class. (Arthur Schlesinger, Jr.'s, *Age of Roosevelt*, and particularly the first two volumes, provides an excellent documentation of this conservative flirtation with "planning." And this fundamental hostility has persisted ever since, forcing the country to blunder into the revolutionary age of automation.

But more than that, this set of attitudes plays an important role in having Americans engage in the wrong debate. They allow people to ignore the fact that the accidental revolution is already a powerful planning agency, and, that in the absence of a conscious and democratic plan, modern technology follows an unconscious and elitist plan of its own. Society is not growing organically, like the oaks and English lawns of the traditional conservative image. It is a human construct, it is accelerating, and if men do not plan the uses of the machines they make, then the machines and their elite guardians will plan the lives of men.

The second criticism of the socialist proposal is both more general and a bit more compelling. A conscious restructuring of society, it is said, will call into life a huge bureaucracy, and this will limit freedom.

In part, this thought rests upon a familiar and naïve assumption: that the present historical choice is between bureaucracy or no bureaucracy. In point of fact, as Max Weber and Schumpeter and many others realized sometime ago, bureaucracies are a characteristic and inevitable mode of the modern age. They are not imported into nations by outcasts and subversives, but are inexorable deductions from the minute division of labor which is of the essence of contemporary technology. The basic issue is whether it is possible to control these bureaucracies, not whether they should exist. And the argument against socialism on the grounds that it represents a bureaucratic danger is really an argument, often unwitting, in favor of the present private bureaucracies and their egotistical planning institutions. Socialism, I would assert, is not an advocate or creator of bureaucracy—the honors in that regard belong to businessmen—but the one political movement that seeks to represent the claim of the individual as against the bureaucracy by making the latter subject to the democratic will.

But this point is more substantial than its proponents usually make it. Max Weber understood that bureaucracy was a fate of the age. But he also felt that there was no way to make the institution responsive. It was of the bureaucratic nature, he said (and the point has been developed previously in these pages), that the subdivision of functions precluded any vantage point of the whole. As a result, the system was massively irrational because there was no way to integrate its highly rational components. Given such a prognosis, there is no future for utopia and little future for democracy.

Weber may have been right. If this turns out to be the case, then socialism and democracy are impossible—and so is any growth in freedom as the West has understood that word. But if there is any hope that Weber's pessimism was wrong, it will come to pass because a way has been found to bring the bureaucracies under democratic control, i.e. to impose a freely chosen purpose upon them. This certainly will not be done by counterposing a myth of landowner or frontier virtues to a horror story of the socialist future and ignoring the present overwhelming fact of bureaucracy.

And perhaps some of the technological developments since Weber's death have undermined at least part of his negativity. Automation and cybernation have struck first in the factory, but they are already beginning to appear as a major factor in the office and on the lower and middle levels of management. This could provide the basis for the dictatorship of the programmers. But, under an utterly different political direction, it might be utilized for a reinvigoration of democracy. If the number of intermediaries between the political decision of the people and its execution can be reduced, if the vast establishment with its prejudices and self-interest can be partly automated, then there might be much less of the Weberian danger.

This possibility depends upon a democratic populace capable and desirous of determining its needs and making them the guiding principle of the economy and society. And here one comes to the really serious objection against the socialist ideal today: that there is no political and social force really interested in taking hold of the advanced nations—the only places where socialism is now possible—and offering them an alternative view of life.

This issue was discussed in the chapter "The Decadence of the Poor." The problem is one of finding a political equivalent of poverty. The workers' movement and its allies provided the West with an internal social dynamic for well over a century. Negroes provided white America with some conscience and consciousness in the fifties and sixties (on the whole, the civil-rights movement in the United States has probably benefited whites more than Negroes; important, but limited, gains in schools and lunchrooms as contrasted with presenting the nation its soul). But if these driven, haunted, and hungering majorities and minorities are to disappear, what group will take their place?

The broad possibilities which will determine the answer to this question have alreay been put forward: the growth of a powerless underclass and a somnolent middle class; the emergence of a new—or old—radicalism through the dislocations that lie just ahead.

There are strong forces militating against the hopeful variants. For one thing, the process of automation and cybernation does not take place in the course of a vast upheaval that goads millions into action. Rather, there has been a gradual chipping away at the factory jobs. Industries, like coal, have been transformed (the United Mine Workers declined from 600,000 to just a bit over 100,000 members in two decades), specific areas have been gutted, and all this in a context of general prosperity.

Another element tended to conceal the magnitude of the change. In the 1950's, jobs in the service industries became more numerous than in manufacturing. This shift transformed the character of the labor force—it signaled a manpower revolution, in the Senate Committee's phrase—but it did not result in thirties-style joblessness. The mass-production jobs which had been the ports of entry to the economy for the old immigrant groups were declining, and this was a blow against Negroes and others at the bottom of the heap. The new employments were often menial and low paid (restaurants, hotels, laundries, hospitals, and the like). Thus, the quantitative figures were disturbing but not tragic, and there was more than a little complacency. But the qualitative shift within the work force quietly brought with it the most serious social problems.

These changes could become more obvious. In 1945, there were no computers in the United States; in 1956, less than a thousand; in 1963, around twenty thousand. By 1967, according to one survey of investment plans, automated machinery would account for only 20 percent of the investment. Obviously, this process still has a long way to go. And it could summon up some of the traditional and practical idealism that accompanies critical social changes.

Under such circumstances, the socialist ideal could once again become a mighty force.

The alternative to this hope is not, these figures should make clear, a continuation of the *status quo*. It is a revolution, but a different kind of revolution. A West without an internal opposition would no longer be the West. Under such circumstances, there would be no group capable of challenging the increasing concentrations of economic and social, which is to say political, power. And something like the Brave New World of Aldous Huxley could be the outcome of the present transformation. Then the Weberian fear of an antihuman, antifreedom reign of the bureaucracies would indeed have come to pass.

It is here that I would locate my own definition of the decadence of the Western tradition. The moment would be announced when there was no longer a basis within society for people to take new ideas passionately and to seek change. It would mean, not a decay from the past, but the rotting of the future.

Marx and the early socialists recognized such a possibility in their minds, if not in their hearts. Emotionally convinced that socialism would inevitably follow upon capitalism, they were profound enough thinkers to realize that there was another possibility, which they called "barbarism." (Engels, the popularizer, was less aware of the option than Marx, the theorist.) Barbarism would come about, they said, through the ruin of all the contending classes. It would be foolish to see in this idea an uncanny anticipation of the present predicament. Yet one element in the formula is particularly apt: that decadance would take the form of a social stalemate.

Today this insight is something more than a nod to the openness and unpredictability of history. It defines a real possibility. The new technology may simultaneously lull the people into privacy while it carries out a public revolution behind their backs. Then men will be as bewildered in the presence of their own genius as, at the beginning of time, they were when confronted with the powers of the natural world. And that is a decadence.

And here it is important to reiterate an idea stated at the very outset of this book, for it marks off a unique aspect of the contemporary decadence. The social revolutions of the past were all accidental, that is, they did not conform to the images the revolutionists projected. But that gap between dream and reality was a function of the general ignorance and level of consciousness. It was life itself that was sad. Today, the problem is not in our stars but in our philosophy. The revolution is happening precisely because society has become so intentionally and carefully competent. History can no longer be blamed; it is man who is in doubt.

Thus it is that in speaking of socialism one can no longer have the faith of the nineteenth-century catechumens. Neither can one look, as some of them did, to an apocalyptic day on which history literally makes it leap from the realm of necessity into that of freedom. If the accidental revolution is to be made conscious and democratic, that will happen in the course of an involved, complex process. It is no longer a question of "seizing" power, for that metaphor implies that the existing power is suitable to the new purpose if only the proper hands are laid upon it. It is rather a problem of transforming power, of changing it, of making new institutions. And no military figure of speech can comprehend such a task.

Since much of the material in this chapter is willfully visionary, it is important to be a little more specific on this point.

There can no longer be any question about the practical feasibility of national economic planning. One of the original arguments against totalitarian Communism was that it would not work. Leaving aside for a moment the fact that the Russian success was purchased at the price of freedom and through a terrible exploitation of the people (and this is a decisive reason for rejecting that society as a model for the future), the brute accomplishments of the Soviet Union demonstrate that an economy can be purposefully mobilized by men. And in the recent experience in that country, there is even the hint of the possibility that the system, in the long run, requires an expansion of liberty.

At least one element in the post-Stalin thaw has been the fact that a sophisticated production process cannot be run on a simple principle of terror. When it is a question of employing forced labor to substitute for machines that do not exist, men can be degraded to the level of "hands" as both the nineteenth-century capitalists and twentieth-century Communists understood. Slaves can dig canals with picks and shovels. But as the productivity level of the nation rises through mechanization, such a technique becomes economically inefficient (it was, of course, inhuman from the start). And slaves cannot run delicate automated machines nor can the interactions of an advanced economy be regulated by military command.

Thus, the Russian rulers have been forced to make certain concessions to the people, to employ the carrot more than the whip. Unquestionably, the Kremlin will resist this trend the moment it calls bureaucratic privilege into question. But I cite the Soviet instance only for the limited purpose of demonstrating that national planning is possible and that it requires, to a degree at least, some kind of willing participation.

Secondly, the Yugoslavian and Polish developments have taken a theory of the thirties and turned it into a practice of the sixties. In the Lange-Lerner thesis, it was pointed out that a planned economy could use a consumer market and a price system as the best way of determining the popular taste. In totalitarian form, this has been done in at least two of the East European countries, and there are tendencies in this direction in Russia itself. Again, the point is not to advocate emulation of the antidemocratic system in those nations, but simply to point out that planning has a wide range of possibilities. Indeed, in a context of democratic planning, the market mechanism could be utilized as a guarantee of individual freedom.

In Western Europe, the postwar years have seen the rise of French "indicative" planning. This approach, as has been seen, does not constitute a challenge to the capitalist economic order and its rule of profit. For that matter, it can be utilized to strengthen the prevailing system, as French bankers and Tory businessmen have obviously realized. But, with this profound limitation, the actual experience of these nations does provide some practical evidence about planning.

The French have proved that it is possible to treat an economy integrally and to orient it toward a certain rate of growth. More than that, in the Fourth Plan and in the preparation of the Fifth, the pressure of the democratic and popular forces has resulted in the introduction of qualitative criteria into the planning mechanism. As a consequence, the category of social investment is taking its place in the economic tables. It will, of course, require more than a little change to fulfill the promise of this beginning (a provocative version of how this could be done was outlined by Mendès-France in his study of *La République Moderne*).

But even the present situation offers positive, hard data on the potential of conscious intervention.

During World War II, the United States made a similar demonstration. Given a military threat that united the people, the economy was directed in the name of the war effort. A priority was given to that one form of social investment the West has thus far recognized with enthusiasm: national defense. Immediately after the war in 1945, a less drastic proposal was made in the Full Employment Bill. Under the terms of this legislation, the President was charged with drawing up a national budget of both the public and private sectors that would annually anticipate the next year's Gross National Product. He was then to estimate the level of unemployment which would be caused by the indicated level of economic activity. If the figure exceeded 3 percent, he was to submit a program of compensatory Federal action along with his report. A conservative Congress could not stand quite so much common sense and rejected the Bill, substituting the pious statements of intent in the Employment Act of 1946, a law which has been ignored since the day it was passed.

More recently, the American Defense Department has given an unwitting illustration of the possibilities of socialism. Presiding over the largest single enterprise in the nation and the greatest amount of funds for social investment, the Pentagon developed a "systems" approach to military procurement. The old, outdated demarcations between the services were, to a considerable extent, abolished. The problem of military capacity was seen as an integrated whole, and expenditures were rationally planned in order to meet global needs.

There is no inherent restriction of the systems approach

to the production of the means of annihilation. It is, for example, quite conceivable that a nation would total up all of its social needs and international obligations, treating them as a whole. Then, after a democratic debate and decision on priorities, the economy could be directed toward the creation of the means of life. The analogy has limits, of course: military patriotism is more developed than brotherhood patriotism; arms needs are more easily measurable than social needs; and so on. The point is simply that there is nothing in human nature or the structure of reality against having a powerful planned and social sector in the economy. It has already been done in the United States.

The instances of planning which I have cited are hardly exhaustive and are certainly not meant as such. But they do illustrate, in a prosaic way well this side of apocalypse, that modern technology can be consciously directed. The problem, once again, is not one of technique, which the advanced societies have in abundance, but of the democratic political will.

For socialism is not a matter of econometric models. These can be prepared, as has been seen, by totalitarians and corporations. The crucial issue, the transformation rather than the seizure of power, concerns the values men impart to their planned technologies. A brave new worlder could specify a certain number of housing units with certain physical characteristics. But a new civilization is not a problem of quantity, of which there will probably be more in any case, but of quality. And that is where freedom is the essence of the socialist proposal.

Perhaps it seems strange in the final pages of a book which has raised issues of God and man to be talking about the way in which public housing is built. But that is precisely the problem: to infuse the minute and calibrated technology, and the growing abundance of statistical and planning data, with the Western spirit, to marry engineering and philosophy. And given the fact that it is still conceivable that this can be done, one cannot simply call the West decadent. The fatalists, like Spengler with his organic metaphor of inevitable social death, rightly understood the potential in this century for ending the Western ideal. What they missed was the possibility of fulfilling it. And there is the contemporary hope.

The fulfillment of this possibility is, of course, a political issue. With so many variables up in the air, it is impossible to set down a program and perspective for the Western nations in this regard. Yet, certain relevant generalizations can be made. In the United States, it is inconceivable that the country can face up to these issues on the basis of politics as usual. The American party system has been structured for some time so as to produce accommodations in the middle of the road and to avoid sharp conflicts. In some ways this trend became particularly marked in the elections of 1964 when Mr. Johnson projected his role as the "President of all the people" against Goldwater extremism. But there is a fateful, and increasingly untrue, assumption underlying such consensus politics in America: that all problems can be solved by conciliation.

If radical options are to intrude in the near future upon all the advanced nations, if the nature of work, the potential of democracy, and the very meaning of economics are in the midst of transformation, then the old wisdom will be inadequate. And what will be required is the appearance of a new party alignment—a new party—in the United States. As of now, there is an American Right and an American Center; but there is not really an American democratic Left. And only the emergence of a democratic Left holds out the possibility of the United States measuring up to its challenge.

For reasons of American history, it is probable that a radical political change will not happen radically. That is to say, if the necessary new party does come, it will not result from the sudden emergence of a full-blown third force, but through the conflict within the present party structure. The potential elements for such a change have already been described: the racial minorities and the poor generally; the labor movement revived; the liberal middle class; both secular and religious humanism. Thus, in looking not to the far distance but the immediate American future, the struggle of the liberal wing of the Democratic Party seems to be the point of departure for any serious hope.

And yet, as all that has been said should make clear, the outcome of this development cannot stop at traditional liberalism. In the process of change, it must become clear that America is having the wrong debate, that the shibboleths about collectivism, balanced budgets, and bureaucracy are without real meaning. For the present premise of most of American politics is that the choice is between a resolute march to the rear in the name of anticollectivism and a cautious confrontation with the future in the name of a mixed economy. In reality, the past which is the dream of the American Right is beyond recall; and the present which is recognized by American liberalism is much more radical than is imagined. At some point, then, a new political movement must begin to talk of a new political program—the democratic and conscious control of a technology that is already collective and bureaucratic.

In Europe, the problem of the first step is somewhat simpler. For in the Social Democratic parties there is an existing force that is committed, in rhetoric at least, to the idea of a new society. There, however, the problem may well be that of breaking through the conservatism of the revolutionary tradition. The main thrust of the traditional socialist ideology was right, but many of the specific deductions from those premises are now wrong. The European Social Democracy is presently faced, not with advocating a distant utopia, but with the democratization and transformation of planning institutions that already exist. And such an achievement is both extremely difficult and quite possible.

In these brief political comments, it is impossible to make judgments about the tactics and specific policies for a problematic future. But the point is that, with all the ambiguities, that future has not been settled; it is not a fate, as in Spengler and other philosophers of decadence. There is no inevitable tomorrow, either for good or for bad. And there is still the possibility that new beginnings can be made.

And so, with half of an apology to Nietzsche, I would end with the idea of the hopeful decadence.

It is possible that it will be with the future as it was with Thomas Mann. Just as he thought he would write a droll comedy about the Magic Mountain, he was thrown sky-high by history, and had his novel and his autobiography rewritten by uncontrollable events, so these last six decades have constantly taken themselves by surprise. Mann could never fully transcend the shock of what happened. He left his magnificent images of disorder, his conviction that a social answer was required, and his inability to find one. The West could end like that.

But at the same time, there is now the material possibility of making the ancient dreams come true. In the West, and in the world, the degrading functions, the inhuman labors, can be done by machines. Men can be released from the scarcity, the hunger, the repetitive routine that have maimed them through the ages. There is—and the moment is utterly unique in history—the imminence of enough for everyone. Such a liberation from economic necessity could be the beginning of man, not his end. To make the transition from the comfortable wisdoms of misery will not be easy, as this book has made plain. But it is possible and that has never been true before.

In some ways, the incredible ambiguity of the present is somewhat similar to the situation described by Charles Dickens in the famous opening passage of *A Tale of Two Cities* (Dickens wrote with bitterness and in a spirit contrary to this writer, yet the words are extraordinarily apt). "It was the best of times, it was the worst of times, it was the age of wisdom, it was the age of foolishness, it was the season of Light, it was the season of Darkness, it was the spring of hope, it was the winter of despair, we had everything before us, we had nothing before us, we were all going direct to Heaven, we were all going direct the other way . . ."

Dickens' age never really resolved those paradoxes. They persist to this day. But now, change is so epidemic and radical that they will not long remain indeterminate. Independent of any political will, a new society is coming. The issue is, what will it be like? And the answer is not yet written, for it will be made by men. It still could be positive, and, if this will be the case, then most of the decadences described here are happy omens.

Keynes was perhaps the first great economist to grasp the modern potential for the end of scarcity (the great socialists had seen the possibility; he analyzed the probability). A man of the business civilization who had come to the aid of capitalism in one of its darkest hours, he nevertheless greeted the prospect of capitalist decadence. The old virtues, like the pursuit of wealth and the social function of greed, were, he said, coming to an end. Then, they would be seen as the vices they truly are. And now, it might be added to his thought, this system which accomplished prodigies is not only no longer necessary, it is ceasing to exist. Its decadence could well be joyous.

Religion should dance on the grave of the God of hunger and fear and human impotence. For if there is divinity, He need not depend on man's suffering, and the task of building Him a house in the modern city will open up the way to the genuine depths of man. Atheistic humanism should rejoice in the passing of the simplistic antifaith. It has turned out that man is more complicated and intractable than was thought, and if that makes the present more difficult it could make the future so much richer.

The socialists should see in the decadence of their old apocalypse a new relevance. For it is no longer a question of yearning for a mystic day on which history will turn a corner. Now, it is literally possible to construct freedom—if the political will can be found in the daily life.

Thus far, this century has been accidental. The most ingenious and calculated period in the history of man, its political and social imagination have not approached the revolutionary intelligence of its technology. So it often seems in these times that there is a new fate, a decadence, abroad. And indeed, if the process does continue along its present course, there will be a decadence that will be simply a death. For although what will follow will be a new social order, it will be fundamentally hostile to the values created over the more than two thousand years of Western man. Casually, heedlessly, the greatest spiritual adventure of humanity will have come to an end. But if the accidental century were to become conscious of itself, the West would then stand on the eve of its fulfillment and could, humanely and democratically, once more become the promise of the entire world.

In these times, something enormous is dying: a good part of the Western tradition and environment. And something enormous is being born. And there is, paradoxically, in the depths of the various despairs of these times the glimpse of the heights of our hope.

INDEX